LIVING BLUE

Helping law enforcement officers and their families survive and thrive from recruitment to retirement

BARBARA RUBEL & JASON PALAMARA

Griefwork Center, Inc.

Kendall Park, New Jersey

Published by Griefwork Center, Inc.
www.griefworkcenter.com

Library of Congress Control Number: 2023945860
Names: Rubel, Barbara and Palamara, Jason
ISBN: 978-1-892906-05-2
ISBN: 978-1-892906-06-9 (ebook)
Subjects: Law Enforcement. Police Psychology.

Cover Design: Kristina Conatser
Interior Design: Kristina Rodriguez
Copy Edit: Erin Leo, Lil Barcaski, and Holly Hudson

Recommended citation: Rubel, B., and Palamara, J. (2024). *Living Blue*: Helping law enforcement officers and their families survive and thrive from recruitment to retirement. Griefwork Center, Inc.

CONTENTS

DEDICATION

Jason: I dedicate this book to my family who has lived blue with me and to my fellow LEOs, both present and those no longer with us. To my parents whose love, support, and example have provided me with the map needed to become the man I am today. To my brothers, Anthony and Adam, who remain my first brotherhood and tribe. To my children who have learned to navigate all that I brought home from work. And to my wife, Veronica, who has loved me through good times and in bad times. Our relationship is what it is today because of your strength and support for someone who didn't always give the same back.

Barbara: I dedicate this book to my mother, a policewoman, and to my father, a sergeant, who died by suicide after retiring from the police force. As a suicide loss survivor, I dedicate this book to blue families who have experienced this devastating loss.

PREFACE

What Sets This Book Apart

Living Blue is a life-changing book that offers a deeper understanding of the impact that vicarious trauma has on law enforcement officers (LEOs) and their family members. This evidence-based guide, rooted in cutting edge research, and personal life experience, focuses on managing symptoms of chronic stress, burnout, secondary trauma, compassion fatigue, and moral injury. *Living Blue* is a blueprint that explores research in police wellness and interventions for supporting LEOs who are vicariously traumatized.

Jason Palamara, a retired Cold Case Homicide detective and Barbara Rubel, daughter of two police officers and a renowned Thanatologist, walk you through the obstacles to well-being. Thanatologists are specialists who focus on managing traumatic death. They use science and applied practice to educate first responders on ways to manage loss and prolonged grief.

Palamara and Rubel share proven techniques to increase officer health and wellness, which also makes this book a valuable tool for mental health professionals who counsel police officers. The book combines stories, research, and introspective prompts, inviting LEOs and their families to discover insight into cultivating a positive mindset to build their resilience. What's more, over 70 law enforcement professionals and experts on wellness share their insight.

The Audience for This Book

Living Blue is an essential guide for law enforcement officers, their families, mental health professionals who support them, and anyone affiliated with police safety and wellness. The content is adaptable enough for new, seasoned, and retired officers. *Living Blue* is written for educational purposes for anyone interested in first responder mental health, and in particular, law enforcement officer well-being.

Chapter 1 Focus: *Managing Law Enforcement Stress.* Insight on this topic will be gained as it relates to local police officers, state and tribal police, federal law enforcement, and public safety directors.

Chapter 2 Focus: *Adverse Childhood Experiences (ACEs).* Police Officer Standards and Training (POST) directors, and academy directors will gain insight on the impact of Adverse Childhood Experiences (ACEs) on an officer's mental health. Trainers and coaches whose clients are law enforcement officers will recognize the relationship between their autonomic nervous systems and social behavior.

Chapter 3 Focus: *Burnout.* Security personnel at higher education institutions and law enforcement executives will learn to identify ways to help employees manage burnout, secondary trauma, compassion fatigue, and empathic distress.

Chapter 4 Focus: *Maladaptive Coping.* Police chiefs, sheriffs, and first line supervisors will glean information on how to mitigate maladaptive coping in officers.

Chapter 5 Focus: *Moral Injury.* Police chaplains will gain valuable knowledge regarding moral injury in law enforcement.

Chapter 6 Focus: *Vicarious Trauma Response.* Civilians, community members, and researchers will find value in learning about a vicarious trauma-responsive approach in policing.

Chapter 7 Focus: *Family Support.* Spouses, partners, parents, and children who are devoted to those who serve will learn about family resilience and work-family synergy.

Chapter 8 Focus: *Women in Law Enforcement.* This chapter is for anyone who wants to support the recruitment, retention, and promotion of women in law enforcement.

Chapter 9 Focus: *LODD.* This chapter provides information to support agency leaders after a Line of Duty Death (LODD).

Chapter 10 Focus: *Suicide.* This chapter is for anyone who wants to learn about suicidal behavior, risk factors, barriers to getting help, and upstream suicide prevention..

Chapter 11 Focus: *Trauma and Grief.* As research broadens the understanding of trauma and grief, command staff will be able to incorporate models of managing loss into police training and curriculum development after reviewing this chapter's information.

Chapter 12 Focus: *Resilience.* Police training managers will gain a broader perspective on building an officer's resilience and ways that they can achieve post-traumatic growth.

Chapter 13 Focus: *Life Post Retirement.* Sooner or later, an officer will retire. We explore life beyond law enforcement and what needs to be done to have a happy retirement.

Learning Objectives

Chapter 1: Law Enforcement Stress
- Identify acute and chronic stressors in policing.
- Describe the benefits of stress inoculation.

Chapter 2: Adverse Childhood Experiences (ACEs) and Wellness
- Identify Adverse Childhood Experiences (ACEs) as a possible predictor of a health risk for adults.
- Describe the polyvagal theory in relation to policing.

Chapter 3: Law Enforcement Burnout
- Examine contributors to empathic distress.
- Explain burnout and secondary traumatic stress.
- Identify effective strategies to manage compassion fatigue.

Chapter 4: Cops and Maladaptive Coping
- Explain how maladaptive coping strategies increases occupational stress.

Identify how culture, stigma, shame, and confidentiality prevent law enforcement professionals from getting help.

Chapter 5: Moral Injury in Law Enforcement

Reflect on contributors to moral injury in policing.

Recognize eight protective factors against moral injury.

Chapter 6: Vicarious Trauma-Responsive Approach in Policing

Examine a vicarious trauma-informed approach to policing.

Describe the significance of internal police peer support programs.

Chapter 7: Law Enforcement Family Support: Spouses, Partners, Parents, and Children

Examine ways to build family resilience.

Select ways to go from work-family conflict to work-family synergy.

Chapter 8: Women in Policing

Describe stressors policewomen encounter throughout their career.

Examine practices to alleviate some of the stress experienced by policewomen.

Chapter 9: End of Watch

Explain eight characteristics of a death notification after a LODD.

Review ways to support bereaved individuals.

Chapter 10: Law Enforcement Officer Suicide

Review how thwarted belongingness, perceived burdensomeness, and hopelessness, are warning signs of suicide.

Discuss how an officer's beliefs and attitudes are barriers to their getting help for suicidal thoughts.

Chapter 11: Grieving on the Job

- Describe Palette of Grief® reactions after a loss.
- Review 25 risk factors that complicate the grief process.
- Compare contemporary mourning models for coping with loss.

Chapter 12: Resilience and Post-traumatic Growth

- Describe post-traumatic growth after a psychological struggle.
- Select eight-character strengths to build psychological resilience.

Chapter 13: Life Beyond Law Enforcement

- Plan for retirement with a long-term wellness strategy.
- Recognize eight elements of resilience that enhance the ability to take action to secure a healthy retirement.

Case Notes

Case Notes are compiled to lay out an officer's case in detail. Case Notes organize everything that they have gathered in an investigation, so it can be put together in their final report. Law enforcement officers (LEOs) can refer back to their notes from interviews, canvasses for video, or witnesses, to re-familiarize themself with what they have learned throughout the investigation and what they need to do next.

Throughout *Living Blue* are **Case Notes** where LEOs, both on the job and retired, share their experiences and suggestions on law enforcement wellness. You will read what a police commissioner, chief of police, assistant chief of police, deputy chief, commander, captain, lieutenant, sergeant, detective, police officer, K9 handler and trainer, and police dispatcher have to say about police stress. Learn about first responder mental health from those who were in the military, FBI, and firefighting. A retired colonel, a fire lieutenant, a former FBI and police hostage negotiation trainer, and a former United States Secret Service agent share ways to build resilience.

Pick up tips to mitigate burnout from police wellness authors, police and public safety trainers, and law enforcement instructors. Gain valuable insight on first responder wellness from a LEO life coach, a transition specialist, a recovery coach, and a transformational life coach. Increase your knowledge about well-being from a psychiatrist, licensed clinical psychologist, suicidologist, family therapist, psychotherapist, grief and trauma specialist, a research professor, and a director of wellness services. To improve overall health, a nutrition specialist and a fitness specialist offer their suggestions.

LORI AAGARD, North Precinct Captain, Seattle Police Department *[pg 177]*

JOHN R. ASHBURN JR., Ph.D, Licensed Clinical Psychologist, Coach and Consultant, LCDR, USN (Retired), Former Director, NYPD Psychological Evaluation Section, Advisory Board member, Forge Health/VFR *[pg 12]*

TIFFANY ATALLA, Director of Clinical Development and Training- First Responder Wellness, Shift Wellness and The Counseling Team International, bestsolutionstherapy.com *[pg 157]*

MEDINA BAUMGART, Psy.D., ABPP, Board Certified in Police and Public Safety Psychology, American Board of Professional Psychology, author, *Surviving Retirement: Finding Purpose and Fulfillment Beyond the Badge [pg 303]*

LISA BERMAN, MD, Psychiatrist, Private Practice and Founder of Inspire Mental Health Services, lisabermanmd.com *[pg 38]*

DIANNE BERNHARD, C.O.P.S. Executive Director, Deputy Chief of Columbia (Retired), Missouri Police Department *[pg 188]*

BARBARA BIGALKE, Founder of the Center for Suicide Awareness *[pg 162]*

GARY A. BOSHEARS, M. P. A., LCC, Chief of Police, Lago Vista Police Department, Texas *[pg 123]*

DR. PAULINE BOSS, Retired Family Therapist, Professor Emerita of Family Social Science at the University of Minnesota, Author, *The Myth of Closure: Ambiguous Loss in a Time of Pandemic and Change* (2022), ambiguousloss.com *[pg 255]*

COMMISSIONER GRAYSON BROSKE, MPA of the Metro Special Police Department Washington, DC *[pg 14]*

DONNA BROWN, Sergeant (Retired), Award-Winning author, *Behind and Beyond the Badge: Stories from the Village of First Responders with Cops, Firefighters, Dispatchers, Forensics, and Victim Advocates [pg 175]*

BRIAN BROWNE, Chief of Police, Laramie Police Department, WY, Father, Husband, Servant *[pg 10]*

CHAD MICHAEL BRUCKNER, Police Life Coach, Army and Police Veteran, Author, *The Holy Trinity of Successful & Healthy Police Organizations: Improving Leadership, Culture & Wellness [pg 119]*

VERA BUMPERS, Chief of Police, Metro Police Department, Houston, Texas *[pg 178]*

ROB CAMPBELL, U.S. Army Colonel (Retired), Author, Speaker, and Leadership Coach, robcampbellleadership.com *[pg 224]*

CHAD CAMPESE, Police Officer, Columbus, Ohio *[pg 51]*

ALEXANDER CASTELLANOS, Police Captain, Miami Florida *[pg 222, 280]*

RYAN M. COLUMBUS, Chief of Police, Tewksbury Police Department, Massachusetts *[pg 121]*

COURTNEY B., Heroes Financial Coaching, heroesfinancialcoaching.com *[pg 309]*

MIKE CRUM, Suicide Interventionist, Marine Corps Veteran, and Violence Prevention Specialist at Fl. Army National Guard *[pg 132]*

DAVID DACHINGER, Fire Lieutenant (Retired), info@responderTV.com *[pg 317]*

TOBY DARBY, Police Captain, City of Glendale, California *[pg 82]*

MAGGIE A. DEBOARD, Chief of Police, Mom, Grandmother and Avid Golfer, President and Co-Founder of the Foundation of First Responder Wellness and Resiliency *[pg 114]*

KAREN DIRIENZO, LICSW, Mental Health Clinician, Burlington Police Department, MA *[pg 84, 306]*

KENNETH J. DOKA, PhD, Senior Vice-President, The Hospice Foundation of America *[pg 256]*

MISTY FIELDS, wholeheartcoachingrenewyourlife.com Grief and Trauma Specialist on LinkedIn, linkedin.com/in/misty-fields-healinggriefandtrauma *[pg 49]*

PATRICK J. FITZGIBBONS, Law Enforcement (Retired), CJEvolution.com *[pg 211]*

JESSICA FLORES, Ten Years Patrol Officer (Retired), Law Enforcement Transition Specialist, Founder of Next Shift, LLC, linktr.ee/next_shift *[pg 308]*

JAMES FLYNN, Recovery Coach *[pg 77]*

JOE FOX, Chief (Retired) NYPD 37 years *[pg 64]*

MICHELE ZANDMAN-FRANKEL AND RANDY FRANKEL, Owners of RevolutioniZe Nutrition, A Nutritional Counseling Company, evolutionizeusa.com *[pg 126]*

MARK L. GAUS, Supervisory Special Agent, FBI (Retired) *[pg 17]*

DAVID GIROUX, Deputy Chief of Police, Commander, Office of Wellness and Safety, Arlington County Virginia Police Department *[pg 314]*

PHIL GOMEZ, Captain, Murrieta Police Department *[pg 25]*

DR. MARK GOULSTON, Psychiatrist, Former FBI and Police Hostage Negotiation Trainer, Author, *Just Listen, and Post-Traumatic Stress Disorder for Dummies,* markgoulston.com *[pg 83]*

NICHOLAS GRECO IV, M.S., B.C.E.T.S., C.A.T.S.M., F.A.A.E.T.S., President and Founder of C3 Education and Research, Inc. *[pg 153]*

SARAH GUENETTE, MA, Trainer, Public Safety Field *[pg 161]*

EVELYN GUTIERREZ, Detective (Retired), NYPD *[pg 169]*

KEN HARKER, Chief of Police in Indiana (Retired, 22 years) *[pg 248]*

JILL A. HARRINGTON, DSW, Creator and Lead Editor, *Superhero Grief [pg 231]*

RAYMOND J. HAYDUCKA, Chief of Police, South Brunswick, New Jersey, 35 Years in Law Enforcement *[pg 117]*

TIMOTHY J. HOOVER, Detective Sergeant, South Brunswick, New Jersey Police Department *[pg 312]*

SAMANTHA HORWITZ, Former United States Secret Service Agent, Co-host, A Badge of Honor Podcast with John Salerno, youtube.com/@ABadgeofHonorPodcast/streams *[pg 281]*

DR. OLIVIA JOHNSON, Founder of Blue Wall Institute *[pg 229]*

JOHN KELLY, Law Enforcement Life Coach, Sergeant (Retired), 30 Year Veteran of Broward County Sheriff's Office, Author, *Surviving Self-Inflicted Wounds: A Deputy's Life of Redemption [pg 209]*

JEFF LADIEU, Captain (Retired), NH State Police, Business Development Manager, Off Duty Management *[pg 319]*

JASON LITCHNEY, Co-Founder of All-Star Talent, allstartalent.us *[pg 17]*

DR. TRISH MAHAN, OTD, MS, OTR/L, CHC, CPC, ELI-MP, CDTS, Registered Occupational Therapist and Transformational Life Coach, youniversalcoaching.com *[pg 277]*

LEAH MARONE, MSW, LCSW, Psychotherapist, leahmarone.com *[pg 133]*

MARLON MARRACHE, Lieutenant LAPD (Retired), Father, Savage Training Group Law Enforcement Instructor, bluconsultinginc.com *[pg 85]*

SHERRI MARTIN, MA, LPCA, National Director of Wellness Services Fraternal Order of Police *[pg 63]*

JON MACASKILL, Navy SEAL Commander (Retired), Founder of Frogman Mindfulness frogmanmindfulness.com *[pg 99]*

SCOTT MEDLIN, Author of *Mental Health Fight of the Heroes in Blue: How to Mentally Survive Working as a Police Officer* *[pg 130]*

BRANDON MEYER, Assistant Chief of Police, Greensburg, Indiana Police Department *[pg 129]*

ADAM A. MEYERS, Founder of Stop the Threat — Stop the Stigma, Former Wisconsin Police Detective, stopthetreatstopthestigma.org *[pg 77]*

EMILY NASH, MA, MFT, Family Coach, Law Enforcement Wellness Specialist, Sergeant's Wife, Groundedme.org, emilynash@groundedme.org *[pg 155]*

ROBERT NEIMEYER, Ph.D., Professor Emeritus at the University of Memphis and currently Director of the Portland Institute for Loss and Transition, portlandinstitute.org *[pg 136]*

NICK PAPROSKI, Director of External Affairs at Connecticut Association of Paramedics and EMTs *[pg 214]*

TIMOTHY PEEK, Deputy Chief, City of Atlanta Police Department *[pg 43]*

MATTHEW PICCOLI, Sergeant, Collier County Sheriff's Office, Florida *[pg 23]*

DR. STEPHEN PORGES, Distinguished University Scientist at Indiana University, stephenporges.com *[pg 46]*

DR. DANIEL REIDENBERG, Psy.D, Managing Director at National Council for Suicide Prevention, Executive Director at SAVE (Suicide Awareness Voices of Education) *[pg 233]*

THOMAS RIZZO, Captain, Author of *COPIKAZE: A Crucible to Manage Mission Impossible [pg 23]*

MIKE ROCHE, Law Enforcement Officer and U.S. Secret Service Agent (Retired), Author of *The Blue Monster [pg 318]*

HERIBERTO RODRIGUEZ, Chief of Police, City of Kempner *[pg 93]*

BONNIE C. RUMILLY, LCSW, EMT-B, Certified EMDR Therapist, and Clinical Director of the Fairfield County Trauma Response Team, Inc *[pg 40]*

JOHN SACCENTI, Served as President of the National Association of Local Boards of Health, Advised the U.S. Surgeon General and the White House on Public Health Policy, Founder and Chief Educator of Career Development Institute, cditraining.org *[pg 18]*

MIKE SCHENTRUP, Captain (Retired), Gainesville, Florida *[pg 307]*

CASSIE SEXTON, Police Dispatcher (Retired), Mindbase Account Executive, getmindbase.com *[pg 120]*

TAMI SHARP, Founder/CEO Law Enforcement Coaching, tami@lawenforcementcoaching.com *[pg 98]*

SHERRI SHEROCK, CHC, CPT, KickSpark Fitness, LLC, linkedin.com/in/sherri-sherock-cfnc-chc-cpt-860b0045 *[pg 48]*

MICHELLE SMALL, Deputy Chief, K9 Handler, Trainer/Instructor at City of Bath, Maine *[pg 219]*

SHAUNA "DOC" SPRINGER, Ph.D., Co-author, *Relentless Courage: Winning the Battle Against Frontline Trauma [pg 220]*

BRANDON STANDLEY, Chief of Police (Retired), Bellefontaine, Ohio Police Department *[pg 304]*

ERNEST STEVENS, Police Officer (Retired), Main Subject Emmy Award winning HBO Documentary, *Ernie and Joe: Crisis Cops*, co-author, *Mental Health & De-escalation: A Guide for Law Enforcement Professionals*, Deputy Division Director, Law Enforcement - The Council of State Governments Justice Center *[pg 213]*

APRIL SWITALA, Sergeant, Bloomfield Township Police Department, Michigan *[pg 176],[pg 313]*

ROSS E. SWOPE, Chief of Police (Retired), Supreme Court of the United States, Author, *Ethics-Based Policing: Solving the Use of Excessive Force [pg 96]*

MIKE TEETER, Captain (Retired), Seattle Police Department, President, Teeter Consulting Group LLC *[pg 80]*

SHAWN THOMAS, Founder of 1st Responder Conferences, Deputy (Retired), King County Sheriff's Office, Seattle, WA, 1strc.org *[pg 44]*

JEFF THOMPSON, Ph.D., Columbia University Medical Center, Department of Psychiatry, NYPD Detective (Retired) *[pg 79]*

CLEE TILMAN, Black & Blue Podcast, youtube.com/@cleetilman9165 *[pg 315]*

MEG TOBIN, LMHC, Licensed Mental Health Counselor, Owner, Breathing Space Psychotherapy, breathingspacepsychotherapy.com *[pg 115]*

ERIC TUNG, Sergeant, Kent Police Department, Peer Support Team Lead, First Responder Wellness IACP 2022 40 Under 40 Honoree, Police 1 Columnist, IG@bluegritwellness *[pg 94]*

JOHN M. VIOLANTI, Ph.D., Research Professor of Epidemiology and Environmental Health, University at Buffalo School of Public Health and Health Professions *[pg 9]*

FRANK VOCE, Founder/President, Reps for Responders, repsforresponders.org *[pg 124]*

DR. VALERIE WOLFE, Lead Psychologist, the Chronic Pain Medicine Department at Kaiser Permanente, Roseville, CA, Private Consulting Business to Improve Sleep, Overall Health and Wellness, drvaleriewolfe.org, drvaleriewolfe@gmail.com *[pg 215]*

DR. TRAVIS YATES, Chief Executive Officer, author of *The Courageous Police Leader: A Survival Guide for Combating Cowards, Chaos, and Lies [pg 320]*

1 | LAW ENFORCEMENT STRESS

DEFINITIONS

MENTAL HEALTH - a state of mind described by emotional well-being, behavioral adjustment, ability to form positive relationships, and cope with life stresses.

WELL-BEING - looking at life in a positive way and thinking that life is going well.

OBJECTIVES

After reading and considering the content of this chapter, the reader should be able to:

- Identify acute and chronic stressors in policing.
- Describe the benefits of stress inoculation.

In My Experience & Lessons Learned

JASON PALAMARA

Detective Jason Palamara—that is who I was for a very long time. As I write this chapter, I reflect on who I am now, out of uniform. At first, when I realized I was no longer a detective, I felt as though I had lost a part of who I was. Now I realize that I did not lose who I was. Rather, I grew into a new version of myself from all I had experienced in my years of service.

1

I was introduced to the NYPD on Tuesday morning, September 11th, 2001. I was in law class waiting to learn the penal law. My instructor told us that he would be right back and that we should remain seated. Although the conversation in the hall was muffled through the door, something was wrong. A few minutes passed before our instructor returned and told us to gather in the hallway so we could report to the auditorium. There was a terrorist attack, and we were getting mobilized to respond. I could only imagine what he would ask us to do and I felt unprepared. I was not ready.

Thinking that this was a training exercise, we went to the auditorium passing every other company doing the same. Once inside the auditorium, my company was met by what looked like everyone inside the building —recruits, instructors, and those who appeared too official for this to be a drill. This is the real thing. The instructor told us that all women and those with children were to stay seated, with everyone remaining to muster outside in the hallway. This directive quickly changed to everyone being told to get ready to be deployed.

I was wearing a recruit cover, had no gun, and in my gray recruit uniform when the realization hit me that this was not a training exercise. Actually, a few officers quit that day. Although feeling unprepared made me anxious, I was excited that I was getting to be a "real cop" so quickly after starting the academy. Soon I was on an MTA city bus lined up outside of the police academy on 20th Street.

We were brought to an intersection by the Midtown Tunnel with our assigned police academy instructor. I was told to direct traffic. I was doing well until I had to direct stressed and traumatized individuals in the street. This authority was thrust upon us recruits without any preparation. Several times, I was yelled at by civilians that I couldn't tell them what to do as I wasn't a *real cop* yet. This was probably why we had been sent out with our instructors.

The following day, I was on a city bus with a fellow recruit to report to Ground Zero. We were to locate the highest-ranking officer, let them know we were recruits from the academy (as if our light gray shirts and McDonald's type covers didn't give us away), and that we were there to assist. I broke my baton holder that morning, so I wrapped the end string around my belt to secure it.

My partner and I weren't standing in front of 1 Liberty Plaza for more than a minute before someone yelled that the building was collapsing. We heard crashing sounds and saw glass falling. Shards of glass and debris were scattered everywhere due to the wind. Instinctively, we all ran. As I ran, the baton now dangling from my belt, hit my knee causing it to swing back up and smack me in the face. This would not be the first time I was physically hurt on the job.

I remember the feeling of eerie calm and acceptance as I ran, believing that I would be crushed from behind at any moment. My partner and I ran a few blocks before reality set in—we were still alive, not beneath a pile of rubble, and if the building had collapsed, we were far enough away to be safe. As we stood catching our breath, a phone rang on the sidewalk beside my feet. I believed that it was a victim's phone. What would I say to the person on the other end? I answered. The voice on the other end said, "You found my phone. Where are you, so I can come get it?" Minutes later, a cop arrived, thanked us, grabbed the phone, and ran off.

I did a lot of running that day. I returned home that night covered in white and gray dust not knowing what I would do the following day. I felt incredibly alone. I was not debriefed at the end of the day. No one spoke to me about how to process my experience. I wasn't prepared for the reality of what was to come. I have never discussed any of my 9/11 experiences until recently. I now realize that not being prepared and destructive coping, such as drinking, can impact job satisfaction whether you are a recruit or a cop ready for retirement.

We can do far more to help law enforcement officers (LEOs) by addressing the sources of their mental and emotional stressors as they occur before they become problems, rather than by trying to fix a growing problem of suicide. We need to encourage more officers to ask for help when they believe they need it. We don't often know we need help until emotional and mental damage to ourselves and our families has been inflicted. It may be more beneficial to state how we should prepare our new recruits for the blue life as "inoculation." This preparation or inoculation of sorts would give our new officers the education they will assuredly lean on as they grow up cop.

I recall a hot summer afternoon towards the end of my day tour. My partner, Kevin, and I were standing in front of the precinct when a 10-85 came over the radio. A 10-85 is a call for assistance "forthwith" right before it changes to a 10-13 officer needs assistance. Without hesitation, Kevin, myself, and every officer hearing the call for help proceeded to run to the location a short distance away.

While running, I was hurtled back to the trauma of 9/11. I realized that my life was at risk every time I secured my vest. So I looked to the senior officers doing this work as an example of navigating this intense new world. But if I had received stress inoculation training I would have learned how to manage the job's physical and mental hazards.

At the scene, we entered the housing development and joined other officers who had already arrived. The elevator was not working, and the call for help was coming from the top floor. Adrenaline pumping, we ran up the stairs. Soon my legs began to feel like rubber, and my feet like weights. After having ran to the building and up the stairs, I was spent. Eventually the rest of the responding officers and I arrived at the top floor. Although tired from the workout, I was thankful that I was there to assist. It all ended well. The officers who had been affecting an arrest, and everyone who responded, were safe.

I wasn't a runner before that day, but I was after it. I needed to focus on my physical endurance and put in the work if I hoped to do something like that ever again. I needed to make changes in my physical health to be better prepared. Not consciously realizing that I was doing it at the time, I decided throughout my career to make what I call "positive progress from pain" by being prepared. The preparation began with developing a flexible mindset from my previously fixed mindset regarding my health, which made me a better officer.

After a year I left uniformed patrol and worked in what was known as the "Conditions Team," before transitioning to the "Crime Team." We wore civilian clothes to fit in and were tasked with making felony arrests. Like the rest of those in "crime", I wore jeans and boots. Wearing boots was not conducive to running long distances. You'd think I would have learned this in my experience of running from the shattered glass during 9/11 and running toward several scenes in my career.

Being in good physical condition was not the end of the lesson. I had to learn how to equip myself with options while adapting and adjusting to the situation, like the time when I was face to face with a robbery suspect who tested my new Timberlands. As I gave chase, the distance between the suspect and I grew. My rubber legs and lead feet returned. My colleagues, who had started their day better prepared than I, arrived in a police van after I called for help over the radio while I was running. I got in front of the suspect and stopped him.

It is important to recognize when we need to lean on others. I also learned a valuable lesson in what it meant to be prepared—sneakers are the way to go.

The life-threatening experience of running after a robber can become a traumatic event. It's not a stretch to say that post-traumatic stress is a real component of our work. Stress and trauma can impact our mental health. We must give that name to what we experience daily if for no other reason than to collectively identify our problem as something recognizable to the mental health community—where there are well-documented unhealthy and healthy coping mechanisms.

Although confidentiality and trust are paramount to officers, they need to trust that seeking help for mental health due to stress and trauma will not be met punitively, and will not negatively affect their career path. For many years this was the norm rather than the exception. Asking for much needed help too often comes with consequences. And where there is focus on sought-after help, it should go beyond mere prevention. Departments need do better while screening new recruits as they process into the ranks of law enforcement. And the responsibility to equip new officers with what they need falls on leadership.

Like a vaccine, educating new officers may not prevent them from getting infected but may mitigate their symptoms should they become ill. We must focus on our LEOs to reduce maladaptive coping as they begin their careers. Recognizing the effects of the trauma an officer will experience as the trauma unfolds will mitigate its hold on the officer. The familiarity and knowledge of what to expect as a result of a traumatic experience can help them choose different ways to cope than the maladaptive coping skills that have become all too common for too long.

Soon after arriving at my first command with the 84th Precinct in Brooklyn, all the new officers fresh out of the police academy were required to undergo brief training from the sergeant about operations. We were told about the residents inside one housing development within our confines.

"Most of the people are good people," she told us. "You will encounter the criminal element that is the minority."

It was a delicate balance between encountering the worst of society and the very best among those who lived there who found themselves swallowed up by all its bad. When crime and despair drown out all that is good, it becomes hard to see the positive, in and outside of work. The lens through which I viewed things became coated in a film of negativity that got thicker over the years.

Later in my career I worked on a difficult case where a teenage girl—Chanel—was found thrown out to the curb as trash, strangled and discarded as if her life meant nothing. I worked on this case every day for years with my partner, Detective Evelin Gutierrez. It ultimately resulted in a positive conclusion. For years, it was difficult for me to manage my emotions when I thought about Chanel. I felt lost within a shell of my old self. I thought about my daughter who was about the same age as the victim. Whenever I looked at the victim's photo, I saw my daughter, which created a need to protect her and my family even more.

Rookie cops focus on learning the job and fitting into a culture that can be intimidating to someone who likely just left years of formal education. The culture curates the persona we adopt to help us satisfy the demands of our new environment. This new persona may conflict with the type of person we were when we entered the job. It may compliment, replace, or damage it, but will assuredly play its part in altering it.

As a detective investigating homicides in the Cold Case Homicide Squad, I looked back on the victim's life and analyzed evidence collected and reviewed past interviews. I saw things from a detached perspective, which gave me a greater chance of success in solving the case. It would be convenient to get in front of things before they occur or, even better, as they unfolded. This was not possible years after a murder had already occurred. However, this is possible when it concerns our mental health and well-being. I found out the hard way that recognizing what I was experiencing gave me a leg up in stopping it from spiraling out of control.

When I became a LEO, I knew nothing about secondary or vicarious trauma, or moral distress, I had not heard those words until two years before retirement while going through peer support and crisis intervention counselor training. The anger I had at times, along with the constant worry about something terrible happening in my life, was me experiencing vicarious trauma. I thought there was something wrong with me. I ran on autopilot and couldn't handle things well.

I never correlated my well-being with work. I found it hard to put the puzzle pieces in their place. I entered this profession as a sponge, absorbing everything I saw and heard from those who walked this path before me. Although it was an intimidating environment, I tried to fit in and learn a tough job under challenging circumstances.

The culture that protects our protectors can do more damage than good. While on the job, we learn to protect our own and keep everything "in house." Whether due to a lack of trust or the belief that no one outside this sacred LEO circle could understand what we are dealing with, we are reluctant to seek professional help or want guidance from anyone who is not a first responder. The flip side to this approach can perpetuate a culture of, "I got this. I'm good." I didn't think about what my quality of life was like for my wife, children, and those on this LEO journey with me. I never paused to be mindful of my overall health.

This mindset that we are the protectors and are there for those that call us for help, and not the other way around, needs to change. The shift started once I questioned and challenged the status quo. Gone are the days where uttering the words "mental health" labels you what we call in the NYPD an EDP or Emotionally Disturbed Person. After 20 years of service, I realized that stress, trauma, empathic distress, moral injury, police culture, and family life impact an officer's well-being.

When you take your first steps through the academy doors, you are provided tools for your mental health "gun belt". If you are a recruit, with the knowledge gained at the academy and the information provided in this book, you will be better prepared, increase your chances of having a successful career, and have a healthy and sustainable family and personal life.

To be a first responder is to be selfless. You place yourself in harm's way and endure what most would do everything they could to avoid. You run towards danger, passing others looking for the very safety you provide. What I hope you glean from this book is the thought that maybe this applies to your safety and well-being, and that you can be the protector of others as well as yourself.

My Story & Evidence-Based Practices

BARBARA RUBEL

"Starting in the academy, incoming police officers should be trained in what trauma looks like and how to respond to it if they see it in themselves, coworkers, or community members. Training should not touch on just the obvious signs but the thousands of subtle cues that may be missed along the way, leading a once stellar officer to get involved in a serious internal affairs investigation. This education should continue throughout officers' careers and include training on how they talk to each other and to the community about their trauma."

—Cathy Bustos, "Police Chief Online

Growing up in Brooklyn, NY, I was the daughter of LEOs. My father was a Sergeant and my mother worked in the Youth Aid Division finding shelter for children whose parents were unable to care for them. This type of assignment was given to women in the 1950s–1970s to keep them from confrontations with a criminal. It's hard to imagine how much the world has changed today when we realize a few short decades ago, this was normal practice.

If you had asked me, as a child, what it meant to be a daughter of two police officers, I would have said, "Proud." I learned from an early age what it means to be a "Blue Family." Reliving the events of my life as I collaborated with Jason in writing *Living Blue* has helped me to realize the incredible gifts my childhood gave me, growing up with two parents dedicated to their community.

On September 11, 2001, somewhat ironically, I started my first day as a bereavement coordinator for Hospice. At 9am, I introduced myself to the nursing director only to be told to go home. A plane had hit a building in New York. Figuring it would probably be fine by tomorrow, she said she would prefer it if I started my job the next day. I drove home disappointed that I would not be meeting my patients that day. I was also teaching a master's level evening course, Health Crisis, at Brooklyn College. I kept asking myself, how do I teach a class about crisis when we were all living in the middle of one?

Jason was dealing with his own crisis. Could police academy basic recruit training prepare Jason, a 22-year-old rookie cop, for what happened on 9/11? For Jason, this real-world police encounter was a traumatic experience. Healing from trauma is promoted when mental health professionals provide early treatment regimens to increase resilience and promote recovery (Franco, 2022). Jason did not get help, was not debriefed, and did not understand healthy ways to promote recovery from the trauma-related stress.

Law Enforcement Stress

Stress is a risk factor for the development of depression (Zheng, 2022). Stress causes mental strain and can make an officer and civilian staff feel unsafe. Hans Selye, founder of the stress theory, notes, "It's not stress that kills us, it's our reaction to it." Law enforcement stress response refers to a series of abnormal psychological, physiological, and behavioral responses (e.g., gastrointestinal discomfort, nervous tension, irritability) due to excessive pressure (Chen et al., 2022).

A review of the literature has revealed that law enforcement personnel frequently experience moments of extreme occupational stress (Greco et al., 2018). However, research on officers, one of the highest-stress occupations, is still lacking despite the expanding body of literature on interventions for high-stress populations like the military and medical professionals (Christopher et al., 2020).

CASE NOTES

John M. Violanti, Ph.D., notes, "While research portrays a rather dim view of police organizations and officer stress, there can be another side to the story. The organization may reduce stress on police officers by virtue of its support and establishment of coherence. A positive oriented paradigm on organizational psychology directly applies to policing, and the influence of the police organization on individual officers may be beneficial under this philosophy.

"The police organization has the capacity to enhance resilience to stress by taking a positive stance toward officers instead of punishment-centered bureaucratic policies. Police organizations can change the course of individual reaction from stress maladaptation to stress adaptation. A policy of social cohesion—instead of separate agendas—among officers and the organization could act to cognitively nullify the stressful experience" *(J. M. Violanti, personal communication, May 9, 2023).*

Contributors to Stress in Law Enforcement

Leading causes of LEO stress are financial problems, poor relationships with a supervisor, witnessing a fatality, unfair promotional opportunities, and a line of duty death (LODD) (Ermasova et al., 2020). Stress is due to constant exposure to violence, abuse, neglect, death, and personal injury, such as confronting a person with a gun or weapon, responding to a murder, being seriously injured on duty, conducting a death notification, or being involved in a high speed pursuit. Officers can experience fatigue from longer shifts, overtime, volatile situations, social media, perceived lack of organizational justice, or internal bias related to gender.

According to the Harris Poll (2022) most Americans (57%) believe that when people talk freely about their mental health, they are brave, and rarely see the conversation as awkward (8%), overly personal (7%), or like they are complaining (6%). Although most people talk about mental health, that is not the case for LEOs. They do not want to be perceived as weak for asking for mental health support and are reluctant to seek out services (Karaffa & Tochkov, 2013). So, leaders must provide tools and strategies to improve their mental health from day one.

CASE NOTES

Brian Browne, Laramie Police Department, WY, Chief of Police, father, husband, servant, notes, "For far too long law enforcement leaders have failed to address employee wellness. We owe it to our officers and their families to talk about the stress and trauma associated with serving our communities. As leaders, we have to provide the tools to improve mental, physical, and emotional health, we have to do better!" *(B. Browne, personal communication, May 16, 2023)* .

The National Wellness Survey for Public Safety Personnel Summary Report (2022) found that common stressors for sworn law enforcement are concerns about COVID-19, negative attitudes from the public about their profession, government officials outside of the agency not understanding what they deal with, responding to critical incidents, and negative media about the profession. Other issues that can influence an officer's stress levels are:

- Organizational practices (e.g., bureaucracy).
- Work schedules (e.g., long work hours, shiftwork, night shift, excessive overtime).
- Potential dangers (e.g., dangerous job risks, violent confrontations with the public, possibility of being injured).
- Trauma (e.g., the body's experience after a critical incident, serious accident, exposure to suffering).
- Co-worker relations (e.g., lack of peer support, fellow officers not doing their job).
- Poor management (e.g., supervisor's discipline style, workplace discrimination, being second guessed, frequent criticism, sexual harassment, lack recognition, denials of requested days off, confidentiality).
- Criminal justice system practices (e.g., unfavorable court decisions).
- Work-family conflict (e.g., marital difficulties, single parent, absence from family functions, disrupted family life, family feels stigma, last minute plan cancellation, second job, events related to work on days off).
- Emotions (e.g., fearful of the worst happening, feel like they are always on the job, inadequate outside of police work).
- Personal issues (e.g., financial problems, unhealthy coping, sleep issues).
- Adverse Childhood Experiences (ACEs) not managed that may impact one's current state.
- Community (e.g., neighbors ask about active investigations, anxious about civilians seeing them in a treatment facility).
- Negative public practices (e.g., calls for defunding the police, negative media coverage).

Safety personnel reported a desire to leave the profession or would not recommend the profession to others. They expressed the work environment, public perception, and management challenges as equally, if not more, problematic than exposure to trauma. The National Wellness Survey for Public Safety Personnel Summary Report (2022) found coping mechanisms moderately associated with depression, anxiety, and PTSD include comfort/stress eating, followed by drinking to numb the pain/stress, using prescription medication to feel better, escaping through television or streaming services, and engaging in unhealthy sexual behavior.

One powerful way to get the most out of this book is to answer the **Law Enforcement Consideration & Personal Insight** questions. Here is the first one:

LAW ENFORCEMENT CONSIDERATION & PERSONAL INSIGHT

Now that you have reviewed the list of issues that can influence stress levels, what has your attention? Have you defined the problem, thought about ways to manage it and evaluated solutions? Or are you complaining, drinking too much and isolating yourself?

If you are a LEO, consider getting a check-up, taking a class on stress management, or getting peer support. If you are a leader, update your agency policies on wellness and identify best practices programs on safety and wellness. If you are a mental health professional, make sure that you are qualified to support LEOs and understand their job-related stressors, the mutual ways that they deal with them, and interventions that work.

CASE NOTES

John R. Ashburn Jr., Ph.D., Licensed Clinical Psychologist, Coach and Consultant, LCDR, USN (Retired), Former Director, NYPD Psychological Evaluation Section, Advisory Board member, Forge Health/VFR, notes, "Today our law enforcement officers are tasked with a seemingly endless (and often competing) range of responsibilities: from social worker to arresting agent, from user of deadly force to EMS provider, all while being under an unprecedented level of scrutiny by the public they're sworn to protect.

"Every year more law enforcement officers die by suicide than die in the line of duty. At the NYPD we found that officer suicides were the result of a wide range of contributing factors, however, these included a dynamic mix of general factors (e.g., occupational stress) combined with specific factors (e.g., seniority, relationship issues).

"Officer wellness programs, referral services, and peer support programs are necessary but not sufficient—we must move past a check-the-box mentality and move towards a comprehensive and integrated set of policies that address officer suicide starting at the training academy, cascading and embedding into day to day operations, and extending from the officer on the beat to the top leadership of the department" *(J.R. Ashburn, personal communication, August 18, 2023).*

Acute Stress

Administration cultural attitudes and civilians in the community are consistent predictors of officer well-being (Patterson & King, 2023). Acute stress, a fleeting emotional or physical response immediately felt after a stressful event, can impact well-being. The most common type of stress is acute stress or short-term stress. A clinician may diagnose an officer with acute stress disorder, a psychiatric diagnosis due to an intense reaction (e.g., intrusive memories, difficulty concentrating) to an overwhelming event (e.g., car crash with child victim) with symptoms lasting from three days to one month after exposure.

Officers feel stress when they respond to a scene where there is use of force, a weapon present, they avoid a car accident, or when call priority is urgent (Anderson et al., 2019). It is stressful to be the first professional who interacts with victims of commercial sexual trafficking (Kenny et al, 2023). Also, it is stressful to serve a warrant, respond to someone suffering, perform a death notification, or respond to a medical emergency. Also, it is stressful to respond to an overdose call and administer naloxone to an opioid user to save their life (Smiley-McDonald et al., 2022).

CASE NOTES

Commissioner Grayson Broske, MPA of the Metro Special Police Department Washington, DC, notes, "In any organization, especially police departments, it functions similarly to a living organism whereby the Chief Executive Officer (CEO) has a top-down fiduciary responsibility to everyone in the organization. If the CEO (head of the organization) does not take care of the hands and the feet that are responsible for the day-to-day operations, then the rest of the organism could perish.

"This is no different in a police department. Members of law enforcement are exposed to a verity of trauma on the job that impacts the organization (fatal car accidents, missing persons, murders, rapes, robberies, officer involved shootings, suicides, etc.). The Chief of Police and command staff must ensure that they are taking care of their officer's physical well-being as well as their emotional well-being so that the organization does not suffer and impact police services to the community" *(G. Broske, personal communication, July 8, 2023).*

Acute Stress Symptoms

Acute stress symptoms can happen minutes or even hours after an event. Although symptom onset occurs quickly, symptoms don't last long, usually ending hours after the event, though they can last 3 to 30 days. Symptoms can include uncontrolled anger, irritability, elevated heart rate, difficulty breathing, sweating, chest pain, headache, neck pain, stomach pain, jaw pain, nausea, and feeling numb. Acute stress can become episodic acute stress due to the frequency of symptoms. Symptoms may be due to daily unreasonable demands or not having the resources to get the job done.

Chronic Stress

When officers and civilian staff have financial problems or an unhappy marriage, they may be on autopilot and not realize that they are dealing with chronic stress. Although acute stress goes away quickly, that is not the case with chronic stress. Continued stressors common in law enforcement, have a significant impact on mental health (Daniel & Treece, 2022).

Chronic stress is everyday unending stress such as dangerous situations, injuries, violence, and having to report about psychologically stressful scenes (Jackman et al., 2020).

Chronic Stress Symptoms

Symptoms linked to chronic stress include cardiovascular disease (e.g., high blood pressure, heart attack, stroke), feeling inadequate to do the job well, absenteeism, turnover, alcohol abuse, sleep disorders, post-traumatic stress, cancer, and suicide. Although symptoms and negative consequences impact an officer's life, they under-utilize stress intervention (Tucker, 2015). Instead, they drink and self-medicate, which are unhelpful coping mechanisms that lead to problems on and off the job (Redman, 2018). Consequently, these coping mechanisms can lead to intense anxiety.

> **LAW ENFORCEMENT CONSIDERATION & PERSONAL INSIGHT**
>
> In what way does your personality have something to do with your ability to manage stress?

Acute Stress and Chronic Stress Can Lead to Anxiety

Anxiety can be described as feeling tension, and worry. The payoff of worrying excessively is feeling tired, shaky, having palpitations, and constantly being on edge. When anxiety does not go away, it becomes an anxiety disorder, a medical diagnosis where symptoms interfere with daily activities, job performance, and relationships (NIMH, 2022). Always under pressure? Personalities that are more competitive, abrupt, and aggressive may experience episodic acute stress more than those who do not have that personality type.

Trauma

Psychological trauma is an emotional response to an extremely negative event (e.g., life-threatening danger, injury, abuse, witnessing a death, LODD) that is now part of one's sensory memory, and needs to be processed and integrated. (Laura, et al., 2016). When a traumatic event occurs, the nervous system responds and attempts to regulate itself. "Individual trauma results from an event, series of events, or set of circumstances that is experienced by an individual as physically or emotionally harmful or life threatening and that has lasting adverse effects on the individual's functioning and mental, physical, social, emotional, or spiritual well-being" (SAMHSA, 2014, p. 7).

Cumulative Career Traumatic Stress

Cumulative trauma due to multiple traumas can range from being on the scene after a single incident (e.g., car crash), repeated and prolonged exposure (e.g., child abuse) or varied and multiple events. The more traumatic incidents experienced, the more likely another event may tip the balance, and even resilient officers may find recovery harder after yet another stressful incident (Laura et al., 2016).

Post-traumatic Stress

Post-traumatic Stress Disorder (PTSD) is a trauma- and stressor-related disorder that usually develops within three months and is diagnosed by a licensed medical or mental health professional. PTSD occurs after experiencing or witnessing a trauma, series of events, or set of circumstances (American Psychiatric Association, 2022). Statistics indicate that 7–8% of those in the general population will develop PTSD. Although there's a lot of talk about PTSD among officers, the numbers are relatively low. Rates of PTSD in law enforcement range 7% to 19% (National Police Support Fund, 2019; Stevelink et al., 2020).

Age, length of service, number of traumatic incidents, social status, and toughness are predictors of developing PTSD. Symptoms include nightmares, flashbacks, anxiety, and uncontrollable thoughts about the event. Symptoms occur for at least one month with at least one re-experiencing symptom, one avoidance symptom, two arousal and reactivity symptoms, and two cognition and mood symptoms (National Institute of Mental Health, 2022a). A study found that support of intimate partners and coworkers predicted lower PTSD symptoms in police officers above cognitive emotion coping strategies (Nero & colleagues, 2022).

CASE NOTES

Mark L. Gaus, Supervisory Special Agent, FBI (Retired), notes, "Strong law enforcement leadership promoting mental health wellness and creating a culture that demonstrates it will be the most effective way to overcome the stigma associated with asking for help. In May, I was rated 80% service connected disability from the VA and 50% of that rating is PTSD. The statistics of harm that come from continuous exposure to trauma and a high stress environment are undeniable and a call to action to take proactive measure to protect the mental health of the law enforcement and first responder community" *(M.L. Gaus, personal communication, October 2, 2023).*

Recruitment and Training

In November 2023, the U.S. Department of Justice awarded over $216 million through the COPS Hiring Program which will put more than 1,700 new police officers in communities across the country. These grants go to nearly 400 police departments to help them hire more officers.

A survey of 4,100 LEOs found the most adverse impacts to recruiting officers were media coverage, lack of police administrator support, legal attacks on qualified immunity, and police reform legislation (Harrison, 2023). Although agencies have recruitment videos, attend job fairs, use social media and offer signing bonuses, 55% of 4,100 respondents in the police study on recruitment noted that these initiatives did not improve recruitment (Harrison, 2023). In particular, Chapter 8 focuses on recruiting women in policing.

CASE NOTES

Jason Litchney, Co-founder of All-Star Talent, notes, "5 best kept secrets in law enforcement recruitment marketing are:

1. **VALUE PROPOSITION:** know what attracted your current officers to your agency. Use survey tools to keep on top of the attract/keep

metrics. Build marketing messaging, imagery and taglines that reso-
nate with your ideal workforce.

2. **KNOW YOUR NUMBERS:** calculate how many applications you will
    need to net the required hires and how much that will cost with the
    current methodology.

3. **MEASURE EVERYTHING:** key performance indicators are the first step
    to building campaigns. Get funding to drive candidates into your
    pipeline. For each dollar spent, track what you received for that dollar.
    Leverage UTM codes in digital marketing. Build a website that cap-
    tures that information. Does your Lateral Officer Facebook Instagram
    campaign perform better than the Nationwide Lateral Officer Goo-
    gle Campaign? What was the cost per application and hire for each
    campaign?

4. **CANDIDATE EXPERIENCE:** ask someone that has no idea about applying
    for a career in law enforcement to 'secret shop' your application pro-
    cess. Do the steps needed to apply make sense to them? Leverage text
    messaging, emails, and automated systems to decrease workloads to
    your recruitment staff while increasing candidate experience.

5. **GET ACTIVE:** set an advertising budget to use on paid sources to amplify
    your message across your target market" (*J. Litchney, personal com-
    munication, September 4, 2023*).

Police training teaches recruits the skills that prepare them to confront a
stressful event, as they experience a stressful event, or in the aftermath of a
stressful event (van der Meulen et al., 2018). The aim is to acquire policing
skills (e.g., physical capabilities, mental resiliency), while focusing on psychological safety and effectively coping with the operational challenges (Di
Nota & Huhta, 2019). Academy training is enhanced with curricula that
builds skills related to empathy, respect, and understanding in police-community interactions (Helfgott et al., 2022).

CASE NOTES

John C. Saccenti developed and wrote all Basic Law Enforcement Training
for the Police Training Commission in the New Jersey Division of Criminal Justice, including the Basic Course for Investigators. He redesigned
and wrote the Basic Course for Police Officers and other major basic and
advanced law enforcement courses. Mr. Saccenti notes, "The preparation

for the stress of being a police officer begins in the selection process. Police officer candidates should undergo both a written and interpersonal psychological assessment by a trained experienced officer. During that interview process, the full extent of the stressors of the profession and the resources available should be discussed. A frank discussion on the personal impact these stressors may have and assurances that many officers have used these resources available in the agency to address them.

"The next intervention for new officers comes at the Academy. All police departments in a state should have a uniform training program mandated through all academies in the state. Complete blocks of instruction dealing with such issues as self-destructive behavior, suicide ideation, marital stress, emotional and physiological impacts of shift work, and the emotional and psychological impact of dealing with the potential carnage they will experience from violent crime and vehicle crashes. Instruction should stress the fact that there is no shame in identifying the adverse impact of these stressors and seeking assistance in dealing with them, but rather recognizing and seeking help is what a true professional does.

"Almost all of our 15 Police Training Commission approved academies in New Jersey train recruits from multiple employing agencies. Therefore, an academy handling officers from multiple agencies cannot address the details of each agency. Such items as agency policies, resources, geographic boundaries are obvious items that must be addressed at the agency level. It is crucial that the agency address the local mental health resources available through the employing agency. If the class is for a single agency this should be covered at the academy. Information relating to mental health, stress, and resources should be testable items and treated with the same gravitas as any other component of the training.

"The next key person in the training process is the field training officer assigned to a rookie to facilitate their transition to the job. A field training officer must be trained on the many aspects of the work, including identifying concerning behavior, counseling a rookie on resources, assuring the officer that they are part of a team, and that help is available if needed. The final support should be a mandatory in-service program reinforcing the warning signs of depression and other emotional and mental health issues on at least an annual basis. This can be handled though roll-call trainings or a separate seminar. Resources available to the officer should also be covered again" *(J. Saccenti, personal communication, May 2, 2023).*

Locus of Control

Classroom and practical training can focus on locus of control, which is the perception of control individuals have over events and outcomes in their environment (Rotter, 1966). Studying for my BS in psychology, I learned about Julian Rotter's studies on locus of control. The first day of class, my teacher asked me if I was going to get an A. I answered, "Yes." Several students answered, "Probably not."

I questioned why they would not believe that they would do well. With an external locus of control, behavior is based on the perception that life outcomes are out of their control. By contrast, I have an internal locus of control and behave based on my internal state. Life outcomes are caused by my actions. I would study and not focus on circumstances outside of my control that would prevent me from doing well. If I didn't study, I would control my own failure.

Testing

Preemployment psychological testing is a tool for recognizing a recruit's personality, attitude, behavioral concerns, and psychopathology (Ellingwood et al., 2018). Although there is no consistency in psychological assessments and tests were not developed using police samples, frequently administered tests are the Minnesota Multiphasic Personality Inventory–2 Restructured Form (MMPI–2–RF), California Psychological inventory (CPI), and the Sixteen Personality Factor Questionnaire (16PF) (Ellingwood et al., 2018). Although individuals who pass the test enter the academy and receive mental strength training, they may have no clue as to how they will handle an event when it happens and not be in control.

As a recruit, Jason went through a hiring process that spanned months. After the application, he completed a personal history questionnaire, a physical abilities test, had a psychological evaluation, and a medical exam. In the academy, he studied history of law enforcement, the criminal justice system, police community relations, the law, communications, vehicle operations, emergency medical care, weaponry, patrol concepts, traffic, criminal investigations, and physical fitness (Police Training Commission, 2022).

Jason's academy classes were behavioral and police science, law, and gym. He also needed classes on managing vicarious trauma (VT), which would have inoculated him from the stressors of the job. As described in chapter 6, VT is defined as adverse changes that occur over time in LEOs when they interact with the suffering and needs of victims and others in the community.

Stress Inoculation

Teaching recruits about stress inoculation and possible challenges that they may face as well as how to manage those stressors before they happen, may mitigate the impact of VT. Although they have a belief of self-efficacy while at the academy, that means little in a stressful event if they are not prepared. Stress inoculation can prepare them for the traumatic situations that lie ahead. A vaccine is an inoculation that benefits the immune system, so it fights off an infection. Like an inoculation prevents against the attack of disease, stress inoculation can prepare the body for an attack of stress.

Fifty years ago, Donald Meichenbaum coined the term, stress inoculation, which is to recognize ways to cope with possible high stress situations. This non-trauma-focused anxiety management program teaches strategies to practice coping skills to manage possible stressors (Meichenbaum, 1974; Meichenbaum & Deffenbacher, 1988).

Stress inoculation training involves keeping track of stress levels and learning problem-solving strategies and coping skills by practicing each skill (U.S. Dept. of Veteran Affairs, 2022). Stress inoculation training teaches recruits in a group setting about the stress response and healthy ways to manage it. It allows recruits to practice newly learned skills inoculating them from stress and trauma that may plague them at certain points in their career.

Stress inoculation training in advance, helps the recruit identify potential traumatic situations they might encounter through imagery and skills training. Stress inoculation training mentally protects them against possible traumatic incidents and builds their confidence as they practice and figure out ways to manage their symptoms. It also teaches coping skills to manage anger-control problems or aggressive behaviors, so the person could be able to manage future job-related trauma and stressors (Meichenbaum, 2007).

In a controlled environment, a police instructor engages a group of recruits by using an interactive stressful or traumatic narrative or video that prompts an emotional reaction. After the traumatic story or video, recruits talk about possible symptoms and ways to cope. This behavioral rehearsal guides them through a real-life scenario, so they can practice what they have learned. Pararescue and combat control already use strategies during stress inoculation training to ensure that they perform well under stress (Robson & Manacapilli, 2014).

Instructors educate them about the stress response, provide behavioral and cognitive skills training (e.g., attention, control), and give opportunities to practice skills under likely stressors (Robson & Manacapilli, 2014). Screening strategies predict battlefield airmen who will have a higher probability of succeeding or be unable to perform in stressful settings. An internal locus of control and being inoculated could possibly help to self-regulate when they are faced with trauma.

> **LAW ENFORCEMENT CONSIDERATION & PERSONAL INSIGHT**
>
> Would stress inoculation have benefited you as a recruit and influenced how you currently manage stress?

Health and Wellness Awareness

At the academy, recruits may not have realized that they:

- Should start taking care of their mental health early on in their career so they retire in a healthier place.
- May struggle with depression at a point in their career.
- Could experience a worsening drinking problem if they already have an unhealthy relationship with alcohol, and their brothers and sisters who are struggling with alcohol use may enable them.
- Might possibly have a substance use problem due to Adverse Childhood Experiences (ACEs) that were never addressed.

- May have a peer who will turn a blind eye to what they see them doing because they think that they are protecting them.
- Most likely will have issues with insomnia due to irregular schedules, shift work, and exposure to trauma.
- May have martial/couple issues due to rotating shifts.
- May experience a moral injury if they commit, witness, or fail to prevent something that goes against their morals.

CASE NOTES

Sergeant Matthew Piccoli, Collier County Sheriff's Office, notes, "As a member of law enforcement, I understand the demands of the job and how mentally taxing it can be. Since the field of law enforcement is extremely demanding and dangerous, I believe high ranking members within the organizational structure need to eliminate mundane mandatory training and introduce a human element to their strict policies to improve morale. Leaders within law enforcement agencies need to remember that police officers are human. For example, many leaders say their officers come first, but these are the same officers working 60 hour weeks to cover short staffing. Do you really care about your officers?" *(M. Piccoli, personal communication, June 8, 2023).*

Philosophers have been studying humans for centuries. We know that humans act humanely as they focus on their best attributes, are self-compassionate and kind to others. Being humane creates a strong foundation for officer well-being.

CASE NOTES

Captain Thomas Rizzo, author of *COPIKAZE: A crucible to manage mission impossible*, notes, "Real resiliency needs to be nurtured within the four walls of an agency before we obsess over the doings within the four corners of our jurisdictions. When administrative ambushes, squad sabotage, and blue/blue bashing remains as the abundance of soil, you cannot be surprised when it bears a bounty of rotten relationships.

"The most amazing buildings will inevitably crumble if they are built upon stilts. Reinforce the foundation of being humane over human WITHIN the building, so that the foundation serves as a viable shelter for what will be encountered outside of the building. That's how you build a BOLD line of resilience over a blurred blue line built to fail" *(T. Rizzo, personal communication, January 12, 2023).*

Mental Health and Well-Being

Well-being is defined as people thinking that their lives are going well (Centers for Disease Control and Prevention [CDC], 2018), and is the balance-point between personal resources and life challenges (Rachele et al., 2013). To change police culture, proactive and ongoing mental health care practices need to focus on psychological equilibrium of officers so they feel balanced (Craddock & Telesco, 2022).

Mental health, an integral component of health and well-being, is a state of mental well-being that allows individuals to cope with stressors, recognize their abilities, learn, and work well, and contribute to their community (World Health Association, 2022). Feeling healthy and full of energy is considered essential to well-being (CDC, 2018).

Life stressors, no matter the occupation, have an impact on well-being (Hill et al., 2018). Command staff and supervisors expect the rise of police leaving the force due to unfavorable public perceptions, low recruitment rates, a lack of mentorship, and defunding of police (Axtell et al., 2022), all of which will impact well-being. When LEOs become discouraged, they may sabotage recruitment, and use messages that indicate that anyone thinking of a career in law enforcement should stay away from policing and look for other opportunities, as it ruins good people and one's faith in humanity (Scheer, 2023).

Given the dearth of research with LEOs and well-being, we can gain insight by looking at studies of healthcare workers as both fields serve the public. For example, factors associated with burnout in healthcare workers that impact well-being are mental health stigma, lack of leadership support, excessive workload and work hours, disconnect between values and key decisions, barriers to mental health and substance use care, lack of culture of collaboration, and vulnerability (Murthy, 2022). Undoubtedly, some of the same factors are present in LEOs.

LAW ENFORCEMENT CONSIDERATION & PERSONAL INSIGHT

Using a scale from 1 (poor) to 5 (well), how would you rate your mental health?

Work-Life Balance

Work schedules impact work-life balance, the ability to recover between shifts, and the ability to maintain a healthy lifestyle, all of which directly attributes to poor health (Poirier et al., 2023). Meaning of the work, and family-work enrichment, can protect employees from the harmful effects of police work while improving their well-being (López-Cabarcos et al., 2023). Overall, organizations should focus on a reasonable workload, and give particular attention to working hours as it affects stress levels and family life (Dodanwala et al., 2022).

CASE NOTES

Captain Phil Gomez, Murrieta Police department, father and husband, notes, "As a 28-year veteran of law enforcement, I believe all first responders need to realize that it is not a matter of 'IF' this career will have a dramatic impact on your mental well-being, it is a matter of 'WHEN' will this career have a dramatic impact on your mental well-being. The faster you accept this fact, the faster you can take proactive steps to protect yourself and those you love. I am currently dealing with my own mental challenges as a result of a very active career. I have personally benefitted from EMDR for dealing with specific incident traumas. I am also benefitting from Neurofeedback Therapy. This is truly a game changer and has made a dramatic difference in my overall mental and physical well-being. This treatment is not very well known in law enforcement, I encourage you to research it if you are not very familiar. My counselor recommended it to me. It is amazing and I truly believe it has saved my life" *(P. Gomez, personal communication, March 12, 2023)*.

THE NEXT STEP

This chapter boosted your awareness of the impact of stress on well-being. In Chapter 2, you will increase your knowledge about the possible impact of ACEs on wellness. Chapter 2 delves into the polyvagal theory, what happens when an officer perceives danger, the Autonomic Nervous System (ANS), and stages of response.

REFERENCES

American Psychiatric Association (2022). What is post-traumatic stress disorder (PTSD)? https://www.psychiatry.org/patients-families/ptsd/what-is-ptsd

Anderson, G. S., Di Nota, P. M., Metz, G. A. S., & Anderson, J. P. (2019). The impact of acute stress physiology on skilled motor performance: Implications for policing. *Frontiers in Psychology,* 10, 2501, 1–11. Sec. Psychology for Clinical Settings. https://doi:10.3389/fpsyg.2019.02501

Axtell, K., Llamas, J., Llamas, M., & Roma, A. (2022) The anatomy of a crisis: Law enforcement leaders' perspective on police enforcement. *The Scholarship Without Borders Journal,* 1(2). https://doi.org/10.57229/2834-2267.1011

Bustos, C. (2023). Trauma-Informed Leadership. *Police Chief Online*, May 24. https://www.policechiefmagazine.org/trauma-informed-leadership/

Centers for Disease Control and Prevention. (2018). Health-related quality of life. *Wellbeing concepts.* https://www.cdc.gov/hrqol/wellbeing.htm

Chen, P-f., Wu, L. (2022). Impact of job demands on police stress response—the roles of basic psychological needs and job autonomy. *BMC Public Health,* 22(2275), 1–10. https://doi.org/10.1186/s12889-022-14758-6

Christopher, M., Bowen, S., & Witkiewitz, K. (2020). Mindfulness-based resilience training for aggression, stress and health in law enforcement officers: Study protocol for a multisite, randomized, single-blind clinical feasibility trial. *Trials*, 21, 236. https://doi.org/10.1186/s13063-020-4165-y

Craddock, T. B., & Telesco, G. (2022). Predicting psychological outcomes in officers exposed to traumatic events. *Journal of the American Academy of Experts in Traumatic Stress,* Winter-Spring, 24-35.

Daniel, A. M., & Treece, K. S. (2022). Law enforcement pathways to mental health: secondary traumatic stress, social support, and social pressure. *Journal of Police and Criminal Psychology*, 37, 132–140. https://doi.org/10.1007/s11896-021-09476-5

Di Nota, P. M., & Huhta, J. M. (2019). Complex motor learning and police training: Applied, cognitive, and clinical perspectives. *Frontiers in Psychology,* 10, 1-20. https://tinyurl.com/4kj9ns7n

Dodanwala, T. C., Santoso, D. S., & Shrestha, P. (2022). The mediating role of work–family conflict on role overload and job stress linkage. *Built Environment Project and Asset Management*, (6), 924–939. https://doi.org/10.1108/BEPAM-12-2021-0153

Ellingwood, H., Williams, K., Sitarenios, G., & Solomon, J. (2018). Psychometric properties of a contextualized, actuarially informed assessment for law enforcement personnel selection: The M-PULSE inventory. *Journal of Police and Criminal Psychology*. https://doi.org/10.1007/s11896-018-9290-0

Ermasova, N., Cross, A. D., & Ermasova, E. (2020). Perceived stress and coping among law enforcement officers: An empirical analysis of patrol versus non-patrol officers in Illinois. *Journal of Police and Criminal Psychology*, 35, 48–63. https://doi.org/10.1007/s11896-019-09356-z

Franco, F. (2022). Resilience and complex post-traumatic stress disorder (C-PTSD). *Journal of the American Academy of Experts in Traumatic Stress*, Winter-Spring, 60–63.

Greco, G., & Fischetti, F. (2018). Physical, technical and tactical training and stress management in law enforcement. *Journal of Physical Education and Sport*, 18(2), 555–560. https://doi:10.7752/jpes.2018.02080

Harrison, B. (2023). What police officers love and hate about their jobs. Key takeaways for police leaders from Police1's hour annual state of the industry survey. Police1, *What Cops Want in 2023*, 44–13.

Helfgott, J. B., Hickman, M. J., Strah, B. M., Atherley, L. T., Kosson, D. S., & Dorscher, E. (2022). The relationship between personality traits and the effectiveness of guardian law enforcement training. *Journal of Forensic Psychology Research and Practice*. htttps://doi:10.1080/24732850.2022.2028392

Hill, P. L., Sin, N. L., Turiano, N. A., Burrow, A. L., & Almeida, D. M. (2018). Sense of purpose moderates the associations between daily stressors and daily well-being. *Annals of Behavioral Medicine* 52, 724–729. https://doi.org/10.1093/abm/kax039

Jackman, P. C., Henderson, H., Clay, G., & Coussens, A. H. (2020). The relationship between psychological well-being, social support, and personality in an English police force. *International Journal of Police Science & Management* 22, 183–193. https://journals.sagepub.com/doi/10.1177/1461355720907620

Karaffa, K. M., & Tochkov, K. (2013). Attitudes toward seeking mental health treatment among law enforcement officers. *Applied Psychology in Criminal Justice* 9(2), 75–99.

Kenny, M. C., Helpingstine, C., Long, H., Earl, N., & Malik, F. (2023). Commercial sexual trafficking of males: A pilot training with law enforcement. *Criminal Justice Studies*, https://doi:10.1080/1478601X.2023.2167079

Laura, U., Friedhoff, S., Cochran, S., & Pandya, A. (2016). *Preparing for the unimaginable: How chiefs can safeguard officer mental health before and after mass casualty events*. Washington, DC: Office of Community Oriented Policing Services. https://ovc.ojp.gov/sites/g/files/xyckuh226/files/media/document/mv_safeguard_officer_mh_mass_casualty-508.pdf

López-Cabarcos, M. Á., López-Carballeira, A., & Ferro-Soto, C. (2023). How to prevent hostile behaviors and emotional exhaustion among law enforcement professionals: The Negative Spiral of Role Conflict. *International Journal of Environmental Research and Public Health*, 20(1), 863. https://doi.org/10.3390/ijerph20010863

Meichenbaum, D. (1974). *Cognitive-behavior modification*. Morristown, NJ: General Learning Press.

Meichenbaum, D. H., & Deffenbacher, J. L. (1988). Stress inoculation training. *The Counseling Psychologist*, 16(1), 69–90.

Meichenbaum, D. (2007). Stress inoculation training: A preventative and treatment approach. In P. M. Lehrer, R. L. Woolfolk, & W. E. Sime (Eds.), *Principles and practice of stress management*, 497–516. The Guilford Press.

Murthy, V.H. (2022). *Addressing health worker burnout: The U.S. surgeon general's advisory on building a thriving health workforce*, 1–76. https://www.hhs.gov/sites/default/files/health-worker-wellbeing-advisory.pdf

National Police Support Fund (2019). *Why high rates of PTSD in police officers?* https://nationalpolicesupportfund.com/police-officers-experience-high-rates-of-ptsd/

National Institute of Mental Health [NIMH] (2022). *Anxiety disorders*. https://www.nimh.nih.gov/health/topics/anxiety-disorders

National Institute of Mental Health [NIMH] (2022a). *Post-Traumatic Stress Disorder* https://www.nimh.nih.gov/health/topics/post-traumatic-stress-disorder-ptsd

National Wellness Survey for Public Safety Personnel Summary Report. November 2022.

Nero, J. W., Campbell, M. A., Doyle, J. N. & Meagher, J. (2022). The link between social support and psychological vulnerability among Canadian police officers. *Journal of Police and Criminal Psychology* 37, 377–391. https://doi.org/10.1007/s11896-022-09505-x

Patterson, S., and King, W. R. (2023). Culture and well-being among sworn officers: an empirical examination. *Policing: An International Journal*, 46(1), 179–193. https://doi.org/10.1108/PIJPSM-06-2022-0078

Poirier, S., Allard-Gaudreau, N., Gendron, P., Houle, J., & Trudeau, F. (2023). Health, safety, and wellness concerns among law enforcement officers: An inductive approach. *Workplace Health & Safety*, 71(1), 34–42. https://doi:10.1177/21650799221134422

Police Training Commission (2022). *Basic course for police officers*. https://www.state.nj.us/lps/dcj/njptc/pdf/Basic-Course-for-Police-Officers-BCPO.pdf

Rachele, J., Cockshaw, W., & Brymer, E. (2013). Towards an operational understanding of wellness. *Journal of Spirituality, Leadership and Management*, 7(1), 3–12. http://www.slam.org.au/wp-content/uploads/2014/02/JSLaMvol7no1_Rachele.pdf

Redman, V.P. (2018). *Macro-level predictors of assaults against police in Kentucky*. Electronic Theses and Dissertations. Paper 3025. 1–96. https://doi.org/10.18297/etd/3025

Robson, S., & Manacapilli, T. (2014). Enhancing performance under stress: Stress inoculation training for battlefield airmen. Defense Technical Information

Center (n.d.). RAND Project Airforce. https://apps.dtic.mil/sti/citations/ADA605157

Rotter, J. (1966). Generalized expectancies for internal versus external control of reinforcement. *Psychological Monographs* 80(1), 1–28.

Scheer, C. (2023). Dealing with toxic messages that sabotage police recruitment. Police1, *What Cops Want in 2023*, 20–24.

Selye, H. (n.d.). Institute of Neuromuscular Medicine. https://www.inmmed.com/blog/stress

Substance Abuse and Mental Health Services Administration. (2014). SAMHSA's Concept of Trauma and Guidance for a Trauma-Informed Approach. HHS Publication No. (SMA) 14-4884. Rockville, MD. https://store.samhsa.gov/sites/default/files/d7/priv/sma14-4884.pdf

Smiley-McDonald, H. M., Attaway, P. R., Richardson, N. J., Davidson, P. J., Kral, A. H. (2022). Perspectives from law enforcement officers who respond to overdose calls for service and administer naloxone. *Health Justice* 10(9), 1–13. https://doi.org/10.1186/s40352-022-00172-y

Stevelink, S. A. M., Opie, E., Pernet, D., Gao, H., Elliott, P., Wessely, S., ... Greenberg, N. (2020). Probable PTSD, depression and anxiety in 40,299 UK police officers and staff: Prevalence, risk factors and associations with blood pressure. *PLoS ONE* 15(11), e0240902. https://doi.org/10.1371/journal.pone.0240902

The Harris Poll (2022). Public perception of mental health and suicide prevention survey results September 2022. https://suicidepreventionnow.org/static/executive-summary-2022-9c5a59e0f8016f1803570b11cfd3cb29.pdf

Tucker, J. M. (2015). Police officer willingness to use stress intervention services: the role of perceived organizational support (POS), confidentiality and stigma. *International Journal of Emergency Mental Health and Human Resilience*, 17(1), 304–314.

U.S. Department of Veteran Affairs. PTSD. National Center for PTSD. *Stress Inoculation Training (SIT) for PTSD*. https://www.ptsd.va.gov/understand_tx/stress_inoculation_training.asp

van der Meulen, E., Bosmans, M. W. G., Lens, K. M. E., Lahlah, E., Van der Velden, P. G. (2018). Effects of mental strength training for police officers: A three-wave quasi-experimental study. *Journal of Police and Criminal Psychology*, 33, 385–397. https://doi.org/10.1007/s11896-017-9247-8

World Health Organization [WHO]. (2022). *Mental Health*. https://www.who.int/news-room/fact-sheets/detail/mental-health-strengthening-our-response

Zheng, Z., Guo, C., Li, M., Yang, L., Liu, P., Zhang, X., Liu, Y., Guo, X., Cao, S., Dong, Y., Zhang, C., Chen, M., Xu, J., Hu, H., & Cui, Y. (2022). Hypothalamus-habenula potentiation encodes chronic stress experience and drives depression onset. *Neuron*, 110(8), 1400-1415.e6. https://doi.org/10.1016/j.neuron.2022.01.011

2 | ADVERSE CHILDHOOD EXPERIENCES (ACES) AND WELLNESS

DEFINITIONS

ACEs - Adverse Childhood Experiences are stressful events that can happen before the age of 18.

POLYVAGAL THEORY - relationship between the autonomic nervous system and social behavior.

OBJECTIVES

After reading and considering the content of this chapter, the reader should be able to:

- Identify Adverse Childhood Experiences (ACEs) as a possible predictor of a health risk for adults.
- Describe the polyvagal theory in relation to policing.

In My Experience & Lessons Learned

JASON PALAMARA

I can still see myself the days following 9/11, covered in white and grey dust as shattered glass falls around me. At certain points throughout my career I did not feel prepared. That feeling has impacted my mental health and wellness. Although daily preparation before I began my tour of duty was probably not needed to get through the day, being prepared for anything that could occur during my shift was essential.

I don't know any officer who gets into their patrol car or begins their foot patrol, no matter the command, without their gun belt. You will never see an officer on patrol without one. Some officers feel comfortable having only their service weapon on their gun belt for regular patrol. Other times, they bring their "off duty" weapon for details (e.g., parades, special events etc.).

An "off duty" weapon is a firearm authorized by the department to be carried while not working, as well as while working, if preferred. Every officer has their own idea of what is appropriate for their situation. Their gun belt is relative to what makes them feel safe, and may be different for the colleague standing next to them. This is determined by past experiences, advice from fellow officers, and their personality.

Once the work day was over, I let go of my focus on being prepared. I needed a break. My mind wanted to leave "self-preservation" mode. Left to our own decision-making skills, at times we officers, on or off duty, decide to step into the "foot patrol" of life unprepared and expect that if something does happen or we hit a few speedbumps, that we will be able to handle anything that comes our way.

Most often, we can handle these rib shots of life. However, we won't be able to handle them if we don't focus on our wellness and improving our emotional safety. We cannot give that which we ourselves do not have. This is also true in what we give ourselves. If we have not sought out and acquired the skills to close the cycles of our stressful events, we carry them into every facet of life, which impacts more than just ourselves.

Within the police department there were always telephone numbers provided for emotional assistance or substance use, flyers disseminated on how to cope with the job's stresses, and trainings posted on our intranet.

Yet, when speaking of officer wellness throughout my career, despite the resouces available, I still felt that I was isolated and alone in my own world. To take advantage of the resources too often carried with it a stigma I was unwilling to accept.

There were visits from the Employee Assistance Unit explaining what to do if we needed to reach out for help. Telling us, "The Helpers," that we may be the ones in need of help is not always received well or for that matter entertained as an option. For example, we would call the place they sent us if we were suspected of having a problem with alcohol "The Farm," and the stigma of being labeled as someone who spent time on "The Farm" made most of us reluctant to seek any kind of help—if we could even bring ourselves to admit that help was in fact what we needed.

Before an officer begins their tour maintenance is performed on their Radio Motor Patrol (RMP)—checking tire pressure, the Mobile Data Terminal (MDT), and vehicle emergency devices. If while on patrol an officer experiences a mechanical issue, they put on their emergency lights while awaiting help. It is more difficult to handle a blown tire while traveling at a high rate of speed than giving it the attention it deserves before beginning your shift. Just like the patrol car, it is more difficult to give yourself the attention you deserve after you begin your journey than while still "parked." When you experience the difficulties of this job, don't be afraid to switch your hazards on and accept a helping hand.

You will learn in this chapter how Adverse Childhood Experiences (ACEs) that were not addressed as a child may possibly impact an officer's mental health. ACEs can lead to increased social problems such as alcoholism, addiction, and suicide. I know that studies on police wellness are focusing on revamping mental health screenings of incoming cadets to focus on ACEs, but I am unsure if officers will self-disclose their ACEs during that time.

During my psychological exam while applying for the police academy, I was asked, "Jason, how were you affected growing up with a mother who suffered with physical health?" and "Jason, how did losing your grandparents at a young age affect you?" In preparation for my psychological exam, I was told by officers to be cautious in what I shared as it would negatively affect my chances of getting hired. "Think about how you are going to answer the questions they ask", I was told. "Don't be an open book!"

Although I had no ACEs, if I did, I wouldn't share the details of childhood abuse, neglect or household dysfunction during my psychological exam.

My responses were coated to sound like what I thought the interviewer wanted to hear. There are things that I never shared. I wanted to be a cop. I wasn't going to let an answer—even if it was the truth—ruin my chances of becoming a police officer.

A system is only as good as the quality of the information provided to it, and how that information is then administered. If officers knew that it was okay to have struggled with the death of a family member, maybe they would be provided tools to assist them as they inevitably are exposed to death as a normal part of an officer's life. If I felt that I could tell my investigator that it was tough to see my mother suffer, and still is, and not be fearful that it would jeopardize my chances of getting hired, it would have helped me learn skills to manage my reactions after witnessing suffering throughout my career.

Being made to feel comfortable sharing from the first interview, and then through the academy and job itself, rather than feeling honesty about one's feelings would be met punitively, will assist in nurturing and helping to grow the human behind the badge.

We need to recognize how ACEs may possibly impact an officer's well-being. Studies suggest that the increasing number of unaddressed ACEs corresponds to worsening physical and mental health problems, as well as being more prone to PTSD as adults. It is difficult to accept as smart policing the holding back of a candidate simply because they experienced abuse or emotional hardship. An applicant's high ACEs score should not immediately disqualify them from hire.

I am often asked how I got into the wellness space, and what led me to my job as Director of Veteran and First Responder Engagement for a behavioral healthcare company. Although my primary responsibilities involve business development, the best part of my job is the interaction I have with fellow Veterans, first responders, and those that support them.

Every engagement is an opportunity to walk with someone on their wellness journey. Wellness is not a singular self-sustaining thing. It is the result of many parts—a combination of the physical, spiritual, social, intellectual, emotional, mental, occupational, environmental, and financial aspects of one's life. Remove one of these factors, and overall wellness is weaker. Remove concentration in one, and the others will have to compensate.

When we believe that we are the singular reason that our life improves if we keep trying harder, we inevitably fall short and blame ourselves. We can forget what truly creates happiness and leads to wellness, and lose our way when we try to go it alone. My work in wellness was born out of a personal dark struggle which grew into a passion to share what I have learned with others who were struggling—specifically those in the first responder community.

I have had the privilege to meet and work with providers that have hearts of gold and are in the wellness space for the right reasons. However, I have also seen providers operating for financial gain with disregard for the people they purport to be assisting. When LEO wellness enters the realm of needing clinical care (e.g., mental health, substance use services, detox, partial hospitalization, in-patient services), it is important that care is provided by those who understand first responder culture.

Wellness is a team effort. It includes not only those providing services, but also the ones receiving them. It includes all the organizations that support our first responders and their families. I want to help them find people that will become their wellness team and am grateful to never have to look far to find them. I find purpose in every encounter in the relationships built with those in the wellness space who share in the mission of and passion for improving the lives of those that protect us. When the heart is hurt because of the weight of the badge, it is not the time for administration to scramble to figure out why.

Let's start from day one to foster the growth of our officers, so when they face job stressors, they have already been given the tools to face adversity. That's when we will ultimately see our suicide numbers begin to decline. Let us provide them with the tools needed to grow up on the job while not expecting them to be fully prepared for policing stressors and traumas simply by getting sworn in. Debating the reasons why an officer decided to end their life is attempting to understand the problem too late. We need to start by focusing on growing the human as they enter the force rather than trying to fix them once they are emotionally and mentally injured.

My Story & Evidence-Based Practices

BARBARA RUBEL

"We've seen the effects of trauma in an officer who grew up in an abusive household and is then confronted with a call for abused children. The effect of that experience may force unresolved trauma to the surface."

—William Mazur and Joseph Collins,
The New Jersey Police Chief Magazine

Years ago, as a consultant with the Department of Justice, Office for Victims of Crime, I presented a keynote address to victim services providers. A reporter asked if I would agree to an interview for a local television station. The interview went well until he asked me about Adverse Childhood Experiences (ACEs). I was like, "Come again?" *I had no idea what ACEs meant.* That embarrassing moment set me on the path to discover this landmark study.

According to experts, ACEs are predictors of health risks and well-being that can impact quality of life. ACEs are traumatic childhood events that can weaken development associated with chronic health problems, mental illness, and risk-taking behaviors in adults. (Warner et al., 2023)

A child's well-being is impacted by adults in their life. When a child experiences adversity and has not been given the tools to manage that experience, it may impact their ability to function as an adult. Mental health problems may stem from childhood abuse, neglect, or dysfunction. Adults may not realize the link between ACEs and their maladaptive coping. The question needs to be asked whether officers have experienced primary and secondary trauma as a child and whether those ACEs have impacted them as adults.

LAW ENFORCEMENT CONSIDERATION & PERSONAL INSIGHT

If you were emotionally neglected as a child by a parent who was unavailable or critical, how has that impacted your mental health as an adult (e.g., struggle with social relationships)?

36

Approaching Trauma from an ACEs Perspective

In this chapter, we focus on ACES, which can cause mental and physical problems, such as depression, STDs, and alcoholism in adulthood (Felitti et al, 1998). According to the CDC (2021), 1 in 6 adults experienced four or more types of ACEs. These experiences may impact positive (e.g., resiliency) and negative (e.g., use of force) outcomes in officers repeatedly exposed to high stress and trauma (Thompson et al., 2022). For example, those who work with victims (e.g., child exploitation, pornography investigation), need to be aware that PTSD and depression linked with ACEs might impact the assessment of threat and can worsen their emotional regulation (Violanti et al., 2021).

> **LAW ENFORCEMENT CONSIDERATION**
> **& PERSONAL INSIGHT**
>
> Have you considered that you may be struggling with an addiction due to your ACEs not having been worked through?

Addiction and suicide are two of the main health issues associated with high ACE scores. Pre-hire risk factors, such as family of origin, adverse experiences, and substance use, are fundamental to most employee suicides and not exposure to traumatic on-duty critical incidents (Rouse et al, 2015). LEOs may have grown up in dysfunctional families, witnessed violence, lived in an unsafe neighborhood, experienced racism, bullying, or lived in foster care. It is not easy for an officer to recall sensitive periods of development if they have grown up in a toxic environment. The mental health challenges they currently face may be due to those early challenges.

> **LAW ENFORCEMENT CONSIDERATION**
> **& PERSONAL INSIGHT**
>
> Did your ACEs influence your decision to become a LEO?

ACE Study

The Adverse Childhood Experiences Study (ACE Study) focused on traumatic life events before the age of 18 and how those events impact adults. The ACE study has shown us that child abuse and neglect is the single most preventable cause of mental illness, a common cause of drug and alcohol abuse, and contributor to death by heart disease and suicide (van der Kolk, 2014).

CASE NOTES

Lisa Berman, MD, Psychiatrist, private practice and founder of Inspire Mental Health Services, notes, "In my work with adults, so much of what we spend time on is childhood trauma and how it affects us as adults. People often say things like 'that was so long ago. I should be over it by now,' so a lot of the work I do is centered around making space for the effects of that trauma in adult life rather than admonishing oneself for still 'not being over it.' Trauma is life changing, no matter when it happens. It changes the way our brain is wired. To think that it is merely an event that happened in the past is a monumental misunderstanding of the nature of trauma" *(L. Berman, personal communication, July 22, 2023).*

ACES Study Categories

The categories in the ACE study are broken down into abuse, neglect, and household dysfunction.

1. Abuse
   - Were their parents psychologically or physically abusive?
   - Did anyone sexually abuse them?

2. Neglect
   - Did they experience emotional neglect?
   - Did they experience physical neglect?

3. Household dysfunction
    - Did they grow up in a home with alcoholism or drug use?
    - Did they experience the loss of a biological parent?
    - Was there depression or a mental health challenge or crisis in the home?
    - Was their mother abused?
    - Was a family member in jail?

When feeling unsafe, officers needed to be taught how to self-sooth. If they were never taught this skill as a child, they may struggle with self-regulation as an adult.

LAW ENFORCEMENT CONSIDERATION & PERSONAL INSIGHT

What made you feel unsafe on a chronic basis prior to the age of 18?

Departmental Focus on ACEs and Wellness

Although studies show that ACEs are prevalent and impact an adult's mental health, an officer may not correlate their childhood to their current maladaptive behavior. Direct exposure to physical violence before the age of 18 was a significant factor for police recruit emotional distress (Tuttle et al., 2023). A study on ACEs in officers recognizes the necessity to talk about preventative treatment as well as revamping mental health screenings of incoming cadets (Levesque, 2021). Officers with high ACEs significantly report shorter sleep duration and poorer sleep quality (Charles et al., 2022).

Wellness coordinators can provide recommendations for departments to implement screening of ACEs in psychological safety and wellness campaigns. This can help officers see health conditions associated with ACEs such as depression, cardiovascular disease, asthma, arthritis, COPD, and diabetes (Merrick et al., 2019; Waehrer et al., 2020).

Being that scores on ACEs are being used as a vulnerability indicator, trauma-focused therapy can help officers manage their early life events (Tehrani, 2022). Providing them with mental health education enhances their ability to assist members of the public who are suffering from mental disorders, and may also make them more likely to seek treatment for their own conditions (Lane, 2022).

CASE NOTES

Bonnie C. Rumilly, LCSW, EMT-B, Certified EMDR Therapist, and Clinical Director of the Fairfield County Trauma Response Team, Inc., notes, "When working with Law Enforcement Officers, it is important to assess their ACEs score. According to the Adverse Childhood Experiences study, the more difficult the childhood, the higher the score is likely to be on the rating scale, which translates to higher risk for physical and mental health problems later in life. Therapists who specialize in the treatment of Law Enforcement Officers (and other First Responders) understand that many Law Enforcement Officers get into their line of work or career path to bring justice and order to an 'unjust' world.

"Many Law Enforcement Officers had a childhood in which physical, emotional or sexual abuse and/or neglect were present. They may have grown up in a home where one or both parents abandoned them, witnessed domestic violence or had one or two substance abusing parents or guardians in the home. A culturally competent and trauma trained therapist will assess the ACEs score in order to gauge how much exposure to the aforementioned traumas impact the current functioning of the Officer. The ACEs score can also drive treatment goals. Especially in EMDR Therapy, we recognize the past is present and is living in the Officer now in addition to the current stressors or traumas they have faced on the job" *(B.C. Rumilly, personal communication, October 3, 2023).*

Classes and Check-Ups

Police departments are incorporating trauma-informed care into their training. Being trauma-informed describes social, behavioral, and mental health services that recognize an individual's previous experience of trauma (Harris et al., 2001). Trauma-informed agencies are recognizing ACEs in offenders.

So, let's take that a step further and recognize how ACEs may possibly impact an officer's wellness. Officers don't like talking about trauma, especially their own mental health, and are turned off by the phrase "mental health services." Mental health services are often perceived as a reactive, punitive connotation and should be replaced with a proactive, educational connotation (e.g., importance of maintaining good mental health) through annual/bi-annual classes or checkups (Padilla, 2023).

LAW ENFORCEMENT CONSIDERATION & PERSONAL INSIGHT

Do you think the way mental health services are phrased and advertised in your agency has an impact on your decision to use them?

Although there is a vast amount of research on ACEs, it has been largely untapped by law enforcement. However, studies on officers show that they experience high rates of ACEs compared to the general population, and they report exceptionally high levels of childhood emotional abuse (Thompson et al, 2022). Family of origin dysfunction, parentification (e.g., child expected to provide support to parent rather than the other way around), individual attributes acquired through adversity, and experiential motivations were linked to the decision to pursue a career in the helping professions (Bryce et al., 2023).

At this point, we are relying on existing literature on children, adults, and healthcare professionals to understand possible mental health issues in LEOs related to their ACEs. Clearly, there is need for further research on understanding the complex relationship between a LEO's childhood trauma and their overall mental and physical health.

LAW ENFORCEMENT CONSIDERATION & PERSONAL INSIGHT

How did your early life experiences and ACES shape how you currently react to stress and trauma?

Somatic Experiencing

Somatic awareness is being mindful of chronic and traumatic stress, suppressed emotions, and trauma symptoms that have accumulated in the body. In 1977, Dr. Peter A. Levine, created Somatic Experiencing (SE™), a body-oriented approach for those stuck in the fight, flight, or freeze patterns.

This evidence-based therapeutic model can help an officer resolve difficult bodily sensations and recover from their experiences. If officers have a stress disorder or have been traumatized, SE, a form of trauma therapy, can help them release stored trauma and manage their ACEs. Advances in neuroscience have shown the importance of balancing the sympathetic and parasympathetic nervous systems.

A somatic therapist uses mind-body techniques that focus on body sensations to resolve physiological states through breathing and visualization exercises, grounding, and forms of body movement. Somatic experiencing improves body awareness to process trauma, whether it happened as a child or during a shift.

An officer's trauma history moves through their body and can stay there. For example, distressing heart and gut sensations are body signals that they have not worked through a trauma. They can consider what their body is telling them as they create a somatic narrative. Their body keeps a record of every traumatic experience and knows every hurt as it holds their trauma history and responds to their past experiences.

Wellness

Wellness is defined as "the quality or state of being healthy especially as an actively sought goal" (Merriam-Webster, n.d.). A sustainable policing strategy that supports the health and safety of our communities is built on wellness, which is centered on health promotion and disease prevention (Jackson & Theroux, 2023).

Timothy Peek, Deputy Chief at City of Atlanta Police Department, notes, "Regardless of how tough you are, mental illness is real and as such, mental health and wellness is critical to make and keep our bodies and souls healthy and whole" *(T. Peek, personal communication, April 8, 2023).*

The Global Wellness Institute defines wellness as "the active pursuit of activities, choices and lifestyles that lead to a state of holistic health" (par. 2). In a nutshell, ten dimensions of wellness are:

- **EMOTIONAL WELLNESS:** empathy, express emotions that bring about positive behaviors, healthy self-esteem
- **PHYSICAL WELLNESS:** fitness, sleep, nutrition, regular doctor visits, stop smoking
- **SEXUAL WELLNESS:** sexual pleasure, absence of disease, self-determination, access to contraception, safety
- **SOCIAL WELLNESS:** connections, friendships, an intimate partner, provide/receive emotional support
- **INTELLECTUAL WELLNESS:** personal growth, curiosity, prioritize learning new things, time management, problem solving, stay informed, be a critical thinker
- **COMMUNITY WELLNESS:** neighborhood parks and recreation, feel safe, like neighbors, sense of belonging
- **CAREER WELLNESS:** fulfilled by your role, values match that of your employer, work-life balance
- **FINANCIAL WELLNESS:** have enough money to enjoy life, a personal budget, build good credit, have an emergency fund, can pay off debt
- **ENVIRONMENTAL WELLNESS:** enjoys being outside, uses eco-friendly products at home, conserves energy
- **SPIRITUAL WELLNESS:** meaning in life, religious beliefs, sense of purpose

LAW ENFORCEMENT CONSIDERATION & PERSONAL INSIGHT

Based on the ten dimensions of wellness, how well are you?

Improving Wellness Services

There is a crucial need to improve comprehensive services for officers exposed to stress and trauma which can include early prevention assessment and proactive mental health and wellness (Craddock & Telesco, 2022). Most law enforcement personnel publicly address wellness concerns at professional meetings and academic conferences, and most police agencies have wellness coordinators and units (Papazoglou, 2021). Wellness coordinators can inform their agency that conferences improve LEO mental health and make recommendations accordingly.

CASE NOTES

Shawn Thomas is the founder of 1st Responder Conferences and a retired deputy from the King County Sheriff's Office in Seattle, WA. Shawn was on the peer support team for 16 years and was a team lead for several years.

Shawn notes, "Those who attend 1st Responder Conferences two day training around the country are provided wellness education, tools and confidential resources to help get them through these difficult professions. 1st Responder Conferences is dedicated to providing overall wellness for public safety professionals, their families and all of the professions that work with first responders. With a message of optimism and sustainability, the goal is to push past traditional silence and bring wellness to our everyday heroes. 1st Responder Conferences provide a climate that supports health and well-being" *(S. Thomas, personal communication, October 5, 2023).*

Strengthened by the Law Enforcement Mental Health and Wellness Act (LEMHWA), police agencies have increased funding to create programs that provide services that prevent suicide (U.S. Department of Justice, 2023). Signed into law in 2018, LEMHWA protects an officer's well-being by funding improved access to agency mental health and wellness services. This is accomplished through peer support, training, family resources, wellness programs, and suicide prevention. The International Association of Chiefs of Police's (IACP) Officer Health and Wellness Agency established the "Ten Steps to Building a Wellness Program" Assessment Tool and Action Planning Roadmap.

According to IACP (2019) to build a health and wellness program and obtain necessary buy-in, develop a program and team leader and review research, connect with agencies that have similar programs, identify priorities, define mission and goals, develop a plan, build a referral network, and provide training for the program team.

Wellness in a Spiritual Workplace

A spiritual workplace begins with agencies, command staff, and supervisors who create a workplace where the department foundation mirrors an officer's values, attitudes, and behaviors. A spiritual workplace can inspire a LEO to express a sense of gratitude and hope, develop purpose in their work, examine ways to make meaning in their role, achieve personal growth, accomplish their organizational mission, find a deep connection to their job outcome, be attuned with their supervisor, elevate trust among other officers, and express how they value what they personally offer the department.

> **LAW ENFORCEMENT CONSIDERATION & PERSONAL INSIGHT**
>
> If a LEO experienced ACEs, can bullying in the workplace, inconsistent rules, as well as a weak leader's neglect, favoritism and lack of praise, cause psychological harm?

Approaching Trauma from a Polyvagal Perspective

What is Polyvagal Theory?

Polyvagal theory focuses on branches of the nervous system. These states impact physiology, psychology, social engagement, and connectedness. Poly means more than one. Vagal originates from the vagus nerve, and derives from the Latin word, vagus, meaning wandering. Polyvagal theory is the science behind feeling safe and calm which enables an officer to make better choices. It helps them understand that unresolved stress can become stored in their body and directly influence how they regulate emotions and functioning.

Polyvagal theory offers a physiological explanation for an officer's experiences, and a framework as to how they may act in a stressful situation because their actions are autonomic. So, if a mental health professional knows how trauma impacts a LEO's nervous system, they can adapt interventions to be faster and more effective.

CASE NOTES

I reached out to world renowned researcher and professor of psychiatry, Dr. Stephen Porges, who originated the Polyvagal Theory who shared four points:

1. Polyvagal Theory links psychological feelings of safety and threat to our physiological state;

2. Functionally, feelings of threat disrupt the homeostatic processes that support health, growth, and restoration. Transitory disruptions are part of normal life, but chronic disruptions retune the autonomic nervous system (ANS) to be locked in a physiological state that supports threat reactions and severely compromises social behavior, cognitive function, and health. In contrast, feelings of safety are dependent on our ANS supporting homeostatic processes (health, growth, and restoration). When our ANS is supporting homeostatic processes, there is a neurophysiological foundation to feel safe, be social, cooperate with others, solve problems, and to heal on both mental and physical dimensions;

3. We note that for many who have experienced severe adversity, their ANS have been retuned to be locked in a state that supports defense, not sociality, on behavioral, psychological, physiological, and even molecular levels. When in this state of chronic threat, feeling safe, making good decisions, and cooperating and trusting others is compromised; and

4. Not all who experience adversity will experience the same response pattern. Some individuals are fortunate to have flexible and resilient ANS that rapidly return to efficiently regulate homeostatic processes without any long term mental or medical health consequences,

Polyvagal Theory emphasizes the response to the 'traumatic' event and NOT the event. Polyvagal Theory assumes that the link between 'traumatic events' and mental and medical health consequences is mediated by an autonomic state locked into a chronic state of defense" *(S. Porges, personal communication, April 6, 2023).*

What is the Vagus Nerve?

The vagus nerve is the main component of the parasympathetic nervous system, which is a part of the autonomous nervous system (ANS). The vagus nerve is responsible for the relationship between the ANS and social behavior, and influences one's psychological state and ability to emotionally regulate.

Where Is the Vagus Nerve?

The vagus nerve is the longest cranial nerve, which runs in two directions throughout the body. It does not travel through the spinal cord. Rather, it runs from the brain to the neck and abdomen, linking the body systems together through the lungs, heart, stomach, and upward from the diaphragm to connect with nerve fibers in the neck, throat, ears, and eyes. The vagus nerve controls skeletal muscles of the mouth, pharynx, and larynx offering the ability to swallow food and speak.

Naturally Stimulating the Vagus Nerve

When you naturally stimulate your vagus nerve, electrical impulses will travel to your brain. A sampling of ways to stimulate the vagus nerve, manage dysregulated stress responses, and gain emotional control are:

- Alternate nostril breathing, diaphragmatic breathing (e.g., deep breathing, belly breathing) can tone, reset, and strengthen the vagus nerve.
- Eat a whole-foods diet and eat probiotics (e.g., pickles, sauerkraut, yogurt, apple cider vinegar).
- Apply cold compresses to your face and the back of your neck, plunge your face in an ice water bath or place an ice pack on your chest.
- Socialize, laugh, and connect with nature.

CASE NOTES

Sherri Sherock, CHC, CPT, notes, "You can stimulate your vagus nerve, the longest nerve in your body. The vagus nerve connects from the brain to important organs in the body such as your gut (intestines & stomach), and your heart and lungs. It is key for turning on the parasympathetic nervous system 'rest and digest' which has a huge impact on mental health. By stimulating this nerve regularly, it can help the body relax quicker after stressful moments.

"Ways to stimulate the vagus nerve are deep slow breathing, singing, humming, or chanting, gargling, consume probiotics (activate gut with good bacteria), meditation, consume Omega-3 Fatty Acids (activating brain health—fish, nuts, and seeds), exercise, and massage (feet-reflexology)" *(S. Sherock, personal communication, April 2, 2023).*

What Happens When an Officer Perceives Danger?

Dr. Stephen Porges coined the term "neuroception" to describe how situations are neurologically evaluated as safe or unsafe (2022). It refers to unconscious awareness where the autonomic nervous system (ANS) evaluates the environment without conscious awareness. Either side of the vagus nerve (ventral and dorsal) can get stimulated by the environment and social interactions.

Although the officer may not be aware of what is going on in their subconscious, they do notice their body reactions. For example, their heart rate increases or slows down, or they feel an uneasiness in their stomach. The Polyvagal theory describes the relationship between the ANS and social behavior (Restauri et al., 2023).

The ANS is involuntary, works automatically without conscious effort, and is usually outside the control of the officer. However, there is evidence that we do have some control over our ANS response through mindfulness and emotional regulation. The system is designed to unconsciously scan for danger, safety, and threat to keep us safe. Its functions are automatic and can be difficult to control, which results in engagement or becoming withdrawn and disconnected.

Misty Fields, grief and trauma specialist, notes, "The ANS is what allows LEOs to respond in rapidly changing environments. Through training, LEOs will learn about vagal nerve pathways that connect the brain and body, so they better understand their own triggers and reactions, as well as those around them. As they learn to regulate emotionally through stimulating their parasympathetic response, they are able to adapt and recover more quickly from stressful situations and remain socially engaged. This kind of training can result in improved mental and physical health" *(M. Fields, personal communication, April 16, 2023).*

Stages of Response

The brain and spinal cord make up the central nervous system. The peripheral nervous system is made up of a somatic nervous system, which is voluntary. This means the muscles and brain can communicate with each other. When LEOs are overwhelmed, their brain informs their nervous system of a threat. If they understand their nervous system, they might manage the experience and recognize if they are numbing and becoming immobile or in fight or flight.

The ANS controls the glands and internal organs (e.g., heart, lungs, digestive system). The neural circuits are responsible for regulation of the ANS. Unconscious biological states produce three stages of response:

1. social engagement;
2. fight or flight; or
3. freeze, shutting down.

Current research notes three emerging defense responses: collapse, please and appease (or the fawn response), and attach/cry for help. Also, LEOs may remain stuck in their trauma response and disconnect from those around them.

Social Engagement

The biology of social engagement is responsible for the ability to regulate body functioning above the diaphragm, controls face muscles, regulates heart and lungs, and improves digestion, which fosters connection. When LEOs have past unresolved trauma or experience a trauma, the vagus nerve shuts down and cannot shift into rest and digest. The parasympathetic nervous system stimulates the "rest and digest" function. If they determine that there is no threat, their body calms down.

The vagal branch of the ANS responds to environmental clues for physical safety and calms the sympathetic nervous system. The fight response does not become activated. Feeling safe, the body and mind effectively and authentically engage, connect, and interact in the environment. LEOs then can emotionally relate with others, become better listeners, and assess empathy. Words used to describe this state of social engagement are curious, empathetic, creative, or grounded.

> **LAW ENFORCEMENT CONSIDERATION
> & PERSONAL INSIGHT**
>
> How do you know when you are in this state?

Fight or Flight

The human body and brain react to trauma and stress because of its biology that causes it to feel the impact of the severity and repetition of trauma (Javanbakht, 2020). Feeling threatened or unsafe triggers the "fight" or "flight" response to seek safety.

When faced with a real threat, hormones are released to prepare the body to stay or run. The sympathetic nervous system stimulates glands that trigger adrenaline and cortisol. The central nervous system creates the ability to get up and go, run away, and move forward. The brain is alert to danger. Pupils dilate for better vision. The heart and breathing rate increase for energy. The skin becomes flushed as blood shifts to muscles, arms, and legs, which become tense, lock up or tremble, getting ready to respond to the threat.

This response cycle prepares the officer to think quickly as their brain receives more blood flow. The response can last from 20 to 60 minutes after the danger is gone. As a dimension of the ANS, the acute stress response happens automatically in response to an actual threat or is triggered by something that is not a real threat such as a phobia (e.g., fear of an animal, going to the doctor). Words used to describe this state are pounding heart, racing thoughts, or dry mouth.

CASE NOTES

Chad Campese, expert in failure and redemption, husband, father, police officer, Columbus, OH, notes, "When it comes to the stress response we face as officers, we only have three options as the years take their toll. We can freeze, embrace the victim mentality and stay exactly where we're at as we drown in self-pity, anger, and regret. Steadily we push everyone away as our lives slowly implode. We can take flight, running away from real life and the real issues, hoping ignoring them will solve the perceived problem.

"New spouses, new places, new toys and hobbies, even at times a new department or job. But we can never run far enough away from ourselves. We will always catch up. Or we can fight. We can do in our private lives what we were trained to do in our professional careers. Step up, problem solve, and face the giant head on while finding solutions. We signed up to be warriors at work. It's time we were also warriors at home. Our lives, our families, they're worth it. LIFE is worth it. How do I know? Because I was that guy. I jacked it all up, and though it was nothing short of a miracle, I think I've finally come out on the other side. And I hope and pray the same for everyone else. It's so much easier to solve other people's problems. There's nothing harder than looking honestly at our own" *(C. Campese, personal communication, January 31, 2023).*

Freeze State

The parasympathetic nervous system, the dorsal vagal, activates the "freeze" state to survive. This is the stage of shut down where the body, in a defensive reaction activated by a threat, goes numb to self-protect (Roelofs, 2017). The nervous system cannot regulate. The officer pulls away and becomes immobile to self-protect. The dorsal branch regulates organs below their diaphragm, from the back of the brain stem down to the gut, and activates the shutdown of the body. Immobilization is a biological response. When the dorsal vagal nerve has taken over, heart rate and blood pressure decrease with a shift in social behavior.

In a study, LEOs reported their freeze state as standing still, stiffening up, becoming rigid/numb or stopping movement, and regaining a sense of direction by seeking sensory stimuli by scanning their environment, touching their body, walking around the police car and focusing on breathing (Keesman 2022). Words used to describe this state are unable to relate, or shut down.

LAW ENFORCEMENT CONSIDERATION
& PERSONAL INSIGHT

How do you know when you are in this state?

THE NEXT STEP

Thich Nhat Hanh, a Buddhist monk said, "Usually when we hear or read something new, we just compare it to our own ideas. If it is the same, we accept it and say that it is correct. If it is not, we say it is incorrect. In either case, we learn nothing" (Goodreads, n.d.). Maybe after reading this chapter, you have learned something new. In the next chapter, you will increase your awareness of empathic distress, burnout, secondary traumatic stress, and compassion fatigue.

REFERENCES

Bryce, I., Pye, D., Beccaria, G., McIlveen, P., & Du Preez, J. (2023). A systematic literature review of the career choice of helping professionals who have experienced cumulative harm as a result of adverse childhood experiences. *Trauma, Violence, & Abuse*, 24(1), 72–85. https://doi.org/10.1177/15248380211016016

Centers for Disease Control and Prevention (2021). Vital signs. *Adverse Childhood Experiences (ACEs)* Preventing early trauma to improve adult health. https://www.cdc.gov/vitalsigns/aces/index.html

Charles, L.E., Mnatsakanova, A., Fekedulegn, D., Violanti, J.M., Gu, J.K., & Andrew, M.E. (2022). Associations of adverse childhood experiences (ACEs) with sleep duration and quality: the BCOPS study. *Sleep Medicine*, 89, 166–175. https://doi.org/10.1016/j.sleep.2021.12.011

Craddock, T. B., & Telesco, G. (2022). Predicting psychological outcomes in officers exposed to traumatic events. *Journal of the American Academy of Experts in Traumatic Stress*, Winter-Spring, 24–35.

Felitti, V. J., Anda, R. F., Nordenberg, D., Williamson, D. F., Spitz, A. M., Edwards, V., Koss, M. P., & Marks, J. S. (1998). Relationship of childhood abuse and household dysfunction to many of the leading causes of death in adults: The adverse childhood experiences (ACE) Study. *American Journal of Preventive Medicine*, 14(4), 245–258. https://doi.org/10.1016/s0749-3797(98)00017-8

Global Wellness Institute (n.d.). What is wellness? https://globalwellnessinstitute.org/what-is-wellness/?gclid=EAIaIQobChMIuvP23--8-wIVGMmUCR2%20HggirEAAYASAAEgJV_PD_BwE

Goodreads (n.d.). Hanh, T.N. https://www.goodreads.com/quotes/392169-usually-when-we-hear-or-read-something-new-we-just

Harris, M., & Fallot, R. (2001). *Using trauma theory to design service systems: New directions for mental health services.* Jossey Bass.

International Association of Chiefs of Police (2019). *Agency assessment tool and action planning roadmap*, Washington, DC: Bureau of Justice Assistance. https://www.theiacp.org/resources/officer-health-and wellness-agency-assessment-tool-and-action-planning-roadmap

Jackson, L., & Theroux, M. (2023). Police need wellness checks too. *Journal of Community Safety & Well-being*, 8(Suppl 1), S4–S6. https://doi.org/10.35502/jcswb.311

Javanbakht, A. (2020). *The aching blue: Trauma, stress and invisible wounds of those in law enforcement.* Anxiety & Depression Association of America. https://tinyurl.com/c56s3sr6

Keesman, L. D. (2022). "FREEZE?" An analysis of police officers accounts of self-enclosing experiences. *Policing and Society*, 32(8), 981–996. https://doi:10.1080/10439463.2021.2003359

Lane, J., Le, M., Martin, K., Bickle, K., Campbell, E., & Ricciardelli, R. (2022). Police attitudes toward seeking professional mental health treatment. *Journal of Police and Criminal Psychology, 37*, 123–131. https://doi.org/10.1007/s11896-021-09467-6

Levesque, S. (2021). Carrying trauma from birth to work: Adverse childhood experiences in law enforcement officers and their implications. *Criminology Student Work*. 23. https://scholarworks.merrimack.edu/crm_studentpub/23

Mazur, W., & Collins (2023). *The New Jersey Police Chief Magazine*, June. Six trauma management best practices for police organizations: Make mental health a priority to strengthen your personnel's resilience. bit.ly/3R8MR99

Merrick, M. T., Ford, D. C., Ports, K. A., Guinn, A. S., Chen, J., Klevens, J., … Mercy, J. A. (2019). Vital signs: Estimated proportion of adult health problems attributable to adverse childhood experiences and implications for prevention - 25 states, 2015–2017. *MMWR Morbidity and Mortality Weekly Report*, 68(44), 999–1005. https://doi:10.15585/mmwr.mm6844e1

Padilla, K.E. (2023). A descriptive study of police officer access to mental health services. *Journal of Police and Criminal Psychology*. https://doi.org/10.1007/s11896-023-09582-6

Papazoglou, K., Kamkar, K., & Thompson, J. (2021). Law enforcement wellness. *Journal of Community Safety and Well-being*, 6(4), 168–173. https://doi.org/10.35502/jcswb.209

Porges, S. W. (2022). Polyvagal theory: A science of safety. *Frontiers in Integrative Neuroscience*, 16, 27. https://doi.org/10.3389/fnint.2022.871227

Restauri, N., Potigailo, V., & Milla, S. (2023). Onward: Creating conditions for transformation in a parapandemic world. *Journal of the American College of Radiology*, 20(5), 503–509. https://doi.org/10.1016/j.jacr.2023.02.023

Roelofs, K. (2017). Freeze for action: neurobiological mechanisms in animal and human freezing. *Philosophical Transactions of the Royal society B: Biological sciences.* https://doi:10.1098/rstb.2016.0206

Thompson, J., Jetelina, K., & Champine, R. (2022). 144 Prevalence of adverse childhood experiences in a national sample of U.S. law enforcement officers. *Injury Prevention*, 28, A52. http://dx.doi.org/10.1136/injuryprev-2022-SAVIR.133

Tehrani, N. (2022). The psychological impact of COVID-19 on police officers. *The Police Journal*, 95(1), 73–87. https://doi.org/10.1177/0032258X211039975

Tuttle, B. M., Cho, Y., & Waldrop, T. C. (2023). Pre-career exposure to violence as a predictor of emotional distress among police recruits. *The Police Journal*, 96(2), 181–196. https://doi.org/10.1177/0032258X211064712

U.S. Department of Justice (2023). *Law Enforcement Mental Health and Wellness Act (LEMHWA) program.* https://cops.usdoj.gov/lemhwa

van der Kolk (2014). *The body keeps the score: Brain, mind, and body in the healing of trauma.* Penguin Books.

Violanti, J. M., Mnatsakanova, A., Gu, J. K., Service, S., & Andrew, M. E. (2021). Adverse childhood experiences and police mental health. *Policing: An International Journal,* 44(6), 1014–1030. https://doi.org/10.1108/PIJPSM-06-2021-0085

Waehrer, G. M., Miller, T. R., Silverio Marques, S. C., Oh, D. L., & Burke Harris, N. (2020). Disease burden of adverse childhood experiences across 14 states. *PLoSONE15*(1), 1–18, e0226134. https://doi.org/10.1371/journal.pone.0226134

Warner, T. D., Leban, L., Pester, D.A., Walker, J.T. (2023). Contextualizing Adverse Childhood Experiences: The intersections of individual and community adversity. *Journal of Youth and Adolescence,* 52(3), 570–584. https://doi.org/10.1007/s10964-022-01713-2

Wellness (n.d.). https://www.merriam-webster.com/dictionary/wellness

3 | LAW ENFORCEMENT BURNOUT

DEFINITIONS

BURNOUT - a syndrome that has not been successfully managed due to prolonged occupational stress that causes exhaustion.

COMPASSION FATIGUE - comprised of burnout and secondary trauma while helping someone who is stressed, traumatized, or bereaved that impact one's professional quality of life.

SECONDARY TRAUMATIC STRESS - stress reactions that stem from learning about a traumatic incident and helping or wanting to help.

OBJECTIVES

After reading and considering the content of this chapter, the reader should be able to:

- Examine contributors to empathic distress.
- Explain burnout and secondary traumatic stress.
- Identify effective strategies to manage compassion fatigue.

In My Experience & Lessons Learned

JASON PALAMARA

You may have heard the saying, "You drink like a Sailor." While in the Navy, I never fit that mold, whether it was an accurate depiction of the culture or not. As my years on the job as a police officer progressed, it would have been more appropriate for someone to say to me, "You drink like a detective." Sometimes the culture of our organizations can build you up, and potentially, be unhealthy. When cops get together after their shift, at a funeral honoring a fallen brother or sister, or at an organizational function, they drink. "Brother, if you need to talk, I'll always have a cold one waiting for you" is often said to show support. It would serve us best to give that statement a closer look.

As a young cop, I developed my skills first as a patrol officer, and then a detective. And I developed my drinking game that rivaled my Navy years jumping from port to port. Drinking was commonplace on the job—what we did to decompress, to celebrate, and to mourn. Who better understands what that means than someone doing the same job as you? This unhealthy way of processing my workday developed into the way I began to process what happened outside of work. I never gave it a second thought until serious damage had already been done. To shift our culture, we need to discuss the problem with other cops.

Having to respond to a traumatic incident like notifying next of kin of a deceased family member or deescalating a hostile situation are difficult experiences that can cause compassion fatigue (CF), secondary traumatic stress, or vicarious trauma. I often experienced empathetic distress. While being sensitive to what the victim was going through, I felt their pain as I tried to wrap my mind around their trauma. Being empathetic, I numbed the strain as I struggled to process the experience by abusing alcohol. Releasing the mounting pressure of my thoughts in this way helped me reach isolation island. It artificially lightened the load of the weight of the badge.

An all-too-common coping mechanism, once off the clock, for such stresses is turning to alcohol. Unaddressed, this can become more damaging to our emotional and physical well-being than the trauma of the daily activities we experience while we are in uniform. When alcohol becomes a means to an end, it becomes the problem. Law enforcement culture does its fair share of enablement. Together, we de-stress over alcohol, which leads to self-medicating at home with further drinking alone. What we are quick to dismiss as necessary to deal with empathic distress or CF can easily become a problem that we individually and collectively struggle to identify.

It's impossible to train for each job you will respond to, though it is possible to train how to process your thoughts and emotions in a productive and healthy way. As a rookie cop, and then rookie detective, I didn't believe this way of thinking was "a thing." It became "a thing" when years later, I had blocked out expressing and processing what I had experienced and what I had pushed through my "LEO filter," too often a filter of avoidance.

First responders tend to believe this is a healthy way to cope. I often found it hard to focus and look past my current situation. I didn't think of the future as I drank to numb the pain. This isolated me from my family until I realized that changes in my life would only happen if it started with me. I had what I am advocating for, a consistent support structure that can foster positive change.

My expertise was in the hunting of those who took the lives of others. There was no closed door I didn't think could be opened. While opening them at work, I was slowly closing them at home. I didn't know any other way. I was exhausted and had nothing left for those who were waiting for me once I ended my tour. I hadn't yet been introduced to what burnout and secondary traumatic stress were and the impact of CF. I wouldn't make their introduction until much later.

Communicating with victims' families and loved ones consistently contributed to my experience with CF. Although repeatedly hearing and experiencing their pain was a difficult part of the job, I still wouldn't have had it any other way because it was what they needed. What I would have done differently was work towards a better understanding of what the experience was and how I could have effectively processed it. As cops, we have a hard time admitting that we have secondary traumatic stress or empathic strain, let alone know how to recognize traumas and stresses when we are experiencing them.

My Story & Evidence-Based Practices

BARBARA RUBEL

My wife, a firefighter and I, a cop, seemed to handle the stress well.
Of course, these days the stress of the job on the streets is nothing
compared with the stress raining down on them from some city
politicians and certain department administrators.

—Steve Pomper

For most of my mother's 30 years on the police force, she worked as a policewoman in Youth Aid Division 11 in the 78th precinct in Brooklyn, New York. In the 1970s, the department was disbanded, and she was transferred from working with children and families to working as a 911 operator.

One night I woke up to her yelling from her room. She was shouting about trying to get help to someone. I heard her scream, "I can't take ONE more of these calls! I'm a cop—this is not what I signed up for!" She had the highest regard for 911 operators, it just wasn't what she was cut out for. My father, who had retired a few years before, gently said, "It's time to retire, Ida." We went back to bed and the next day, she put in her papers. Empathic strain took its toll as the demands of her job were overwhelming. Although my mother was resilient, she was burned out.

FABULOUS Framework to Manage Burnout

After reviewing years of evidence-based practices, I created the FABU-LOUS framework which focuses on ways to build resilience by putting character strengths into practice to manage one's stressful career (Rubel, 2019; Rubel, 2016). The FABULOUS Framework is an acronym that identifies eight characteristics of resilience for managing burnout, CF, vicarious trauma, empathic distress, moral suffering, and transforms those issues into better job performance and wellness (Parekh de Campos et al., 2023). The protective eight resilience factors are flexibility, attitude, boundaries, being united, laughter, optimism, understanding job satisfaction, and self-compassion (Parekh de Campos et al., 2022; Rubel, 2019). In this chapter, the framework focuses on burnout.

FABULOUS FRAMEWORK TO MANAGE BURNOUT

INSTRUCTIONS: Let's identify eight character strengths that may mitigate the impact of burnout. Review the following burnout symptoms:

BURNOUT SYMPTOMS: cynical, distrust, difficulty concentrating anger, anxiety, powerless, headaches, gastro problems, backaches, ineffective, no accomplishment, lack of motivation, don't enjoy job, poor performance, detachment, shame, sleep problems, chest pain, increased illness, easily irritated, aggressive, mistrust, relationship issues, insomnia, exhaustion, drained, forgetful, high blood pressure.

Now that you have reviewed the many symptoms of burnout, start with #1. Flexibility. Focus on possible causes and risk factors. Next, focus on a character trait, that, when put into practice, helps you to have a flexible mindset. For example:

Resilience competency for Flexibility: being creative helps me to think of different ways to solve a problem.

1. Flexibility

- **CAUSES AND RISK FACTORS:** no input in decision making, don't reframe negative thoughts.
- **RESILIENCE COMPETENCIES:** openness, reflective, critical thinker, creative, inventive.

Resilience competency: (fill-in) helps me to: (fill-in)

2. Attitude

- **CAUSES AND RISK FACTORS:** workforce shortage, financial issues, lack skills for job.
- **RESILIENCE COMPETENCIES:** careful, motivated, agreeable, daring, eager.

Resilience competency: (fill-in) helps me to: (fill-in)

3. Boundaries

- **CAUSES AND RISK FACTORS:** don't set limits, don't say "no," shift work, overtime.
- **RESILIENCE COMPETENCIES:** determined, sense of control, helpful, disciplined, organized.

Resilience competency: (fill-in) helps me to: (fill-in)

4. United

- **CAUSES AND RISK FACTORS:** coworker relationships, protests ineffective leadership.
- **RESILIENCE COMPETENCIES:** attachment to others, collaborative, sociable, outgoing, loyal.

Resilience competency: (fill-in) helps me to: (fill-in)

5. Laughter

- **CAUSES AND RISK FACTORS:** no work-life integration, not appreciated, no employee rewards.
- **RESILIENCE COMPETENCIES:** witty, playful, zest for life, happy, sense of humor, funny, imaginative.

Resilience competency: (fill-in) helps me to: (fill-in)

6. Optimism

- **CAUSES AND RISK FACTORS:** politics, no sense of purpose, lack of control.
- **RESILIENCE COMPETENCIES:** realistic, prudent, trusting, hopeful, religious.

Resilience competency: (fill-in) helps me to: (fill-in)

7. Understanding Job Satisfaction

- **CAUSES AND RISK FACTORS:** lack clear goals, non-engaged, not using skills.
- **RESILIENCE COMPETENCIES:** kindness, skillful, confident, leadership, efficient, brave.

Resilience competency: (fill-in) helps me to: (fill-in)

8. Self-compassion

- **CAUSES AND RISK FACTORS:** critical of self, feel alone when you fail, exaggerate when things go wrong.
- **RESILIENCE COMPETENCIES:** patient with oneself, self-kindness, gentle, humility, tolerant, self-regulation.

Resilience competency: (fill-in) helps me to: (fill-in)

Think positively as you consider the dominant strengths that you have used in the past to manage a stressful situation, and continue to use those strengths to mitigate burnout.

Empathic Distress

Empathy is the capacity to be sensitive to a person's emotional state, which inspires a desire to look out for their well-being (Decety et al., 2021). To be empathic is to sense one's emotions, attitudes, and motivations about their experience and imagine what they are thinking and feeling. Empathy can be experienced affectively, somatically, or cognitively.

- **AFFECTIVE EMPATHY:** aware and sensitive to what the person is going through, understand their experience and aptly respond.
- **SOMATIC EMPATHY:** physically feel their emotions (e.g., fear, anxiety, frown after seeing a victim frown).
- **COGNITIVE EMPATHY:** calmly taking on one's perspective, recognize their thoughts, identify with their feelings and attempt to understand their response.

Although affective empathy is a risk factor for exhaustion and disengagement causing burnout in officers, cognitive empathy is not associated with burnout (Correia et al., 2023). Cognitive empathy can be encouraged in officer selection and training, with no risk of making them more vulnerable to burnout (Correia et al., 2023). Empathy-based strain can bring about adverse occupational health and well-being outcomes, such as burnout, anxiety, and depression (Rauvola et al., 2019). Empathic distress is characterized by a strong, self-related adverse reaction to a person's suffering, and a need to leave the situation to shield oneself from overwhelming negative feelings (Singer et al., 2014; Ashar et al., 2017).

Compassion Fatigue

Compassion refers to understanding a person's distress, recognizing what they are going through and wanting to lessen their suffering. While empathy is the ability to relate to their pain, compassion is the need to help them and alleviate their distress. Compassion fatigue (CF) results from the stress of exposure to a traumatized person rather than from the actual trauma.

CF is the coming together of both occupational burnout and secondary traumatic stress (STS) that causes increased exhaustion, anger, irritability, harmful substance use, absenteeism, reduced feelings of sympathy, empathy, an inability to make decisions, and lack of job satisfaction (Cocker & Joss, 2016). When officers and civilian staff are not familiar with CF or ignore its symptoms, their well-being could be impacted (Papazoglou et al., 2020).

Burnout

The first element of CF is burnout. Burnout is prolonged occupational stress that has not been successfully managed (WHO, 2020) It is a psychological syndrome that is due to chronic workplace stress (Freudenberger, 1974; Maslach, 1976). It is due to an imbalance between job demands and resources.

Excessive workload among officers is a significant predictor of greater emotional exhaustion and depersonalization (McCarty et al., 2019). In policing, both stress and burnout are caused by challenging conditions and working environment, media, and the public perception. Overtime, trauma and conservative-male cultural values (e.g., masculinity, solidarity) increase burnout and adverse behavioral outcomes (Ghazinour et al., 2021).

CASE NOTES

Sherri Martin, MA, LPCA, National Director of Wellness Services Fraternal Order of Police, notes, "Levels of critical stress among members of law enforcement have often been attributed to traumatic scenes experienced during an officer's career, although the profession has long been focused on the impact that critical incidents and trauma have on the well-being of officers, we have not done as good a job with examining other stressors that are parts of a career in law enforcement. Again, surveying members of law enforcement with the 2021 Critical Issues in Policing Survey, the FOP gathered the perceptions and experiences of nearly 6,000 active and retired police officers across the United States.

"When comparing the levels of stress generated by approximately 60 stressors, including not only critical incident stressors related to exposure to trauma, but also organizational and operational stressors, the top-rated source of police stress was staff shortages, classified as an organizational stressor. These findings provide important insight about the most impactful potential focus of wellness services for officers" *(S. Martin, personal communication, April 24, 2023).*

The Fraternal Order of Police partnered with NBC New York to conduct a survey of active and retired sworn officers from across the U.S. (Fraternal Order of Police [FOP] n.d.; Martin, 2018). They found that stressful experiences as an officer cause unresolved emotional issues leading to sleep problems, being easily agitated, withdrawing, recurring, unwanted memories, a change in view of their job and the future, increased jumpiness or watchfulness, and family and relationship problems.

Ninety percent reported stigma as a barrier to getting treatment, 79% reported critical stress at certain points in their career, over 90% reported that the public and the profession are unaware that critical stress is a problem in law enforcement, and 73% reported peer support as the most helpful of treatments.

CASE NOTES

Joe Fox, NYPD Chief, 37 years (Retired), notes, "Law enforcement leaders must recognize that we have a significant number of officers who are quietly 'working while wounded,' regardless of how functional they may appear from the outside. We are responsible for the safety of our officers, and that includes managing the injuries we cannot see. Leaders must openly talk to their officers about mental wellness and proactively provide resources to manage traumatic exposures, even before they occur. Until we can fully acknowledge that we have a growing crisis in our profession, we will never change the culture or eliminate the stigma that exists for seeking help. If we don't take care of them, no one will" *(J. Fox, personal communication, April 17, 2023).*

Occupational and Organizational Stress

Occupational stress is the harmful physical and emotional responses that happen when the job requirements do not match the worker's capabilities, resources, or needs that can lead to poor health and even injury (NIOSH, 2023). Police organizational stressors are inadequate training, perceived inequality, public scrutiny, long hours, on call and specialized duties (Craddock & Telesco, 2022).

Organizational stressors are culture and climate, continuous shifts, inflexible work schedule, and inability to participate in decision-making. Stressors include absence of leadership, lack of recognition, perceived unfairness, and leaders showing favoritism to others. Inadequate resources, time constraints, interpersonal disputes with coworkers and superiors, and a bureaucratic organizational structure that punishes and severely manages individuals also impact well-being (Purba et al., 2019).

Secondary Traumatic Stress

The second element of CF is secondary traumatic stress (STS), which is "the natural consequent behaviors and emotions resulting from knowing about a traumatizing event experienced by a significant other—the stress resulting from helping or wanting to help a traumatized or suffering person" (Figley, 1995, p. 7). It results when an officer learns the details of a person's trauma who they were helping, rather than personally experiencing the event (Essary et al., 2020).

Secondary Traumatic Stress Symptoms

STS symptoms bring about alterations in arousal and reactivity. While PTS symptoms are due to direct exposure, STS symptoms are due to indirect exposure. Symptoms can include changes in cognition and mood, difficulty remembering details of a trauma, guilt or shame when recalling the trauma, feeling on guard, irritable, angry, easily startled, or avoiding people, places, and situations that trigger the memory of the trauma. Three STS dimensions are:

- **INTRUSION:** pounding heart, relive a person's trauma, upset by reminders, nightmares, and distressing thoughts of what happened to the other person.
- **AVOIDANCE:** emotionally numb, little interest in things, less active, discouraged about the future.
- **AROUSAL:** jumpy, lack concentration, easily annoyed, expect bad things to happen, tension and preoccupation with individual or cumulative trauma, trouble sleeping, overly alert.

> **LAW ENFORCEMENT CONSIDERATION & PERSONAL INSIGHT**
>
> Has an ongoing problem finally caught up to you?

Compassion Satisfaction

Compassion satisfaction (CS,) a term introduced by Stamm in 1997, refers to the "satisfaction with and positive feelings of helping, as well as a sense of self-efficacy related to helping" (Christian-Brandt, 2020, p.2). CS becomes a strength that acts as a shield against CF (Grant, 2019). Stress is decreased, and CS is increased when they have recognition from other LEOs and members of the public (Davies et al., 2022).

CS increases when there is appropriate staffing, and when leaders promote a culture of caring, professional development, teamwork, and eliminating mistrust and intimidating behavior (The Center for Victims of Torture (n.d.). CS may lessen the impact of burnout (Ruiz-Fernández et al., 2020). CF and CS among officers is understudied even though they frequently encounter trauma (Andersen & Papazoglou, 2015).

Professional Quality of Life Measure (ProQOL)

The Professional Quality of Life Measure (ProQOL, Version 5) is a self-assessment commonly used to measure burnout, STS, CS and CF (The Center for Victims of Torture, 2021). The scale has 30 questions to assess issues that impact mental health (Stamm 2010). This free measure is used in many law enforcement studies related to mental health.

THE NEXT STEP

This chapter increased your knowledge about empathic distress, burnout, secondary traumatic stress and compassion fatigue. Chapter 5 focuses on maladaptive coping strategies and how culture, stigma, shame, and confidentiality may prevent a LEO from getting help.

REFERENCES

Andersen, J. P., & Papazoglou, K. (2015). Compassion fatigue and compassion satisfaction among police officers: An understudied topic. *International Journal of Emergency Mental Health and Human Resilience*, 17(3), 661–663. bit. ly/3Lja0BV

Ashar, Y. K., Andrews-Hanna, J. R., Dimidjian, S., & Wager, T. D. (2017). Empathic distress is the negative affect arising in response to others' suffering—Empathic care and distress. *Neuron, 94*(6), 1263–1273. https://doi. org/10.1016/j.neuron.2017.05.014.

The Center for Victims of Torture (2021). *Professional Quality of Life. ProQOL, Version 5*. https://proqol.org/proqol-measure.

The Center for Victims of Torture (n.d.). Compassion satisfaction. bit.ly/3RfJrRU

Christian-Brandt, A. S., Santacrosse, D. E., & Barnett, M. L. (2020). In the trauma-informed care trenches: Teacher compassion satisfaction, secondary traumatic stress, burnout, and intent to leave education within underserved elementary schools. *Child Abuse & Neglect*, 110(3), 104437.

Cocker, F., & Joss, N. (2016). Compassion fatigue among healthcare, emergency and community service workers: a systematic review. *International Journal of Environmental Research and Public Health,* 13(6), 1–18. bit.ly/3P5fpxH

Correia, I., Romão, Â., Almeida, A.E. & Ramo, S. (2023). Protecting police officers against burnout: Overcoming a fragmented research field. *Journal of Police and Criminal Psychology*. https://doi.org/10.1007/s11896-023-09584-4

Craddock, T.B., & Telesco, G. (2022). Predicting psychological outcomes in officers exposed to traumatic events. *Journal of the American Academy of Experts in Traumatic Stress*, Winter-Spring, 24–35.

Davies, L. E., Brooks, M., & Braithwaite, E. C. (2022). Compassion fatigue, compassion satisfaction, and burnout, and their associations with anxiety and depression in UK police officers. *The Police Journal.* https:// doi:10.1177/0032258X221106107

Decety, J., & Holvoet, C. (2021). The emergence of empathy. *Developmental Review*, 62, 100999. bit.ly/44YCzfb

Essary, J. N., Barza, L., & Thurston, R. J. (2020). Secondary traumatic stress among educators. *Kappa Delta Pi Record*, 56(3), 116–121.

Figley, C. R. (Ed.). (1995). *Compassion fatigue: Coping with secondary traumatic stress disorder in those who treat the traumatized*. Brunner/Mazel.

Fraternal Order of Police (FOP). (n.d.). *Report on FOP/NBC survey of police officer mental and behavioral health*. https://fop.net/officer-wellness/survey/

Freudenberger, H.J. (1974). Staff burn-out. *Journal of Social Issues*, 30(1), 159–165. https://doi.org/10.1111/j.1540-4560.1974.tb00706.x

Ghazinour, M., & Rostami, A. (2021). Social ecology of police resilience. In M. Ungar (Ed.), *Multisystemic resilience: Adaptation and transformation in contexts of change*, 181–196. Oxford University Press.

Grant, H. B., Lavery, C. F., & Decarlo, J. (2019). An exploratory study of police officers. *Frontiers in Psychology*, 9. https://doi:10.3389/fpsyg.2018.02793

Martin, S. (2018). National officer wellness committee and NBC *Report on FOP/ NBC survey of police officer mental and behavioral health*. https://tinyurl.com/2ut7mnwz

Maslach, C. (1976). Burned-out. *Human Behavior* 5(9), 16–22.

McCarty, W. P., Aldirawi, H., Dewald, S., & Palacios, M. (2019). Burnout in blue. *Police Quarterly*, 22, 278–304. https://doi.org/10.1177/1098611119828038

National Institute for Occupational Safety and Health (NIOSH). (2023). *Stress at work. Job Stress*. https://www.cdc.gov/niosh/topics/stress/default.html

Papazoglou, K., Marans, S., Keesee, T., & Chopko, B. (2020). Police compassion fatigue. *FBI Law Enforcement Bulletin*, 1–9.

Parekh de Campos, A., Boysen, R., & Coyle-Saeed, S. (2022). *Loss, grief, and bereavement, 5th ed*. Elite Learning. Colibri Healthcare.

Pomper, S. (2021). Healthy Homes Allows Peace Officers' Mental Health to Thrive. *National Police Association*. https://tinyurl.com/y283mn4n

Purba, A., & Demou, E. (2019). The relationship between organisational stressors and mental wellbeing within police officers: a systematic review. *BMC Public Health*, 19, 1286. https://doi.org/10.1186/s12889-019-7609-0

Rauvola, R. S., Vega, D. M., & Lavigne, K. N. (2019). Compassion fatigue, secondary traumatic stress, and vicarious traumatization: A qualitative review and research agenda. *Occupational Health Science*, 3, 297–336. bit.ly/3sKw5Ty

Rubel, B. (2019). *Loss, grief, and bereavement: Helping individuals cope.* (4th ed.). SC Publishing, Elite Healthcare.

Rubel, B. (2016). *Death, dying, and bereavement: Providing compassion during at time of need* (3ed). Western Schools.

Ruiz-Fernández, M. D., Ramos-Pichardo, J. D., Ibáñez-Masero, O., Cabrera-Troya, J., Carmona-Rega, M. I., & Ortega-Galán, Á. M. (2020). Compassion fatigue, burnout, compassion satisfaction and perceived stress in healthcare professionals during the COVID-19 health crisis in Spain. *Journal of Clinical Nursing*, 29, (21–22), 4321–4330.

Singer, T., & Klimecki, O. M. (2014). Empathy and compassion. *Current Biology*, 24(18), R875-R878. https://doi.org/10.1016/j.cub.2014.06.054

Stamm, B. H. (2010). The concise ProQOL manual, 2nd edition. Pocatello, ID.

Stamm, B. H. (1997). Work related secondary traumatic stress. https://www.researchgate.net/publication/290118676

World Health Organization [WHO] (2020). Burnout an 'occupational phenomenon': International classification of diseases. https://www.who.int/news/item/28-05-2019-burn-out-an-occupational-phenomenon-international-classification-of-diseases.

4 | COPS AND MALADAPTIVE COPING

DEFINITIONS

MALADAPTIVE COPING - a counterproductive action used to deal with stress or a difficult situation, which limits the ability to adapt and ultimately impacts well-being.

OBJECTIVES

After reading and considering the content of this chapter, the reader should be able to:

- Explain how maladaptive coping strategies increases occupational stress.
- Identify how culture, stigma, shame, and confidentiality prevent law enforcement professionals from getting help.

In My Experience & Lessons Learned

JASON PALAMARA

Rather than a singular event, a culmination of stressful and traumatic events over the course of my career have impacted my functioning and physical health and have strained relationships. Trauma can be explained as a culmination of what we see and experience as a LEO that builds up over the course of our career. When left unaddressed, we slowly buckle under the weight of our traumas. We aren't quick to talk about trauma-related stress.

Stigma and confidentiality are obstacles in getting help. Stigma is imbedded in our culture surrounding speaking about our mental health. Stigma is what a LEO looks to avoid by not talking about something because they fear that they will get "jammed up," put on the "rubber gun squad"—get stripped of their gun and shield and placed on administrative duty until cleared again for "full-duty" status. It is easier to keep quiet and not be labeled as damaged goods which seems to stay with you through your career.

Not discussing my personal issues with someone brought with it more stress. I felt a quiet shame that was left to mature. It began to eat away at all that was good in my life. How could I not have everything together? Confidentiality should be the bedrock that all else is built upon. Without it, especially in law-enforcement, an unstable environment remains.

Although the problems I caused were mine to fix, I didn't know how to fix them. I felt ashamed. I operated through *all or nothing* thinking. There was no in-between. Countless times my wife told me, "Jason, things are not always black and white. They are sometimes gray." I wasn't about to talk to the ones who I had hurt. I did not want to traumatize them by listening to me share my trauma. I was avoiding doing so for myself as well as for them.

Staying at work, and alcohol once off the clock, were my holistic approach to mitigating the effects of the weight of the badge and everything wrong in life. Liquor was my elixir and a false embodiment of a solution and temporary remedy that had prolonging qualities—numbing the pain and allowing me to escape to my island vacation for brief periods of time. As the numbing wore off, I returned asking myself what was it that I needed and what stopped me from changing. I then took control and reduced the visits to my island.

Would you allow a perpetrator on the street to take control of your gun in a fight of your life? You would battle them while calling over your radio for back up. You have the power to lift yourself from your struggles. Great strength can come from a great struggle. It will not be easy, but neither is fighting a guy who outweighs you, is taller than you, and high on PCP. You'll do it though, won't you, because your life depends on it.

I often used breathing exercises to calm my body and mind and focused on my Christian faith. Author and lecturer, Alan Watts said, "Muddy water is best cleared when leaving it alone" (Goodreads, n.d.). I read how the brain is affected by our thoughts, actions, and food choices. So, I thought about what I was doing all those times the urge hit to drink. Then, when I poured myself a drink, I asked myself what could I do instead?

I had shut my wife out for too long. Also, I couldn't have a good workout if I was drinking and eating garbage. I was using maladaptive coping mechanisms to deal with the everyday bad experiences of the job. But, I was able to turn that around. . . and so can you! My wife and I got back in the gym, which helped us to grow in our relationship. We found our rhythm again, grew in our faith, and saw the positive results of doing the simplest things together.

Hunting murderers needed my every thought and nothing less. Always looking to be one step ahead had put me one step behind my health and well-being, and another step back from a healthy family life. My wife and children got what was left, which wasn't much. I worked around the clock through some intense investigations. I became more attached to victims and their families than my own, used maladaptive coping mechanisms, and was on a crash course due to stress, trauma, burnout, and secondary traumatic stress. It took work to change this dynamic.

If you and the members of your department are like mine, if a fellow officer has died by suicide, you would rally the troops and do what you could to ensure that they were properly honored, and their surviving family members were taken care of emotionally and financially. If you could be that supportive after the fact, why not explore what you can do to help someone who is not coping well before a suicide occurs?

My Story & Evidence-Based Practices

BARBARA RUBEL

"Not why the addiction but why the pain."
—Gabor Maté

Years ago, I presented a workshop at the American Association for Suicidology conference and met Dr. Edwin Shneidman, a distinguished suicidologist. He told me that we must look at physical pain as much as mental pain when we talk about suicide. After retiring from the force, my father suffered with severe back pain. In keeping with a stiff upper lip notion of masculinity, he chose not to meet with a pain doctor, try pain medications, or even talk to his family. Instead, his maladaptive way of coping was to write a suicide note and take his life three weeks before becoming a grandfather to triplets. We got the message that he was suffering, but unfortunately for all of us, not soon enough.

Maladaptive coping, which is not a mental illness, is a counterproductive action such as self-harm, binge eating, substance abuse or, in extreme cases, suicide used to deal with stress or a difficult situation, which limits the ability to adapt. Instead, LEOs should use adaptive coping strategies, such as problem solving, getting enough sleep, seeking peer or professional support, limiting alcohol intake, and exercising, which can help them avoid the fate of my father.

Maladaptive Coping and ACEs

If an officer has not worked through their experience of abuse, neglect, or household dysfunction as a child, it may impact their behavior as an adult. Their current maladaptive strategies could possibly be due to the overwhelming stress they experienced as a child (e.g., family conflict, poor treatment, unvalidated emotions (Wadsworth, 2015). If officers have built unhealthy emotional walls around themselves because they did not feel safe or had no boundaries as a child, these walls may keep them from feeling safe or loved as an adult. ACEs may directly influence emotion regulation and the types of coping strategies adults use, which can lead to even greater physical and emotional stress vulnerability (Sheffler et al., 2019).

An attachment injury early in life can make them be on high alert all the time. LEOs may drink too much, feel emotionally numb, daydream excessively, or take unnecessary risks. They may feel sick, can't shake off persistent thoughts, or feel angry. They may find it hard to solve problems never having learned healthy ways to cope. "There is broad understanding within the field that alcohol abuse, divorce, hypertension, and depression are occupational hazards that equal or surpass threats of violent encounters opposed by patrolling and fighting crime" (Spence et al. (2019), p. 25 para 3).

In July 2019, the Officer Safety and Wellness Group (OSW) assembled. During this meeting, the OSW Group made several recommendations for future research as well as program and policy changes departments can consider safeguarding officer wellness (Bradley, 2020). Although these five questions need to be explored in the research, we can discuss them in relation to maladaptive coping.

1. How pervasive a problem is pre-existing or unresolved trauma in LEOs?
2. What is the nature and extent of early life traumatic experiences on LEOs?
3. How many LEOs have experienced either physical or sexual abuse as children?
4. What impact, if any, did that have on their decision to become a LEO?
5. Does the nature of police work trigger previous trauma for some officers?

LAW ENFORCEMENT CONSIDERATION & PERSONAL INSIGHT

What behaviors do you want to increase (e.g., mindfulness, emotion regulation) and what behaviors do you want to decrease (e.g., addiction, acting without thinking)?

Maladaptive Coping and Police Organizational Stress

My father used situational avoidance when he did not go to the doctor to manage his pain, perhaps fearing he would hear bad news about his health. As a retired sergeant, he kept a lot to himself. He used a common form of cognitive avoidance: denial. The last time I spoke with him, I was in the hospital awaiting the birth of triplets, and on complete bed rest. He was looking forward to being a grandpa. Although mental illness, a personality trait, or an ACE may cause an officer to use avoidance coping, in my father's case, he had chronic pain issues after 21 years of service.

Organizational stress and conservative-male culture are predictors of mal-adaptive coping (Gutschmidt et al., 2022). Officers may attempt to survive with repeated maladaptive thoughts and behaviors and get used to living in a maladaptive stress response (e.g., binge eating, self-harm, anger). Those who use maladaptive coping such as denial, blame, and negative distraction are more vulnerable to developing psychological stress when faced with job demands (Kaur et al., 2013). Maladaptive coping behaviors due to law enforcement stress that are repeatedly cited by research include alcoholism, abuse of medications or illicit substances, isolation, depersonalization, avoidance of outside of law enforcement connections, negative perception of others, and pornography.

Avoidance Coping

When a LEO denies or minimizes something, so they don't have to confront the problem, they are using avoidance coping. Procrastination is linked to anxiety, depression, and low self-esteem. It is an avoidance coping strategy, and is associated with poor mental health (e.g., depression, anxiety, stress symptoms, disabling pain in the upper extremities), unhealthy lifestyle behaviors (e.g., poor sleep, physical inactivity), and negative levels of psychosocial health factors (e.g., loneliness economic difficulties) (Johansson et al., 2023).

LAW ENFORCEMENT CONSIDERATION & PERSONAL INSIGHT

What are you avoiding and more importantly, why are you avoiding it?

Alcohol Use

Some officers believe that a few drinks with peers can temporarily ease anxiety—racing thoughts, chest pain, or feeling jittery. Although a drink temporarily numbs anxiety, in the long run, this maladaptive coping behavior can make problem-solving an issue and make anxiety worse. It is customary for officers to meet at the bar. When an officer excessively drinks, their health suffers from unintentional injuries, high blood pressure, liver cirrhosis, or cancer. Alcohol can be a poison, especially when mixed with drugs—an interaction that can kill. Being in denial or not being truthful about their consumption can interfere with their wellness.

CASE NOTES

James Flynn, Recovery Coach, notes, "In my sobriety, I have had the pleasure of getting to know four different police officers who were in recovery from alcoholism. One was my boss, one was my temporary sponsor, another was an acquaintance that I frequently heard share in meetings, and the last one was someone I worked with in treatment. Fun fact, in NYC, years ago they used to have an A.A. meeting called Cops and Robbers. The meeting was frequented by cops who were in recovery, and those whose stories included a fair amount of criminal justice involvement. The focus was on the participant's similarities rather than their differences" *(J. Flynn, personal communication, January 12, 2023).*

Culture, Stigma, Shame, and Confidentiality

There are many obstacles and stigmas. Accordingly, evidence-based wellness and stress reduction begins by changing the culture, reducing stigma and shame, and maintaining confidentiality.

CASE NOTES

Adam A. Meyers, founder of Stop the Threat — Stop the Stigma, former WI police detective, notes, "Public safety professionals who openly seek help for their mental health often face personal or professional criticism, discrimination, and sometimes termination. This should not deter them from seeking help, but it does. Mental illness is not a flaw in character or a sign of personal or professional weakness. Public safety leaders must take a helpful approach when anyone in their command is struggling from mental health issues.

"Leaders should establish peer support groups and actively participate in them. Leaders, 'Are you a part of the problem or the solution?' Public safety professionals need to be able to trust the leaders and colleagues of their departments to recognize the obstacles and stigmas associated with mental health. They need to feel comfortable and confident that if they are involved in a critical incident and later struggle with mental health issues from the incident, that help will be available with no strings attached" *(A.A. Meyers, personal communication, December 29, 2022).*

Police Culture

Culture is a combination of knowledge, beliefs and behaviors that involve ethnic heritage, racial, religious, geographic, or social groups, including personal identification, language, thoughts, communications, actions, customs, beliefs, values, and institutions (NIH, 2021). Culture includes personal traits, gender, sexual orientation, physical qualities, and religious practices (Hunter, 2022). There is a common theme woven through police culture that centers on beliefs, attitudes, and norms. Generally, police culture is characterized by skepticism and suspicion of the public, assessing individuals in terms of a potential threat, a "we versus they" mentality toward the public, and peer group loyalty (Paoline, 2001).

Police culture emphasizes being "overtly masculine, politically conservative, communally isolated, cynical, action-oriented, and extremely loyal to other officers" (Raganella et al., 2004, p. 282). Police culture is frequently portrayed as cynical with pervasive toxic masculinity and where mental illness stigma adds a burden to those already struggling with mental health issues (Demou et al., 2020).

Some male officers believe that they must conform to social status and masculinity norms and don't admit they have a problem that might impact negatively on their career (Sitko-Dominik, 2022). Stereotypical femininity norms that contradict patterns of male behavior are sharing emotions, disclosing difficulties, and expressing the need for support or professional help.

A study found that 43% to 60% of public safety personnel (e.g., police officers, correctional workers, firefighters) would never, or only as a last resort, seek professional mental health care (Carleton et al., 2020). The emphasis needs to be framing the message that getting help might make them feel stronger and reaching out is an act of toughness. Fellow officers and supervisors should not doubt the authenticity of those with poor mental health or make accusations that inhibit disclosure and help seeking behaviors (Bell et al., 2022).

Departments can provide early, dedicated support, respect confidentiality, connect employees with resources, make accommodations, maintain a strong connection between employees and the organization, have vocal leadership support, and share stories of lived experience that normalize human challenges (Workplace Suicide Prevention & Postvention Committee, 2022). To enhance well-being, departments can:

- Adopt organizational policies on wellness.
- Protect professional development training budgets.
- Offer training on managing STS.
- Create a vicarious trauma-informed workplace.
- Establish an organizational culture of peer support.
- Have social networks for self-disclosure.
- Create a spiritual workplace where employees feel positive energy and connection toward the agency.
- Be consistent while cultivating mutual colleague recognition and support.
- Praise employees for their contribution.
- Be a role model and demonstrate the importance of choosing a balanced lifestyle.
- Create partnerships and form new alliances to share practices to promote high standards of policing that have a direct impact on their role.

CASE NOTES

Jeff Thompson, Ph.D., Columbia U. Medical Center, Department of Psychiatry, NYPD Detective (Retired), notes, "A title or rank doesn't define police leadership—especially when it comes to suicide prevention, resilience, and well-being. Changing culture and fighting stigma must start with you so, make your own mental health a priority. That's not selfish, it's smart and it's something you deserve. Inspire others by your actions because we're all in this together" *(J. Thompson, personal communication, January 3, 2023).*

Police culture is viewed as being unaccepting of weakness and encourages officers to bottle up their feelings and avoid seeking help for mental health concerns (Porter & Lee, 2023). The culture of masculinity, cynicism and solidarity are associated with mental health problems at work (Velazquez & Hernandez, 2019). Police culture may view officers with problems as weak and unfit for duty, and that receiving psychiatric counseling may hinder career progress (Burns et al., 2020).

Police organizations are facing a mental health crisis of epic proportion, and a fundamental change in the police culture must occur (Craddock & Telesco, 2022). Change must include leadership who recognize that LEOs are not faking being sick, they are faking being well (Edwards, 2023). Seven practices for leaders to strengthen police employee-employer relations and improve an officer's well-being are:

1. **COMMUNICATION.** Listen properly, consider their body language, tell stories, and remain calm.
2. **EMOTIONAL INTELLIGENCE.** Understand their emotions as well as the officer's emotions. Be self-aware, empathetic, have impulse control, the ability to problem-solve, and remain optimistic.
3. **VULNERABILITY.** Admit that they make mistakes, are learning and growing.
4. **AUTHENTICITY.** With modesty and humility, they make decisions that reflect their values.
5. **GROWTH MINDSET.** Embrace challenges and recognize that they are a source of growth.
6. **EMPATHY.** While sensing an officer's needs, they understand and respond appropriately.
7. **ACCOUNTABILITY.** They own their actions, decisions and their mistakes (Edwards, 2023).

CASE NOTES

Mike Teeter, Retired Captain, Seattle Police Department, President, Teeter Consulting Group LLC, notes, "In Law Enforcement, as in many professions, it is easy to point the finger at our leadership as the source of the problems in our organizations. Through 21st Century Police Leadership training (21CPL), mandated for all new mid-level managers and above in Washington State, we take a different approach.

"Whatever your position in your organization, there are things you can do now to improve the experience and engagement and well-being of the people on your team. Building meaningful relationships with your people comes first, as the members of your team need to know that their leaders know them and care about them as people. Communication is another key, making sure we keep those within our area of influence informed about the what and the why of significant decisions and changes impacting on them and their work. The last key element we focus on is culture.

"By culture, I mean building a culture where people on our teams can share opinions about upcoming decisions, where we actively work to mentor and develop them, where all are treated with dignity and respect and where we approach leadership from a values-based, servant-oriented perspective. Using these principles, many law enforcement leaders are already making this profession and their workplaces better and reducing the organizational stress their teams experience" *(M. Teeter, personal communication, January 14, 2023).*

Stigma

Viktor Frankl (1996) said, "Everything can be taken from a man but one thing: the last of the human freedoms—to choose one's attitude in any given set of circumstances, to choose one's own way." Leaders and officers can choose a social attitude that continues the stigma or choose a path toward wellness. Stigma, a negative social attitude, is linked to an attribute that implies social disapproval that may lead to being discriminated against (APA, n.d.). Being that the word, stigma, originated from the Greek word, "mark," they may feel that using these services would mark them as weak. Perceived stigma can reduce help-seeking behaviors that increase the risk of suicidal behavior (Carpiniello et al., 2017).

A barrier in accessing mental health is a reluctance for LEOs to discuss a psychological issue with peers because of a cultural taboo associated with this type of discussion (Bell & Eski, 2016). The likelihood of their voluntarily utilizing stress intervention services would increase if they perceived their organization was in support of these services, but if they perceive being stigmatized, there is a significant decline in using them (Tucker, 2015). It is stressful to consider general mental health care due to fear of a fitness for duty evaluation (FFDE) or the possibility of losing their job (Fox et al., 2012; Padilla, 2016).

Based on a national study of U.S. law enforcement, over 90% of officers perceive stigma as negatively influencing help-seeking behavior, and when they access services and find them effective, levels of stigma are extremely high (Drew & Martin, 2021). They are negatively impacted by perceptions of stigma when contacting support services (Acquadro Maran et al., 2022). When leadership and management address wellness, there is a potential to create a work environment where mental health stigma is reduced and where employees feel able to seek psychological help (Wild et al., 2020).

CASE NOTES

Toby Darby, Police Captain at City of Glendale, CA, notes, "I have been in law enforcement for 29 years. The law enforcement culture has always been to suppress and hide your feelings after dealing with a critical incident. I, personally, didn't want to look weak not only to my peers, but my superiors. I think some good advice to law enforcement leaders would be to show some vulnerability before, during and after a critical incident. If an officer saw that their leaders were open to peer counseling, or were very supportive and encouraging after an incident, then the officer will more than likely feel safe to talk about what they are going through. A leader who is open and talks about their feelings is also very beneficial" *(T. Darby, personal communication, March 20, 2023)*.

Shame

Shame is a common feeling connected to PTS symptoms, including dissociation, which include changes and disturbances to consciousness, memory, self-identity, and bodily and environmental experiences (Kouri et al., 2023). Being that shame is a deeply engrained emotion, avoidance strategies don't work. It's hard to get over embarrassment. Officers may feel as if fellow officers are sneering, or supervisors are being condescending. Becoming resentful can give rise to black and white thinking, a type of thought pattern that makes them reason through absolutes. They may not share their suffering due to a social taboo which makes them avoid painful thoughts, especially if they do not want to burden others (Busch, 2020).

If they experience shame and fear rejection, they may act in ways that bring about more feelings of shame, which may cause them to cope in unhealthy ways. As a result, they may constantly worry about rejection and think that there is something wrong with them. They may fear that they will be perceived as weak by other officers (Brough et al., 2016). Perhaps they don't get help because they're using the same maladaptive coping methods, judging or enabling each other. LEOs may get help if they realize that other officers experience the same symptoms (Queirós et al., 2020).

CASE NOTES

Mark Goulston, psychiatrist, former FBI and police hostage negotiation trainer and author of *Just Listen*, notes, "Guilt is feeling you have done something wrong; shame is feeling there is something wrong with you" *(M. Goulston, personal communication, May 14, 2023).*

Therapy can alleviate deep-rooted issues of shame and self-blame. I reached out to therapists from different trauma modalities, including cognitive behavioral therapy (CBT), dialectical behavior therapy (DBT), emotion-focused therapy (EFT), and eye movement desensitization and reprocessing (EMDR). I was told that a LEO may not realize that shame is universal and may believe that they are defective. The consensus was that officers can focus on the origin of where the idea of their being defective came from.

LAW ENFORCEMENT CONSIDERATION & PERSONAL INSIGHT

If you feel shame in your body, how can you regulate your state (e.g., walk, jog in place, do pushups, adjust posture) to shift your mindset?

Confidentiality

Although stigma is an obstacle to help-seeking among officers, worries about confidentiality is also an obstacle (Newell et al., 2022). Confidentiality is paramount being that stigma is a barrier to seeking support (Watson et al., 2018). Departments need to provide confidential access to culturally competent public safety clinicians whether they are in private practice, in-house, or telehealth.

CASE NOTES

Karen DiRienzo, LICSW, Mental Health Clinician, Burlington Police Department, MA, notes, "As a co-responder clinician, I have had the privilege to ride alongside officers in their cruiser, a unique place for a civilian to be. The talks in the cruiser to and from calls—the chatting about the daily demands of the job, the past calls that they will never forget, the unknown of the scene we were heading to—gave me an inside view of the first responder culture and their resilience. As time went by, conversations slowly progressed to beyond the job—family stress, marital issues and financial pressures. They talked and I listened.

"Many in this profession are reluctant to seek therapy or mental health support. They rely on their character strengths and each other to manage their job and stress. There needs to be a feeling of true connection and trust, what I call 'the glue,' for an officer to feel safe to share; no therapeutic relationship or treatment modality will be successful without it.

"The stigma for reaching out for help will melt away when an officer knows that the clinician understands their job, is not offended by their language and dark humor, will not flinch as they hear the details of a horrific scene that has forever left an imprint on them, and will not judge. I want that officer who needs help to know that their confidentiality will be protected. We are out there and ready to listen" *(K. DiRienzo, personal communication, March 1, 2023).*

Officers need good leadership and management at the group level, with a supportive organizational environment and team support regarding mental health (Wild et al., 2020). Comments provided by officers to me:

- "I would be humiliated if they found out."
- "I am not going to be branded as weak."
- "I know that my partner wouldn't want to work with me if he knew."
- "I was bullied on the job and did nothing about it. I'm retired now and it still bothers me."
- "I won't tell you what happened. I will tell you this. If it got out, I would lose my job."

Barriers in accessing mental health services are that LEOs don't believe that they have a problem, are concerned about confidentiality, believe that psychologists cannot relate to policing, or may be stigmatized that they are not fit for duty (Jetelina et al., 2022).

CASE NOTES

Marlon Marrache, Lieutenant LAPD (Retired), father, Savage Training Group Law Enforcement Instructor, notes, "If there was the availability of reaching out twenty-five years ago to a law enforcement liaison that has the best interest in you, has the police compatibility, understands the everyday life of a patrol and/or detective meaning, they have the same experience and circumstances as you did or do, you would be able to have officers and detectives show up to work emotionally healthy.

"Further, there are a lot of LEOs that still have trauma in which they feel like there is no closure because they simply hesitate to open up, especially the ones that have been involved in an officer-involved shooting. Thus, it is germane that today's law enforcement officer to seek and talk to a professional" *(M. Marrache, personal communication, July 21, 2023).*

THE NEXT STEP

This chapter increased your awareness of maladaptive coping. In Chapter 5, we highlight how to manage moral distress in a healthy way and explore symptoms and protective factors against moral injury. The chapter focuses on how mindfulness meditative practices, trauma-sensitive mindfulness, therapy, and pastoral intervention are strategies to manage moral injury.

REFERENCES

Acquadro Maran, D., Magnavita, N., & Garbarino, S. (2022). Identifying organizational stressors that could be a source of discomfort in police officers. *International Journal of Environmental Research and Public Health*, 19(6). https://doi:10.3390/ijerph19063720

American Psychological Association. Dictionary of Psychology. (n.d.). Stigma. https://dictionary.apa.org/stigma

Bell, S., & Eski, Y., (2016). "Break a Leg—It's all in the mind": Police officers' attitudes towards colleagues with mental health issues. *Policing: A Journal of Policy and Practice*, 10(2), 95–101, https://doi.org/10.1093/police/pav041

Bell, S., Palmer-Conn, S., & Kealey, N. (2022). "Swinging the lead and working the head"—An explanation as to why mental illness stigma is prevalent in policing. *The Police Journal*, 95(1), 4–23. https://doi.org/10.1177/0032258X211049009

Bradley, Kelly D. (2020). *Promoting Positive Coping Strategies in Law Enforcement: Emerging Issues and Recommendations*. Officer safety and wellness group meeting summary. Washington, DC: Office of Community Oriented Policing Services. https://tinyurl.com/5n7r3r4u

Brough, P., Chataway, S., & Biggs, A. (2016). You don't want people knowing you're a copper! A contemporary assessment of police organizational culture. *International Journal of Police Science & Management*, 18(1) 28–36.

Burns, C., & Buchanan, M. (2020). Factors that influence the decision to seek help in a police population. *International Journal of Environmental Research and Public Health*, 17(18). https://doi.org/10.3390/ijerph17186891

Busch, B., & McNamara, T. (2020). Language and trauma: An introduction. *Applied Linguistics*, 41(3), 323–333. https://doi.org/10.1093/applin/amaa002

Carleton, R. N., Afifi, T. O., Turner, S., Taillieu, T., Vaughan, A. D., Anderson, G. S., Ricciardelli, R., MacPhee, R. S., Cramm, H. A., Czarnuch, S., Hozempa, K., & Camp, R. D. (2020). Mental health training, attitudes toward support, and screening positive for mental disorders. *Cognitive Behaviour Therapy*, 49(1), 55–73. https://doi.org/10.1080/16506073.2019.1575900

Carpiniello, B., & Pinna, F. (2017). The reciprocal relationship between suicidality and stigma. *Frontiers in Psychiatry*, 8, 35. https://doi.org/10.3389/fpsyt.2017.00035

Craddock, T. B., & Telesco, G. (2022). Predicting psychological outcomes in officers exposed to traumatic events. *Journal of the American Academy of Experts in Traumatic Stress*, Winter-Spring, 24-35.

Demou, E., Hale, H., & Hunt, K. (2020). Understanding the mental health and wellbeing needs of police officers and staff in Scotland. *Police Practice and Research*, 21, 702–716. https://doi.org/10.1080/15614263.2020.1772782

Drew, J. M., & Martin, S. (2021). A national study of police mental health in the United States: Stigma, mental health and help-seeking behaviors. *Journal of Police and Criminal Psychology*, 36, 295–306.

Edwards, G. (2023). I'm not faking being sick, I'm faking being well: The need for leadership in mental health for policing. *Journal of Community Safety & Well-being*, 8(1), 550–556. https://doi:10.35502/jcswb.294

Frankl, V.E. (1996). *Man's Search for Meaning*, Beacon Press.

Fox, J., Desai, M. M., Britten, K., Lucas, G., Luneau, R., Rosenthal, M. S. (2012). Mental-health conditions, barriers to care, and productivity loss among officers in an urban police department. *Connecticut Medicine*, 76(9), 525.

Goodreads, (n.d.). Watts, A. https://tinyurl.com/yrdkjk4f

Gutschmidt, D., & Vera, A. (2022) Organizational culture, stress, and coping strategies in the police: an empirical investigation. *Police Practice and Research*, 23(5), 507–522. https://doi: 10.1080/15614263.2021.1958683

Hunter, J. J. (2022). Clinician's voice: Trauma-informed practices in higher education. In T. R. Shalka & W. K. Okello (Eds.), Trauma-informed practice in student affairs: Multidimensional considerations for care, healing, and wellbeing. *New Directions for Student Services*, 177, 27–38. Wiley. https://doi.org/10.1002/ss.20412

Jetelina, K.K., Molsberry, R.J., Gonzalez, J.R., Beauchamp, A.M., & Hall, T. (2020). Prevalence of mental illness and mental health care use among police officers. *JAMA Network Open*, 3(10), e2019658. https://doi:10.1001/jamanetworkopen.2020.19658

Johansson, F., Rozental, A., Edlund,K., Côté, P., Sundberg, T. Onell, C., Rudman, A., & Skillgate, E. (2023). Associations between procrastination and subsequent health outcomes among university students in Sweden. *JAMA Network Open*, 6(1).

Kaur, R., Chodagiri, V.K., & Reddi, N.K. (2013). A psychological study of stress, personality, and coping in police personnel. *Indian Journal of Psychological Medicine*, 35(2). 141–147.

Kouri, N., D'Andrea, W., Brown, A. D., & Siegle, G. J. (2023). Shame-induced dissociation. *Psychological Trauma: Theory, Research, Practice, and Policy*. https://doi.org/10.1037/tra0001428

Maté, Gabor, (n.d.). *Goodreads*. https://tinyurl.com/2reknpna

National Institute of Health [NIH]. (2021). *Cultural respect*. https://www.nih.gov/institutes-nih/nih-office-director/office-communications-public-liaison/clear-communication/cultural-respect

Newell, C.J., Ricciardelli, R., Czarnuch, S.M., & Martin, K. (2022). Police staff and mental health: barriers and recommendations for improving help-seeking. *Police Practice and Research*, 23(1), 111–124. https://doi:10.1080/15614263.2021.1979398

Padilla, K. (2016). Stress and maladaptive coping among police officers (Master's thesis, Arizona State University).

Paoline, E.A. (2001). *Rethinking Police Culture: Officers' Occupational Attitudes*, LFB Scholarly Publishing.

Porter, C. N., & Lee, R. (2023). The policing culture: An exploration into the mental health of former British police officers. *Current Psychology*. https://doi.org/10.1007/s12144-023-04365-y

Queirós, C., Passos, F., Bártolo, A., Marques, A.J., DA Silva, C.F., & Pereira, A. (2020). Burnout and stress measurement in police officers. *Organizational Psychology*, 11(587), 1–23. https://doi.org/10.3389/fpsyg.2020.00587

Raganella, A.J., & White, M.D. (2004). Race, gender, and motivation for becoming a police officer. *Journal of Criminal Justice*, 32, 501–513.

Sheffler, J.L., Piazza, J.R., Quinn, J.M., Sachs-Ericsson, N.J., & Stanley, I.H. (2019). Adverse childhood experiences and coping strategies. *Anxiety Stress Coping*, 32(5), 594–609. https://doi:10.1080/10615806.2019.1638699

Sitko-Dominik, M.M., & Jakubowski, T.D. (2022). Traditional male role norms, social support, and symptoms of post-traumatic stress disorder among male polish police officers. *Journal of Police and Criminal Psychology* 37, 392–406. https://tinyurl.com/2tu2t3wp

Spence, D.L., Fox, M., Moore, G.C., Estill, S. & Comrie, N.E.A (2019). *Law Enforcement Mental Health and Wellness Act: Report to Congress*. Washington, DC: U.S. Department of Justice. https://cops.usdoj.gov/RIC/Publications/cops-p370-pub.pdf

Tucker, J. M. (2015). Police officer willingness to use stress intervention services. *International Journal of Emergency Mental Health and Human Resilience*, 17(1), 304–314.

Velazquez, E., & Hernandez, M. (2019). Effects of police officer exposure to traumatic experiences and recognizing the stigma associated with police officer mental health. *Policing: An International Journal*, 712–724. https://rb.gy/mjjwx

Wadsworth, M. E. (2015). Development of maladaptive coping: A functional adaptation to chronic, uncontrollable stress. *Child Development Perspectives*, 9(2), 96–100.

Watson, L., & Andrews, L. (2018). The effect of a Trauma Risk Management (TRiM) program on stigma and barriers to help-seeking in the police. *International Journal of Stress Management*, 25(4), 348–356. https://doi.org/10.1037/str0000071

Wild, J., Greenberg, N., Moulds, M. L., Sharp, M-L., Fear, N., Harvey, S., Wessely, S., & Bryant, R. A. (2020). Pre-incident training to build resilience in first responders: Recommendations on what to and what not to do. *Psychiatry* (83)2, 128-142. https://doi: 10.1080/00332747.2020.1750215

Workplace Suicide Prevention & Postvention Committee (2022). Mental health promotion and suicide prevention in the workplace. *United Suicide Survivors International*, Denver, CO. https://archive.hshsl.umaryland.edu/handle/10713/19711

5 | MORAL INJURY IN LAW ENFORCEMENT

DEFINITIONS

MEDITATION - a formal practice where attention is focused on bringing awareness to your body to calm your mind.

MINDFULNESS - non-judgmental awareness in the moment where you pay attention to your body and breath allowing your mind to rest from worry.

MORAL INJURY - when fundamental moral principles are compromised because of something you did or did not do, something that was done to you, or something that you witnessed, and this causes moral feelings like guilt or shame.

OBJECTIVES

After reading and considering the content of this chapter, the reader should be able to:

- Reflect on contributors to moral injury in policing.
- Recognize eight protective factors against moral injury.

In My Experience & Lessons Learned

JASON PALAMARA

My police career began with my assumptions of the world being shaken due to the attacks of September 11th. By the end of my career, the assumptions I preferred to hold of the world appreciating and valuing police work, were disrupted due to the public's growing disdain for it and us. It grew harder for my colleagues and I to perform our jobs. We thought about how we would take care of ourselves and loved ones while protecting the public as we dealt with the Covid-19 pandemic.

As officers and in the position of the public's protector, it was difficult to witness those losing their life to Covid and being unable to prevent heartache caused by a disease we had yet to fully understand. We were directed to follow and enforce rules and regulations that often conflicted with our morals, values, and beliefs. Lines were being drawn and officers were losing their jobs. This injurious environment created personal and career chaos for many.

As a Veteran and LEO, I had been accustomed to a hurried lifestyle. I needed to learn how to be still, and how to be okay with being still knowing that it would help me to quiet things down. Being still enabled me to see and hear a lot more than my own voice. When we learn to slow down and be more present through practices such as mindful meditation, breathing exercises, and prayer, the more joy we tap into (Comer, 2019). Jaeda DeWalt writes,

> *"The calm within the storm is where peace lives and breathes. It is not within perfect circumstances or a charmed life. It is not conditional. Peace is a sacred space within, it is the temple of our internal landscape. We are free to visit it whenever we seek sanctuary. Underneath the chaos of everyday living, peace is patiently awaiting our discovery" (Goodreads.com, n.d.).*

On average, officers have a career lasting two decades. They experience traumatic incidents, consistent threats to life, moral injury (MI), and a plethora of other things. They need supervisors, peers, and resources to help prevent them from reaching the point of no return. Many times, I have been asked if I retired because of the challenges of the work. I hadn't, but many have and many more will. NYPD officers are resigning at a record-breaking pace, and they are having a hard time reconciling both organizational and personal conflict because of this work (Balsamini et al., 2023). We need to strive for a collaborative effort with an outlook that is specific to each person. As the culture begins to change, it will become commonplace that asking for help shouldn't be stigmatized.

If you went out on patrol without your service weapon, and got into a shooting, you wouldn't question why you weren't able to defend yourself. The same principle applies to being able to defend yourself from, and effectively manage, life's stressors. You must prepare and strengthen yourself for your loved ones, but also for yourself. A good way to do that is through mindfulness and meditation.

I never had the opportunity to participate in mindfulness training while on the job. It can be as simple as looking down at your feet, planting them solidly on the floor, being connected to the earth, and telling yourself, "I am grounded and connected to that which is bigger than I am". Saying it and seeing it helps you to believe it, which helps release you from the grip of chaos. When I started doing this, I began to ask why I was making my problems bigger than my place in this world. I focused on beautiful things in my life rather than giving my attention to what was not. This is a choice you can make.

While you are running and in your personal spin cycle, take a moment to pause. Use your senses to observe what is happening. Be aware of what you hear, see, smell, taste, and feel. Appreciate the stillness for a moment as the world around you continues on. Allow things to just be while you observe them. This space is there for you when you feel there is nowhere to rest. The next time you turn in for the night and begin to lose yourself in the rush of thoughts about your day, what will happen tomorrow, and all the to-dos, feel the tension you are holding onto. Take a deep breath. Allow your body to sink down. Let your head rest on the pillow. Don't allow the tension to have control over you.

Cases can't be solved unless facts and evidence are discovered and uncovered. What are you missing in life because the next important thing, case, or career advancement chase, is robbing you of time spent going within? We are officers. We have the ability to have a heightened sense of what is happening around us, seeing ten steps ahead and the skill to mitigate danger before it develops. How is that working for you? Bring awareness to what you hold in your body and mind in a non-judgmental way. It brings with it the space needed to shift your responses to it.

You don't have to sit in the locker room with your legs crossed while humming to find stillness. Your partner may, and should, make fun of you for this! Surveil yourself as you would a perp walking down the street. If you are feeling angry, ask why without blaming yourself. We reconstruct what happened and discover the unknown because of a good interrogation or interview. Would you allow a perpetrator to say they didn't do it, and let that be the extent of your inquisition?

As cops, when we begin to apply the skills employed in our work to ourselves, the discovery it allows is endless. Situations may be outside of your control. Decisions must be made. But the place in which you make them will determine their effectiveness and ultimately how you feel because of them. Practicing mindfulness, meditation, or other modalities where you can detach from what may have a grip on you, begins the growth necessary to handle what this blue life throws at you. In the NYPD, we were allowed a "wash-up" period before the end of our tour. Are you allowing yourself the same? Take as many as you need throughout the day. Refocus on what is serving and not serving you, and what makes you a better you.

My Story & Evidence-Based Practices

BARBARA RUBEL

Moral Injury in Law Enforcement

LEOs can experience moral distress, an ethical pain or negative feelings, when they know the right thing to do, but are unable to do it due to constraints beyond their control. The necessary conditions for moral distress are a combination of a moral event, psychological distress, and a direct causal relation between them both (Morley et al., 2019). Where moral distress refers to an ethical problem, moral injury (MI) lasts longer than moral distress and refers to how the problem produces serious harm.

MI is the psychological distress that results from committing, failing to stop, or witnessing acts that violate one's own moral standards or beliefs

(Plouffe et al., 2023). Although a consensus definition has yet to emerge from the literature, labels also include moral conflict, inner conflict or moral dilemma. Perceived betrayals and transgressions can violate deeply held expectations as to what is right.

When core principles that guide officers are violated, MI can occur. Morally injurious events (PMIEs) happen when a person perpetuates, fails to prevent, bears witness to, or realizes acts have deeply transgressed their moral beliefs and experiences (Litz et al., 2009). Psychological trauma is due to events that shatter one's assumptive world about what is right or wrong and disrupts their moral identity (Kvitsiani et al., 2023).

MI can occur after a trauma and make an individual feel shame because they know what they need to do, but are not able to do it. If they have been diagnosed with PTSD, they may also experience MI. In fact, a study of LEOs suggests that MI predicts PTSD (Papazoglou et al., 2020). High risk groups for MI are veterans, healthcare workers, and first responders (Norman et al., 2023). A study on veterans found that MI is felt when they see things that are morally wrong, witness an immoral act, behave in a way that violates their morals, fail to do something that they feel they should have done, feel betrayed by a leader who violates their moral beliefs, or they are betrayed by others who they once trusted (Richardson et al., 2020).

CASE NOTES

Heriberto Rodriguez, Chief of Police at City of Kempner, notes, "Officers need to know that they are safe in our command. We love them and we care for them. I will always encourage my people to get help and I will help find it if they need my assistance" *(H. Rodriguez, personal communication, April 17, 2023).*

Core Values and Moral Injury

Core values are guiding principles related to beliefs and practices that rarely change. Values can energize and influence overall behavior. Values such as lawfulness, courage, justice, balance, and insightfulness help shape our view of the world. If you are helping an officer who is struggling with MI, these questions sketch out ideas about their values:

- What do their core values (e.g., hard work) mean to them?
- What evidence do they have that they are living their values (e.g., commitment, bravery) as they do their job?
- If they have an inherited value passed down from someone in their family or from their culture (e.g., service to others), what does that inherited value mean to them?
- Do they share the same values (e.g., loyalty) as their personal heroes?
- Do their values (e.g., authenticity) help them realize what they need for themself to mitigate the impact of MI?
- What highest priority in life drives their behavior at home and at work?
- Are their core values (e.g., citizenship, influence, contribution) in line with their department?

Moral Injury Symptoms

MI impacts emotional, physical, cognitive, behavioral and spiritual well-being. Symptoms can bring about a religious struggle with faith, lost purpose or inability to make meaning of one's role. Officers can lose trust in the system and in themselves as their sense of self suffers.

CASE NOTES

Sergeant Eric Tung, Kent Police Department, Peer Support Team Lead. First Responder Wellness, IACP 2022 40 Under 40 Honoree, notes, "To be a good cop, you need to be well. You need to take care of yourself, your mind and body. To neglect any aspect of your health is to ignore a chance to be optimal: and our community needs you to be optimal" *(E. Tung, personal communication, January 12, 2023).*

Officers may have a lack of self-forgiveness if they feel individually responsible. MI can create feelings of shame, guilt, and betrayal (Jinkerson, 2016). They may experience anger, trust issues and not forgive others who were responsible for what occurred (Barnes et al., 2019). Optimism, cognitive flexibility, active coping skills, a supportive social network, attending to physical well-being, and having a personal moral compass promote resilience (Iacoviello & Charney, 2014).

LEOs face MI whether they are disappointed in leadership, feel betrayed by supervisors, or policies that go against their moral compass. Although understanding MI may be crucial to understanding and reducing the alarmingly high prevalence of police suicide (Barr, 2020; Thoen et al., 2020), the associations between MI, suicidal risk, and psychological conditions that increase suicide remains unaddressed (Levi-Belz, 2023).

**LAW ENFORCEMENT CONSIDERATION
& PERSONAL INSIGHT**

Have you blamed yourself or experienced trust issues due to MI?

FABULOUS Framework to Manage Moral Injury

Researchers have confirmed that cognitive flexibility, a positive attitude, maintaining boundaries, feeling connected, having a sense of humor, being optimistic, job satisfaction, and self-compassion, enhance wellness. The FABULOUS framework focuses on wellness and resilience (Rubel, 2019), and in this chapter, the framework highlights concepts related to MI. The following eight principles are general guidelines for supporting LEOs who are interested in mitigating the impact of MI:

- *Flexibility* to change the way things are done in the department so trust is ensured, and core values are not violated;
- *Attitude* to identify ways to maintain a positive approach when betrayed by others;
- *Boundaries* to examine limits of acceptable behavior when seeing something that is morally wrong;
- *United* or having relationships with family, friends, and fellow service members when someone violates your beliefs and expectations as to what is right;
- *Laughter* to maintain a healthy perspective to increase happiness when experiencing a lack of self-forgiveness;
- *Optimism* when betrayed by leaders, and to realistically prepare for the best possible outcome;

- *Understanding* job satisfaction despite feeling guilty for not providing the right amount of support or acting in a way that violated your values;
- *Self-compassion* when you feel shame after you commit, witness, or fail to prevent something that goes against your moral beliefs.

LEOs need encouragement, especially when faced with a moral issue. To manage MI, they can put protective resilience factors, such as being calm, empathetic, grateful, hopeful, open-minded, or spiritual, into practice.

The Moral Injury of Ineffective Police Leadership

Agencies need to provide clear policies, have leaders who set a high bar for ethical behavior, and shift the culture to put mental health first (Stemig, 2023). Working under ineffective leadership is a potentially morally injurious event (McEwen et al., 2021). Officers can experience MI when their job stressors are ignored, exacerbated, or prolonged because of ineffective leaders (Simmons-Beauchamp & Sharpe, 2022). MI can occur when a leader fails and betrays what is right (Shay, 2014). This can bring about a violation of trust, as the leader's actions are non-congruent with an officer's values (Roth et al., 2022).

CASE NOTES

Ross E. Swope, Chief of Police (Retired), Supreme Court of the United States, author of *Ethics-Based Policing*, notes, "There are never enough officers, even when fully staffed. Unfilled vacancies can significantly exacerbate the situation. There is some level of minimum staffing required to serve and protect effectively. What are you going to do now: forced overtime, change or cancel days off, deny annual leave?

"Short-term band aid, long-term disaster. What is the disaster—morale killer, resignation motivator, performance drag, cynic booster, team divider. An enlightened leader knows what this does to those under their charge and must put forth all effort to avoid this. Staff with volunteers not with mandatory call ups" **(R.E. Swope, personal communication, July 10, 2023).**

A breach of trust can be morally assaultive, which impacts an officer's mental health (Papazoglou et al., 2020b). When the department requires them to carry out enforcement measures that conflict with their values, they may suffer MI, which makes them feel guilt or shame (Blumberg et al., 2020). Also, if they are ordered to enforce actions that go against their moral beliefs, they can lose respect for their supervisor.

Ineffective leadership can occur due to an individual's traits and behaviors, such as being self-centered, arrogant, closed minded, a micromanager, having a poor work ethic, putting political concerns above safety and welfare, failing to act when appropriate, failing to interact successfully with others, unproductive communication, and lack of integrity (Schafer, 2010).

Ineffective leaders reward loyalty to their own agendas, berate employees in front of lower ranking officers, are dishonest, mismanage resources, cause a critical front-line staffing crisis, minimize concerns about the lack of resources and training, fail to act in a way that creates an unhealthy workforce unable to effectively cope with line-of-duty deaths, only address staffing shortages after a death, or lead through personal bias and moral ambiguity (Simmons-Beauchamp & Sharpe, 2022).

LAW ENFORCEMENT CONSIDERATION & PERSONAL INSIGHT

Has an event caused you to experience MI?

Meditation Can Mitigate Moral Injury

Meditation, which comes under the umbrella of mindfulness, reduces chronic stress and increases well-being (Dahl et al., 2015). Meditation is a practice that brings awareness to the body to calm the mind and include mindfulness of breathing, compassion, or showing oneself loving kindness, and use of mantras or phrases.

Abraham Maslow, a psychologist, known for Maslow's hierarchy of needs, said that to be in the present moment is a key element of mental wellness. Mindfulness allows for an accepting attitude that is usually cultivated through meditation (Oyler et al., 2022). Being mindful may be a protective factor from perceiving events as morally injurious, which may result in enhanced mental health (Senger et al., 2022).

Being mindful is a helpful practice when facing anxieties while acknowledging that this time will pass (Behan, 2021). John Kabit-Zinn defined mindfulness as a non-judgmental awareness in the moment where you pay attention to your body and breath, which allows your mind to rest from rumination and worry and be wise while understanding oneself (Mindful Staff, 2017). Mindfulness-based interventions (MBIs) include a group-based weekly class composed of meditation practices such as body scan, mindful movement, sitting and walking meditation, experiential inquiry-based learning, or exercises (Crane et al., 2016).

Mindfulness meditative practices that can lessen MI are gratitude, prayer, making meaning, having purpose, and self-compassion. Mindfulness-based stress reduction (MBSR) programs, which combine meditation, yoga and psychoeducation, can reduce stress, burnout, and compassion fatigue. Evidence is mounting for the effectiveness of mindfulness-based therapies in promoting well-being in high-stress employment (Trombka et al., 2021).

CASE NOTES

Tami Sharp, founder and CEO of Law Enforcement Coaching LLC, daughter of an outpost Deputy Sheriff who served 23 years as an officer, notes, "Have external support. Gone are the days of suck it up buttercup. Find culturally competent, professional wellness resources which will provide you with an outlet and support system throughout your career. Try different people, products, solutions.

"Open yourself up to trying a variety of resources that will help you feel like you are operating from a well-balanced, healthy, confident space. There is no limit to how many resources one person should be using. Find what works best for you and then share that knowledge and encourage others to explore support as well. Normalize talking about wellness" *(T. Sharp, personal communication, March 23, 2023).*

Trauma-Sensitive Mindfulness

Practicing mindfulness enables detachment from work, reduces psycho-logical work–life conflict, and enhances work–life balance satisfaction (Althammer et al., 2021). Interventions based on mindfulness are meant to raise awareness of internal signs of stress and to promote the use of techniques to lessen its effects (Cohen et al., 2019). Mindfulness thera-pies are increasingly mentioned in the literature as a way to foster psycho-logical well-being, particularly in LEOs (Chopko, 2022; Withrow, et al., 2023). LEOs reported a considerable reduction in aggression and scores on depression (Khatib et al., 2022).

Mindfulness is not a standardized practice within preventive stress inter-ventions intended for pre-traumatic officer or recruit training (Murray, 2020). Being that a mindfulness method can trigger panic, trauma mem-ories, or discomfort, increased awareness of one's thoughts, emotions, and sensations is important (Binda et al., 2022). However, police mindful-ness training (MT) is a promising strategy for the dangers faced by LEOs (Christopher et al., 2016; Christopher et al., 2020). In a therapeutic con-text, a LEO may be able to manage their distress, which may not be the case if they are doing mindfulness in a group or without a trained clinician (Farias & Wikholm, 2016).

MBIs may reduce law enforcement organizational, operational, physical, and psychological strain, and are effective in reducing an officer's stress-re-lated outcomes (e.g., PTSD symptoms, negative affect, burnout, sleep dis-turbances, anxiety), while increasing emotional intelligence, self-compas-sion, mindfulness, positive affect, and sleep quality (Grupe et al., 2021; Vadvilavičius et al., 2023). An MBI for anxiety or stress must have a teacher who understands trauma. Yoga or another somatic experiencing approach might feel safer for them.

CASE NOTES

As a retired Navy SEAL Commander, and now working as a mindfulness and performance coach, Jon Macaskill has seen firsthand the power of mindfulness in enhancing resilience, particularly in high-stress professions like law enforcement and military. Jon notes, "Promote mindfulness train-ing. Chiefs must lead the way in incorporating mindfulness and resilience training as part of the regular training regimen. Regular mindfulness practice enhances self-awareness and emotional regulation, and is key to managing high-stress situations.

"Foster an environment where mental health discussions are encouraged, not stigmatized. Make mental health resources readily available and create a culture of support that understands the unique stressors in law enforcement work. Time away from the line of duty is essential for recovery and resilience. Chiefs should encourage officers to take regular time off and promote activities that enhance work-life balance and well-being" *(J. Macaskill, personal communication, July 8, 2023).*

Interventions

Therapies to manage MI include adaptive disclosure therapy, MI reconciliation therapy, spiritually integrated cognitive processing therapy, prolonged exposure, and healing through forgiveness therapy. Pastoral care interventions include pastoral narrative disclosure, and MI group or structured pastoral care.

Here are some key points and insights from the chapter:

1. **DIFFICULTY IN DISCUSSING MI:** Moral injury can be challenging for LEOs to talk about, primarily due to fear of judgment from others. The stigma and potential negative reactions from society can add to the emotional strain.
2. **IMPACT ON WELL-BEING:** MI can lead to intense emotional pain, potentially resulting in feelings of undesirability, self-condemnation, and a desire to avoid living due to suffering and emotional distress.
3. **LOSS OF MEANING:** LEOs may experience a loss of meaning in their lives, which can manifest as a spiritual or religious struggle. They may struggle with thoughts that they are evil and are unable to forgive themselves.
4. **RECLAIMING IDENTITY:** To move forward and heal, LEOs need to reclaim their identity as moral beings. This involves re-engaging with their pre-trauma sense of self and striving to regain a sense of goodness as ethical individuals.
5. **MAKING AMENDS:** LEOs can make symbolic amends through activities like volunteering, philanthropy, or monetary donations.

6. **IMPORTANCE OF RELATIONSHIPS:** Family, friends and social connections help LEOs manage MI. Support from loved ones and a sense of responsibility for those who depend on them can be important sources of strength.

7. **REALIGNING WITH VALUES:** Realigning one's life and actions with core values is crucial for healing. This process involves identifying personal goals and engaging in meaningful activities that activate positive emotions.

THE NEXT STEP

The chapter underscores the challenges of MI and suggests strategies for coping and healing, including reclaiming a sense of moral identity, making amends, nurturing relationships, and realigning one's life with core values. It acknowledges the profound emotional and psychological impact of MI and the importance of addressing it to support the well-being of LEOs. Chapter 6 concentrates on a vicarious trauma-informed approach to policing.

REFERENCES

Althammer, S. E., Reis, D., van der Beek, S., Beck, L., & Michel, A. (2021). A mindfulness intervention promoting work–life balance. Special Issue: *Positive Psychology Interventions in Organizations*, 94(2). 282–308. https://doi.org/10.1111/joop.12346

Balsamini, D., Marino, J., McCarthy, C., & Vago, S. (2023). NYPD cops resigning in new year at record-breaking pace—with a 117% jump from 2021 numbers. The New York Post. https://nypost.com/2023/03/10/nypd-cops-resigning-from-force-in-2023-at-record-pace/

Barnes, H. A., Hurley, R. A., & Taber, K. H. (2019). Learning to forgive moral/ethical transgressions by self and others. Moral Injury and PTSD: Often co-occurring yet mechanistically different. *The Journal of Neuropsychiatry*, 31(2), 98–103. https://neuro.psychiatryonline.org/doi/full/10.1176/appi.neuropsych.19020036

Barr, L. (2020). Record number of US police officers died by suicide in 2019, advocacy group says. *ABC News*. https://tinyurl.com/2shbfjzy

Behan, C. (2021). The benefits of meditation and mindfulness practices during times of crisis such as COVID-19. *Journal of the American Academy of Experts in Traumatic Stress*, 4, Winter-Spring, 54–56.

Binda, D. D., Greco, C. M., & Morone, N. E. (2022). What are adverse events in mindfulness meditation? *Global Advances in Health and Medicine*, 11, 1–3. https:://doi: 10.1177/2164957X221096640

Blumberg, D. M., Papazoglou, K. & Schlosser, M. D. (2020). Organizational solutions to the moral risks of policing. *International Journal of Environmental Research and Public Health*, 17, 7461, 1–26. https://tinyurl.com/37bybdty

Chopko, B. A., Adams, R. E., Davis, J., Shea, M. Dunham, P., & Patrick, A. (2022). Associations between mindfulness, post-traumatic stress disorder symptoms, and post-traumatic growth in police academy cadets: An exploratory study. *Journal of Traumatic Stress*, 35(3). 967–975. https://doi.org/10.1002/jts.22803

Christopher, M. S., Goerling, R. J., Rogers, B. S., Hunsinger, M., Baron, G., Bergman, A. L., & Zava, D. T. (2016). A pilot study evaluating the effectiveness of a mindfulness-based intervention on cortisol awakening response and health outcomes among law enforcement officers. *Journal of Police and Criminal Psychology* 31(1), 15. https://tinyurl.com/2s3p96rn

Christopher, M., Bowen, S., & Witkiewitz, K. (2020). Mindfulness-based resilience training for aggression, stress and health in law enforcement officers. *Trials* 21(236). https://tinyurl.com/yc852n2p

Cohen, I. M., McCormick, A. V., & Rich, B. (2019). Creating a culture of police officer wellness. *Policing: A Journal of Policy and Practice*, 13(2), 213–229. https://doi.org/10.1093/police/paz001

Comer, J. (2019). The Ruthless Elimination of Hurry. WaterBrook.

Crane, R.S., Brewer, J., Feldman, C., Kabat-Zinn, J., Santorelli, S., Williams, J.M.G., & Kuyken, W. (2016). What defines mindfulness-based programs? The warp and the weft. *Psychological Medicine*, 47, 990–999. https://doi:10.1017/S0033291716003317

Dahl, C. J., Lutz, A., & Davidson, R. J. (2015). Reconstructing and deconstructing the self: Cognitive mechanisms in meditation practice. *Trends in Cognitive Science*, 19(9), 515–523. 10.1016/j.tics.2015.07.001

Dewalt, J.(n.d.) Quotes. dewaltads. https://www.goodreads.com/quotes/1028750-the-calm-within-the-storm-is-where-peace-lives-and

Farias, M., & Wikholm, C. (2016). Has the science of mindfulness lost its mind? *BJPsych Bulletin*, 40(6), 329–332. https://doi: 10.1192/pb.bp.116.053686

Grupe, D. W., McGehee, C., Smith, C., Francis, A. D., Mumford, J. A., & Davidson, R. J. (2021). Mindfulness training reduces PTSD symptoms and improves stress-related health outcomes in police officers. *Journal of Police and Criminal Psychology* 36, 72–85 https://doi.org/10.1007/s11896-019-09351-4

Iacoviello, B. M., & Charney, D. S. (2014). Psychosocial facets of resilience. *European Journal of PsychoTraumatology*, 5, 23970.

Jinkerson, J. D. (2016). Defining and assessing moral injury: a syndrome perspective. *Traumatology* 22, 122–130. https://doi:10.1037/trm0000069

Khatib, L., Glaser-Reich, J., Mosbey, D. Oliva, V., Riegner, G., Dean, J. G., Harth, N. M., & Zeidan, F. (2022). Mindfulness meditation training reduces aggression and improves well-being in highly stressed law enforcement officers. *Journal of Police and Criminal Psychology*. https://doi.org/10.1007/s11896-022-09554-2

Kvitsiani, M., Mestvirishvili, M., Martskvishvili, K., & Odilavadze, M. (2023). Dynamic model of moral injury. *European Journal of Trauma & Dissociation*, 7(1), 100313. https://doi.org/10.1016/j.ejtd.2023.100313

Levi-Belz, Y., Ben-Yehuda, A., & Zerach, G. (2023). Suicide risk among combatants: The longitudinal contributions of pre-enlistment characteristics, pre-deployment personality factors and moral injury. *Journal of Affective Disorders*, 324, 624–631. rebrand.ly/epx4dsx

Litz, B. T., Stein, N., Delaney, E., Lebowitz, L., Nash, W. P., Silva, C., & Maguen, S. (2009). Moral injury and moral repair in war veterans: A preliminary model and intervention strategy. *Clinical Psychology Review*, 29(8) 695–706, https://doi.org/10.1016/j.cpr.2009.07.003.

Maslow, A. (n.d.). BrainyQuote. rebrand.ly/1y26tbx

McEwen, C., Alisic, E., & Jobson, L. (2021). Moral injury and mental health: A systematic review and meta-analysis. *Traumatology*, 27(3), 303–315. https://doi.org/10.1037/trm0000287

Mindful Staff (2017). Jon Kabat-Zinn: Defining Mindfulness. What is mindfulness? The founder of mindfulness-based stress reduction explains. *Mindful.* https://www.mindful.org/jon-kabat-zinn-defining-mindfulness/

Morley, G., Ives, J., Bradbury-Jones, C., & Irvine, F. (2019). What is "moral distress"? A narrative synthesis of the literature. *Nursing Ethics*, 26(3), 646–662. https://doi: 10.1177/0969733017724354

Murray, E. (2020). *FBI Law Enforcement Bulletin.* U.S. Department of Justice. Building police officer psychological capital to mitigate stress. https://leb.fbi.gov/articles/featured-articles/building-police-officer-psychological-capital-to-mitigate-stress

Norman, S. B., Griffin, B. J., Pietrzak, R. H., McLean, C., Hamblen, J. L., & Maguen, S. (2023). The Moral Injury and Distress Scale: Psychometric evaluation and initial validation in three high-risk populations. *Psychological Trauma: Theory, Research, Practice, and Policy.* https://doi.org/10.1037/tra0001533

Oyler, D. L., Price-Blackshear, M. A., Pratscher, S. D., & Bettencourt, B. A. (2022). Mindfulness and intergroup bias: A systematic review. *Group Processes & Intergroup* Relations, 25(4), 1107–1138. https://doi.org/10.1177/1368430220978694

Papazoglou K., Blumberg, D. M., Chiongbian, V. B., Tuttle, B. M., Kamkar, K., Chopko, B., Milliard, B., Aukhojee, P., & Koskelainen, M. (2020). The role of moral injury in PTSD among law enforcement officers: a brief report. *Frontiers in Psychology,* 11, 310.

Papazoglou, K., Blumberg, D. M., Kamkar, K., McIntyre-Smith, A., & Koskelainen, M. (2020b). Addressing moral suffering in police work: theoretical conceptualization and counselling implications. *Canadian Journal of Counselling and Psychotherapy*, 54(1), 71–87. https://cjc-rcc.ucalgary.ca/article/view/68490

Plouffe, R. A., Easterbrook, B., Liu, A., McKinnon, M. C., Richardson, J. D., & Nazarov, A. (2023). Psychometric evaluation of the moral injury events scale in two Canadian Armed forces samples. *Assessment*, 30(1), 111–123. rebrand.ly/r8ovou4

Richardson, C. B., Chesnut, R. P., Morgan, N. R., Bleser, J. A., Perkins, D. F., Vogt, D., Copeland, L. A., & Finley, E. (2020). Examining the factor structure of the moral injury events scale in a veteran sample. *Military Medicine*, 185 (1–2), e75–e83. https://doi.org/10.1093/milmed/usz129

Roth, S. L., Andrews, K., Protopopescu, A., Lloyd, C., O'Connor, C., Losier, B. J., Lanius, R. A., & McKinnon, M. C. (2022). Development and preliminary evaluation of the moral injury assessment for public safety personnel. *Traumatology*, 1–8. Advanced online publication. https://doi.org/10.1037/trm0000367

Rubel, B. (2019). *Loss, grief, and bereavement: Helping individuals cope.* (4th ed.). SC Publishing, Western Schools.

Schafer, J. A. (2010). The ineffective police leader: Acts of commission and omission. *Journal of Criminal Justice*, 38, 737–746. https://doi:10.1016/j.crimjus.2010.04.048

Senger, A. R., Torres, D., & Ratcliff, C. G. (2022). Potentially morally injurious events as a mediator of the association of gratitude and mindfulness with distress. *Psychological Trauma: Theory, Research, Practice, and Policy.* https://doi.org/10.1037/tra0001233

Shay, J. (2014). Moral injury. *Psychoanalytic Psychology*, 31(2), 182–191. https://doi.org/10.1037/a0036090

Simmons-Beauchamp, B., & Sharpe, H. (2022). The moral injury of ineffective police leadership: A perspective. *Frontiers in Psychology,* 13, 1–6. rebrand.ly/g60v1os

Stemig, S. (2023). *Culture of Wellness Toward Resiliency* (Thesis, Concordia University, St. Paul). https://digitalcommons.csp.edu/criminal-justice_masters/27

Thoen, M. A., Dodson, L. E., Manzo, G., Piña-Watson, B., & Trejos-Castillo, E. (2020). Agency-offered and officer-utilized suicide prevention and wellness programs: a national study. *Psychological Services*, 17, 129–140. https://doi.org/10.1037/ser0000355

Trombka, M., Demarzo, M., Campos, D., Antonio, S B., Cicuto, K., Walcher, A.L., García-Campayo, J., Schuman-Olivier, Z., & Rocha Neusa, S. (2021). Mindfulness training improves quality of life and reduces depression and anxiety symptoms among police officers. *Frontiers in Psychiatry*, 12, https://doi.org/10.3389/fpsyt.2021.624876

Vadvilavičius, T., Varnagirytė, E., Jarašiūnaitė-Fedosejeva, G., & Gustainiene, L. (2023). The effectiveness of mindfulness-based interventions for police officers' stress reduction: A systematic review. *Journal of Police and Criminal Psychology.* rebrand.ly/8rdp2b0

Withrow, A., Russell, K., & Gillani, B. (2023). Mindfulness training for law enforcement to reduce occupational impact: A systematic review and meta-analysis. *The Police Journal*, 0(0). https://doi.org/10.1177/0032258X231156710

6 | VICARIOUS TRAUMA-RESPONSIVE APPROACH IN POLICING

DEFINITIONS

VICARIOUS TRAUMA - adverse changes that occur over time in officers when they observe and interact with the suffering and needs of victims and others in the community.

VICARIOUS TRAUMA-INFORMED APPROACH - educating command staff, supervisors, officers and their families about loss, trauma, psychological safety, health and wellness to prevent suicide.

OBJECTIVES

After reading and considering the content of this chapter, the reader should be able to:

- Examine a vicarious trauma-informed approach to policing.
- Describe the significance of internal police peer support programs.

In My Experience & Lessons Learned

JASON PALAMARA

*"We never found his head. Did he ever tell you
what he did with my son's head?"*

—Desire, mother of 19 year old homicide victim

This was the conversation I was having while driving a victim's mother and son to court for the Grand Jury proceedings for the arrest of the individual who had murdered and dismembered their loved one. We hadn't. I knew this was true after reviewing crime and autopsy photos more times than I wished to. I had asked the victim's killer that very question. Possibly part of the norm for this type of work? Yes. Normal in general for most people? Absolutely not.

When other detectives you work with experience similar situations, there remains a sense of normalcy behind these stories that, left unexamined, grow to a warped perspective of things. This normalization begins to shape how you see life and your place in it. I was always fearful of the worst-case scenario in almost every situation. Ultimately, how I processed other events in my life was negatively impacted as a result.

"That's nuts. Don't tell anyone that shit bro!" was a response I got from a friend who I told about the conversation I had with the victim's mother.

Through the lens of my experience, the most common forms of trauma-related stress are from seeing, and being directly involved in, human experience in ways unfamiliar to most outside of this work. No one should have to observe the aftermath of a suicide, of a horrific vehicle accident, a murder, or listen to painful stories from those that have had heinous acts done to them. After you compassionately support them, you go home, and try to get a restful night's sleep.

For most of my career, I equated trauma to something more physical in nature. It wasn't until later that I recognized different forms of trauma. With further education, my role as a NYPD Peer, Crisis Intervention Counselor, and my current role with a behavioral health organization, I now understand what was not so clear to me in my earlier years.

As a young cop, trauma was what others experienced. I assumed that whatever I experienced was what I was supposed to be exposed to and a normal element of my profession. It was just part of what occurred on the job, and more importantly because of it. Towards the end of my career, and after developing a better understanding of trauma, I realized that I fit into a descriptor that I had reserved for those I was entrusted to serve and protect.

Many times I experienced vicarious trauma (VT), which impacted more than my mental and physical health. It impacted how I viewed myself and the ones closest to me. I realized that I should not blame myself, or think what I was experiencing meant that there was something wrong with me; was something I caused; or something I didn't have the ability to fix. VT was damaging my health and impacting the lives of everyone around me.

This is where bad things happen. My work experiences changed my perceptions about my world. I was looking through a destructive lens, and viewed the world as if it was a timer. I waited to hear the end bell ring as the ticking was getting louder and drowning out all that was good in my life.

One time, as a detective, I responded to the home invasion of an eighty-two-year-old victim. This woman was hog tied with duct tape, beaten, and robbed in her home. She had lost her husband many years prior and lived alone with her family of cats. I sat next to her on the bed as she cried through retelling her account of what had happened. I imagined a detective sitting next to my mother doing the very same thing I was doing. A lengthy investigation resulted in multiple arrests and a friendship built out of a terrible situation.

The thoughts of these cases and many others were uninvited guests in my head. They affected my physical and mental health in ways for which I was not prepared. It took a while for me to realize that there are protective factors that mitigate VT. For me, those factors became my intentional choice to seek out the good in the worst of situations.

This victim became my buddy. She helped me process my exposure to her trauma more than I believe I had helped her process hers. I became hyper focused on changing how I was as a dad and son. I looked to create shared experiences with my family and was grateful for them and the time we had together. I still do this today with a lot less catastrophizing.

Some thoughts are still there, but I have turned them into more of a snapshot in time. An album of sorts that I will be thankful I have when our shared time here on earth is no more. Having a mentor is one way to deal with VT. Mentorship comes in the form of those you read, listen to, and can work with. If your department does not have a mentorship program, then be intentional about seeking out those that challenge you to grow.

Although it is beneficial to learn from a senior officer, it is equally important to have someone with an outside perspective from the law enforcement world.

Organizational interventions, having a good relationship with a supervisor and a peer support member could benefit those who are suffering from VT. Peer support is one way to prepare for what LEO life will inevitably throw at you. Whether it is formal services offered by your department or simply seeking out a fellow colleague that you trust to unpack what may be weighing you down. This is the prep work I am talking about. Building the habit of talking to your support network as common practice will create an environment of acceptance should you hit a rough patch. Believing it is okay to ask for help having never practiced doing so can be a monumental task during troubling times.

It is one thing to actively seek out support but another when it comes and finds you without solicitation. Our LEO supervisors can create an environment where sharing the human behind the badge is encouraged. You do this by intentionally showing interest in those you lead. Taking the time to learn the birthdays of those in your squad and putting calendar reminders in your phone takes little effort. Your phone will do the work for you and alert you when it's time.

Little things done intentionally for those you lead shows them that you took the time to care. That is leadership. That is being human. Management must get involved and remember that they were once in the shoes of the officers they are entrusted to support. Their title does not insulate them from the same pain a patrol officer is exposed to. It would be prudent to make sure budgets allow for programs and services that address the very specific needs discussed in this book.

Supervisors can lessen VT by being vulnerable and sharing their own experiences with their officers who look to them for support and guidance. A while ago, a friend that is an ATF agent spoke to me about his experience with his leadership following a mass shooting. He and other agents were told that a government agency was coming to provide them with support as a result of exposure after responding to an incident.

After their leaders prepared them, they probably let their guard down and considered being open about how the incident had affected them. However, a few days before the agency arrived, leadership informed them that it was going to be an investigative session, a questioning of how they did what they did, what they may have done wrong, and what could have been done better. Now, it was a finger pointing event.

I share this with you as an example of what not to do as a leader or supervisor. Show your people that you care from the very beginning. Our heroes are not perfect and do the best with what they have and what they know in the moment. Start with care and the rest will be much easier. Additionally, peer-to-peer programs can also mitigate vicarious trauma by supporting the feeling of family and understanding. They enforce the feeling that one is part of a tribe and around those that "get them."

Recently, I spoke with a cop who completed his initial intake assessment for mental health services. He asked me, "am I going to get to speak with you again?" If this doesn't drive the need for peer support home, I don't know what will! If I could go back to July 2, 2001, I would pull myself out of the line waiting to begin my processing into the police department and tell myself that everything will be okay.

I would tell myself that I should surround myself with those that challenge me. I would tell myself that I am creating the ability to become a better version of myself. I would give myself a hug and tell myself that the pain will come hard and disguise itself in many ways, but that there is happiness and peace on the other side of it. I would tell myself that what I am about to endure does not define me or my life. Rather, it makes it more than I can possibly fathom at the moment.

You are of no use to anyone if you are not consistently strengthening who you are at your core. It is easy to put on your uniform and hide what lurks inside. This will work for a short while, but the monster will rear its ugly head whether you are ready for it or not and in whatever form it wants. It may show itself as the end of your marriage, the loss of relationships, a health condition that could have been mitigated if only you took better care of yourself. The list is endless.

I was in ASIST—Applied Suicide Intervention Skills Training—while learning to become a crisis intervention counselor. I was in a mock scenario talking to a woman who was standing on a bridge ready to jump. It was really my instructor standing on a chair on a stage. Although a veteran of the NYPD, I felt nervous in this pretend encounter inside of a small room watched by fellow trainees. The weight of every word I spoke had the potential to be what causes this person to either jump, give life another shot, or at the very least, give the Emergency Service Unit (ESU) an opportunity to grab them from behind.

This training would have been valuable as a new officer because it prepares you for a lifesaving situation. It helps immerse you in the pain of another human being. It reminds you that we are all human and vulnerable. The understanding and education received there and through the NYPD peer training and courses like Mental Health First Aid, ended up being instrumental in my growth. These trainings should be experienced department wide.

Employee Assistance Units (EAU) are staffed with those trained to assist officers when struggling with health and wellness and with those who have struggled themselves. My entire day revolved around homicide investigations. Everything an EAU officer does revolves around assisting a fellow officer with resources when they feel like there is nowhere else to turn or that no one else will understand what they are going through.

When you have reached a point that seems impossible to overcome, and that no one will understand, when giving up seems like a better option than not, consider this a good time to speak with your EAU. Though I wasn't aware of wellness apps for first responders while on the job, there are several that offer confidential wellness services on personal finances, health and wellness, relationships, or share ways to connect to peer support services.

Let the will and determination you put forth in being that first responder to everyone else, replicate itself for you. You are not called a "Second Responder." You're a "First Responder." Put yourself first. You can be first to both those you serve and to yourself without giving anything up. I was privileged to be a part of the NYPD's Health and Wellness Section, Peer Support Program in my final years. It's through such programs that I believe we are changing the way we look at taking care of our officers, and therefore our officers may begin to change how they look at taking care of themselves.

Taking care of yourself should also include focusing on your nutrition. When I was on uniformed patrol early in my career, my partner liked to go on his traditional White Castle run. A *crave case*, a box that contained thirty sliders, is all he needed to get our tour started! When working late tours, it was often difficult to find restaurants with healthy options. There was a time when I could polish off a Dunkin' dozen without back up needed. This soon caught up to me and the notches in my gun belt. What you put into your body will affect your health and ultimately how you feel. Garbage in, garbage out.

We are going to start to see more training like this where you can be yourself yet not feel like you are exposed and compromising your cover. The anxiety of feeling judged by our peers is real. We are often our harshest critics. The LEO life is competitive, and we feel that displaying any perception of weakness puts us at a disadvantage. Not putting yourself and your well-being as a top priority *will* put you at a disadvantage. Those same critics are suffering in silence right along with you.

For all my undercovers out there, you know there is valuable intelligence gained while cloaked in anonymity. Barbara was one of the first compassion fatigue and vicarious trauma experts to present a program in the Metaverse, a virtual reality platform where one can remain anonymous. Maybe initially engaging in this way can be the catalyst for you exploring what help looks like. Gather your information, assess, and then make your decision to get more involved.

My Story & Evidence-Based Practices

BARBARA RUBEL

"Even when there is no immediate threat, our body may remain tight and on guard, our mind narrowed to focus on what might go wrong. When this happens, fear is no longer functioning to secure our survival. We are caught in the trance of fear and our moment-to-moment experience becomes bound in reactivity."

—**Tara Birch**

If your life were a movie, is there a scene you'll never forget? For me, it is the scene where I am a little girl who sees her father's head and face covered in blood. My father was a police sergeant in Brooklyn, New York. I was a child of the '60s playing stoop ball with my friends when I noticed his squad car pull up to our home. As he stepped out of his car, his face and uniform covered in blood, my legs went weak, and it felt like my stomach hit the ground. "Daddy!" I shrieked. Although he told me that he was okay, I was confused and very upset. We went inside where he sat down in the kitchen and I watched my mother carefully and methodically tweeze shards of glass from his head, the remnants of a glass bottle that was thrown at him.

As I reflect back on this time, I wondered why my father didn't go to the hospital. Why did my parents not shield me from the horror of witnessing each piece of glass being removed? It never occurred to them the impact this might have on their child. After calmly chatting about the incident with my mother, he got into the squad car and went back to work, and my mother told me to go outside and play. At dinner, my parents discussed the incident, but with the same levity as if he had helped an old lady cross the street or a cat had gotten stuck up a tree, not that he'd been violently assaulted.

I now realize that my father was primarily traumatized, and I was vicariously traumatized. I learned early in life that officers talk to other officers about things that happened to them—but that's it. Although it is not typical for them to discuss the details of incidents with their spouse or partner, especially their children, my mother was a policewoman.

My parents regularly discussed their jobs at the kitchen table in front of me. The police family is a combined identity because of shared experiences that produces a shared perception that police are the only ones who understand police (Brough et al., 2016). Being in law enforcement, my parents understood the stressors of the job. I was a child and could not understand why anyone would want to throw a glass bottle at my father. He took his trauma home. Although many years have passed, I still vividly remember that day.

LAW ENFORCEMENT CONSIDERATION & PERSONAL INSIGHT

Has something happened during a shift that brought up a trauma from your childhood?

Vicarious Trauma for Law Enforcement

The American Psychological Association (2021) defines trauma as an emotional response to a terrible event that includes initial reactions (e.g., shock, denial) and longer-term reactions (e.g., flashbacks, headaches, nausea, strained relationships). Being that the event is perceived as distressing, it affects functioning (Dombo et al., 2019). Too much for an officer's system to process while it is happening, it shapes their sense of safety in the world.

Events can occur in a rural area where officers know the victims as well as the criminals. Their emotional response could then have more of a personal impact. The way an officer in a department in a rural area in the south deals with cumulative stressors and trauma is not the same as an officer in a department in a large city in the east.

Vicarious trauma (VT) develops when there is an extended encounter with trauma, which requires emotional labor to manage the distressing impact (Moran et al., 2020). Witnessing of, or learning about, a traumatic experience can produce an empathic response that can have a damaging impact on health, which can lead to individual and organizational burdens if changes are not made due to organizational barriers and cultural issues (Hallinan et. al., 2021).

To change the culture or eliminate the stigma, we first must recognize the impact of VT. VT was first defined as an inner transformation of a trauma provider due to a cumulative and empathetic engagement with another person's trauma (Pearlman & Mac Ian, 1995). LEOs may be exposed to violent or gruesome death, homicide, suicide, mass casualty or mass fatality, a situation that poses a threat to their life or of serious bodily harm, or an act of criminal sexual violence (Bureau of Justice Assistance, 2022a). VT is the adverse changes that occur over time when observing and interacting with the suffering of victims and others.

CASE NOTES

Maggie A. DeBoard, Chief of Police, mom, grandmother and avid golfer, president and co-founder of the Foundation for First Responder Wellness and Resiliency, notes, "Law enforcement leaders must recognize that we have a significant number of officers who are quietly 'working while wounded,' regardless of how functional they may appear from the outside. We are responsible for the safety of our officers, and that includes managing the injuries we cannot see.

"Leaders must openly talk to their officers about mental wellness and proactively provide resources to manage traumatic exposures, even before they occur. Until we can fully acknowledge that we have a growing crisis in our profession, we will never change the culture or eliminate the stigma that exists for seeking help. If we don't take care of them, no one will" *(M. Deboard, personal communication, January 2, 2023).*

Vicarious Trauma Symptoms

Trauma is the root of many chronic diseases, such as weight gain, digestive disorders, chronic pain, premature aging, allergies, addictions, exhaustion, and autoimmune disorders. When a person experiences trauma, their psychological responses are regulated by the nervous system. Initially, they may experience sadness, confusion, numbness, or anxiety. Delayed reactions may include nightmares, avoidance of emotions, flashbacks, and fatigue. These physical, emotional, and mental reactions are very similar to VT reactions.

VT impacts a LEO's sense of safety and self-efficacy and causes them to change the way they look at the world. VT symptoms are like a victim's traumatic memories (Jenkins & Baird, 2002). Symptoms include rage, being overprotective, hypervigilant, feeling numb, an exaggerated startle response, rapid heartbeat, aches and pains, trouble concentrating, powerlessness, and decreased interest in intimacy.

CASE NOTES

Meg Tobin, LMHC, a Licensed Mental Health Counselor and owner of Breathing Space Psychotherapy, notes, "Turning to a trauma therapist can be a deeply meaningful step for Law Enforcement Officers, who so often carry the heavy burden of society's most challenging and heart-wrenching moments. The impact of this work is far-reaching, touching not only their professional life but also infiltrating the sanctuary of their homes and relationships. They also face the silent struggle of vicarious trauma, an emotional weight absorbed from the painful experiences of the people they are sworn to protect and serve.

"Therapists skilled in techniques like EMDR, Somatic Experiencing, EFT Tapping, and Brainspotting offer more than just coping strategies; they offer a path to emotional freedom. These approaches focus on how the body and mind hold onto traumatic experiences, helping officers release these emotional knots and find peace. Ketamine-Assisted Psychotherapy is also one modality that is emerging, offering a ray of hope for many, and in my experience, showing quick and promising results for those grappling with acute trauma symptoms.

"In essence, a trauma therapist can provide these brave men and women with a vital set of emotional tools for healing, not only enhancing their ability to serve their communities but also enriching their lives outside the uniform. It's not just about surviving each shift; it's about truly living, both on the job and off" *(M. Tobin, personal communication, September 1, 2023).*

Vicarious Trauma Self-Efficacy

Thirty years ago, Bandura defined self-efficacy as the belief in one's ability to perform a specific task. LEOs must have confidence in their ability to manage the challenging demand of policing in a traumatic situation but also cope with their own VT symptoms. Self-efficacy describes the level of confidence about one's abilities to cope with a stressful or challenging demand (Luthans et al., 2007). Self-efficacy may reduce feelings of insecurity, loss of control, uncertainty about highly complex work experiences, or role conflict due to a leader's passivity in decision-making (López-Cabarcos et al., 2023).

Vicarious Trauma-Informed Approach to Policing

Although an obstacle to wellness is overcoming bureaucracy, agencies can take a proactive approach to VT-informed practices by focusing on the LEO, the department, the entire agency, and blue family. Leaders are realizing the importance of a culture of building resiliency no matter the focus area. Police enforcement officials are identifying mental health issues and promoting access to services given community expectations and agency needs (U.S. Department of Justice, 2019). These officials are focusing on a VT approach, which involves educating command staff, supervisors, officers, and their families about the impact of loss and trauma and the importance of psychological safety, health and wellness to prevent suicide.

Leaders are also recognizing that a VT-informed approach puts the LEO at the center of issues related to well-being, and that they need to be involved in the development of wellness policies. It is paramount to translate evidence-based research into actionable practices. When officers are trauma-informed they can better serve those in the community who have experienced trauma.

A VT-informed approach focuses on an organization that understands the impact of VT by recognizing symptoms and having a plan of action to integrate safety, health, and wellness into policies and practices to maintain the mental health of LEOs. Although there is a great amount of literature that focus on VT in healthcare professionals, the issue is understudied among officers and specifically detectives, although they have repeated contacts with victims of violent crimes (Morabito et al., 2021). We need more studies on VT-informed approaches in policing.

CASE NOTES

South Brunswick, New Jersey Police Chief Raymond J. Hayducka, 35 years in Law Enforcement, notes, "All police officers put their lives on the line every day to protect and serve our communities. We are the first to respond to a scene and regularly encounter some of the most traumatic events affecting communities. The emotional and mental toll of this work can build and significantly impact an officer and their family.

"It is essential that a 'Culture of Resiliency' is created and maintained within every law enforcement agency in the country. The responsibility for establishing this culture of safety and wellness within a law enforcement agency requires leadership that starts with the Chief Executive of the agency. This responsibility also needs to be shared with every member of the agency, including union leaders, frontline supervisors, training personnel, and human resources staff.

"Every agency should have the resources and programs set forth by policy to address officer wellness issues. These wellness issues and resources are, but not limited to, contracted mental health professionals, physical fitness, nutrition assistance, peer to peer assistance, financial planning assistance, and a family support program. We need to take care of our people so they can take care of our communities" *(R.J. Hayducka, personal communication, July 6, 2023).*

Psychological Safety

Psychological safety (PS) can be defined as feeling safe when taking interpersonal risks at work (Frazier et al., 2016). PS factors in engagement, wellness, well-being, post-traumatic growth, and mental health (Edmondson & Bransby, 2023; Porges, 2022; Sullivan et al., 2018; Morton et al., 2022). When a department is psychologically safe, officers think that their supervisor and fellow officers are supportive and trust that they won't be punished for speaking up. They engage in constructive conflict or confrontation and speak their mind as they respect each other's competence and feel positive toward each other (Newman et al., 2017).

Every agency needs to establish and implement ways to assist the law enforcement staff, particularly those who frequently deal with child abuse and trauma. This is crucial from the perspectives of social justice and public health (Beer et al., 2022). Agencies show employees that they are valued when they offer routine mechanisms of support throughout their careers, not only when they are exposed to trauma or begin to show signs of trauma (U.S. Department of Justice, 2019).

Supervisors Can Make or Break Psychological Safety

The relationship an officer has with their supervisor enhances psychological well-being, while poor management weakens it and puts them at a higher risk of negative mental health outcomes (Farr-Wharton, 2021). First-line supervisors need the resources and services to promote wellness while paying attention to their subordinates' needs, and knowing when they could benefit from additional support or referral to appropriate services (President's Task Force on 21st Century Policing, 2015).

Chad Michael Bruckner, Police Life Coach, Army and Police Veteran, and author, *The Holy Trinity of Successful & Healthy Police Organizations: Improving leadership, culture & wellness*, notes, "I recommend evaluating candidates from a totally different lens than we previously have. Instead of how many arrests or SWAT experience someone has (really irrelevant to WHAT KIND of leadership capabilities), I recommend evaluating EQ and soft skills. IQ gets us hired but EQ gets us promoted.

"When we install leaders who lead from the heart, they're emotionally intelligent enough to know they don't know everything. A healthy ego will enable the Chief Executive to surround himself with the brightest and most capable junior leaders. When we hire Chiefs based on their soft skills and leadership potential, we're creating an organization culture where we advocate to 'get things right,' regardless of 'who's right'" *(C.M. Bruckner, personal communication, July 11, 2023).*

For example, operational stress may be caused by friends and family not understanding policing or fatigue. Organizational stress may be caused by inconsistent leadership style or staff shortages. A cause of police professional stress, which mediates the indirect causal relationship between organizational and operational stress and job satisfaction, is a lack of social support from a supervisor (Acquadro Maran et al., 2022).

First-line supervisors who focus on helping officers break maladaptive coping patterns and make mental health a priority save lives. They ask officers questions about traumatic experiences, validate what they are going through, identify what is at stake if they don't change their behavior, and get them needed support. A proactive supervisor listens to and supports an officer, gets them the resources needed so they don't have long-term mental health problems, and maintain an attitude that it is brave to talk about mental health.

Perception of being satisfied with the job is based on the level of information and communication from the organization and management, the working conditions and relationships between the employee, colleagues and direct supervisors, job demands, decision range, hours, vacation time, benefits, and compensation (Lepold et al., 2018).

Supervisors need to acknowledge the psychological impact of operational stress (e.g., exposed to death, violence, trauma, human suffering, shift work, inadequate sleep, and compromised relationships with the public) on officers (Purba & Demou, 2019; SantaMaria et al., 2018). To improve life satisfaction, police administrators should work to reduce job stress while increasing job involvement, job satisfaction, and organizational dedication which could benefit the officers, the agency, and the community (Lambert et al., 2021).

CASE NOTES

Cassie Sexton, Retired Police Dispatcher, emphasizes, "Law Enforcement is used to being the hero and saving others, usually the first to help and last to seek help. When we do finally raise our hand for help, we really should have five years ago. We should be normalizing and encouraging our Law Enforcement to be asking for help, and taking care of themselves, that's real bravery and strength" *(C. Sexton, personal communication, January 23, 2023).*

While focusing on bravery and strength, supervisors have to figure out the strategies to overcome barriers to access mental health resources such as ensure confidentiality, provide accessible, uncomplicated resources, and provide police-specific services (Newell et al., 2022). Four ways departments can focus on empowerment and growth are by:

1. Adopting a non-punitive response to members who ask for help.
2. Encouraging recruits and seasoned officers to continually utilize their information-seeking skills to empower themselves.
3. Reinforcing that stress managed well can create growth.
4. Focusing on how well-being is an opportunity for growth, rather than focusing on how well-being is about change.

LAW ENFORCEMENT CONSIDERATION & PERSONAL INSIGHT

How does your supervisor inspire good officers to stay in law enforcement, even during today's increasing social tensions?

Public safety officers often don't have appropriate resources or support, which leaves them at higher risk for long-term mental health consequences (Bureau of Justice Assistance, 2022). Supervisors, as problem solvers, recognize that occupational stressors in police work increase the risk for poor mental well-being, which can affect professionalism, organizational effectiveness, and public safety (Purba et al., 2019).

Whether an officer reports to a Sheriff, Chief, Captain, Detective or Sergeant, they need to trust that they have similar struggles with stress, anxiety, or insomnia. Supervisors can get in touch with their attitude about wellness, model healthy coping mechanisms, communicate frequently about peer support, and create psychological engagement focusing on strengths and well-being within the framework of family, friendships, and community.

The Family-Centered Shift

Living Blue is not just about the law enforcement professional, it is also about the family. In fact, a police department is more than a community, it is family. A family-centered shift focuses on an officer who makes sound decisions while at work, realizing that the outcome of those decisions can impact their family, and treats the needs of those at work and at home equally based on their needs. To develop a healthy workforce, a department can shift to a family-centered approach. For example, agencies can put together a wellness day for officers and families. Chiefs and supervisors should attend with their families.

CASE NOTES

Ryan M. Columbus, Chief of Police, Tewksbury Police Department speaks directly to the leaders when he says, "We talk a lot about earning the trust of the community in policing and working hard every day to achieve that. In leadership we need to take that same approach and work hard to earn the trust of our officers; that we will be there for them in a time of crisis. Everyone should have a voice in the organization, from the officer two weeks out of the academy to the 25-year veteran. Courage is seeking help.

Leaders must create an environment where it is safe to do so. How do we achieve this? We have to earn it!

"Every leader in this profession will come across someone who is suffering in their agency, and how you handle that situation will be the tone you set for your agency. Trust me, everyone is watching. It takes time and effort to break down the barriers of mistrust in the "administration," but we must work at it. Mistrust in the administration in this profession goes back decades; it isn't personal. Work to break down this barrier by being open and honest. Create a Peer Support Unit.

"I'm amazed how many officers want to help their colleagues. We placed signs throughout our station that state, 'its ok to not be ok.' I have spoken to officers about how some calls that I have been on have affected me and that therapy is helpful. We have implemented the ability to earn wellness days (up to 4 per year) and 90% have used them. This is voluntary and through their own therapist.

"To see so many officers using this program, it shows this is needed. I help people in my agency, some have worked out and some have not, but the people see we care because we have proven that. Let's take care of people and be there for them when they need help as we would want them to be there for our community. It's easy to deem these big city problems, but it's in every agency" *(R.M. Columbus, personal communication, January 23, 2023).*

Wellness Programs

Senior police administrators and supervisors recognize the need for training to provide a supportive environment (Baek et al., 2021) that includes building employee strengths, motivating them, authentically caring about their well-being, building trust in leadership, and instilling connection to the organization's culture (Witters & Agrawal, 2022).

CASE NOTES

Chief of Police Gary A. Boshears, M.P.A., LCC, Lago Vista Police Department, Texas, notes, "I think it is important for Chiefs to realize that we are the drivers of the culture in our departments. We can't have a one-time training class, seminar, or briefly talk about a wellness or resiliency program and expect it to benefit our officers if we don't anchor those practices in the culture of our department. It is our responsibility as the chief executive of the department to ensure that our department has a culture of wellness and resiliency at all levels of the department.

"Starting when officers are recruited and, until the day they retire, we must give them tools to manage the day-to-day stressors of the job and we must ensure they not only have those tools but that the department supports them using those tools. When our officers go out into the communities, we want our citizens to have the best version of that officer. When our officers go home at the end of their shift, we want their families to have the best version of that person.

"Every officer will one day leave our agency and we want them to be a better person because of their time at our agency. Building a culture of wellness in a police organization might involve a culture change, perhaps even a significant culture change for individuals who are longstanding with the agency. Expect some resistance and some pushback and understand that not everything is going to be easy but, in the long run, your agency, your officers, and your communities will be in a better place" *(G.A. Boshears, personal communication, July 18, 2023).*

Officer wellness programs focus on enhancing resiliency (Council on Criminal Justice, 2021). A wellness program that boosts resilience, also boosts ethical decision-making (Blumberg et al., 2020). A VT-informed wellness program is an agency's approach towards establishing a healthy workplace by integrating mental health practices within the work schedule and during personal time. But smaller agencies face difficulties due to a lack of mental health service providers with which to partner (Bureau of Justice Assistance, 2022).

Wellness programs already in place are critical incident support management, engagement, and well-being programs such as stress management, psychological first aid (PSA), psychological services, peer support, holistic wellness programs, weekly yoga classes, and resilience building training.

These programs enhance engagement, which is an actively involved state of being enthusiastic, inspired, with positive energy, a sense of empowerment, and feeling completely connected with work and others (Hilliard et al., 2019). Online training focuses on substance misuse, sleep, relationship problems and financial wellness. However, Taylor and associates (2022) found that 62% of U.S. agencies don't offer wellness services.

Agency provided accessed services are a substance abuse program, peer support, online self-care training/program, suicide awareness and prevention education/program and peer support, in person training/program for mental and physical care, employee assistance programs (EAP), psychological or psychiatric services, debriefings with a manager or work colleague, mental health first-aid training, and chaplaincy services (Drew & Martin, 2023).

The #1 ranking accessed external service is general practitioners (Drew & Martin, 2023). Least-accessed services are substance abuse programs, and annual mental health and wellness checks (Drew & Martin, 2023; Bonner & Crow, 2022). Although most departments have some type of wellness program, most do not have a comprehensive wellness program that offers service in five major areas of health: stress management, mental health, alcohol/drug use, nutrition/diet, and physical fitness (Filkins, 2021).

Leaders can consider hiring full-time wellness team members to confidentially focus on exercise, diet, sleep, stress management as well as financial management. All studies point to exercise as one of the best ways to manage job stressors. Undoubtedly, exercise could improve coping after critical incidents, reduce stress and low mood, and improve problem-solving and use of resources (Wild et al., 2020).

CASE NOTES

Frank Voce, founder/president of Reps for Responders, was an Eagle Scout, a volunteer firefighter in his late teens, and played high school and college football. Frank majored in Criminology and spent a great deal of time at the gym training for powerlifting competitions. He even competed in the

World Association of Benchers and Deadlifters (WABDL) competition in Las Vegas. He came in second place in the deadlift in his weight class and age group. In 2015, Frank graduated from the police academy. Although he struggled with alcohol in 2018–2019, he has been sober since September 2019. Frank realized he needed to reach out for help to improve mentally and physically. Physical fitness was key to survive and thrive on the job.

Frank Voce notes, "Being an active first responder, I believe firmly in physical fitness. Not being physically fit can lead to heart disease. As a LEO, you have enough to worry about such as not knowing what is going to happen with each call, the overtime, the missing family events, the dangers of the job and organizational stressors.

"With physical fitness on your side, at least you have less chance of being obese, having high blood pressure, mood swings, chronic illness, high cholesterol, or type 2 diabetes. Here are a few suggestions to try: running, walking, hiking, climbing, swimming, or biking. Consider weight training, which includes Powerlifting movements, CrossFit movements, Strongman Movements, Bodybuilding Movements, and Kettle Bells. Get into sports such as basketball, baseball, football, frisbee, rowing and more. From dancing to mixed martial arts, you choose! Fitness is a huge outlet. I refuse to be a statistic to this job and so should you" *(F. Voce, personal communication, August 15, 2023).*

Nutrition Wellness Program

Nutritional wellness begins by learning about healthy food choices and its impact on physical and mental health. Every officer has dietary needs from weight loss to specific diets such as diabetic, gluten-free, or lactose-free. They must also be mindful of their cholesterol, fat, or sodium restrictions.

LAW ENFORCEMENT CONSIDERATION & PERSONAL INSIGHT

What healthy food choices (e.g., grilled chicken, carrots, oranges, hummus, peanut butter) would you consider snacking on during your break?

It is challenging for an obese officer to complete on-duty tasks such as running, pulling, pushing, lifting, and carrying (Dicks et al., 2023). Studies have found that obesity in LEOs is due to lack of physical activity, poor nutrition, short sleep cycles, and working longer hours or the midnight shift. Their innate preference for the times of day when they like to sleep or when they are most alert or active is known as their chronotype. Obesity is linked to a mismatch between chronotype and work schedule.

According to IACP Center for Officer Safety and Wellness (n.d.) there are several ways first-line supervisors can provide education and support to improve officer nutrition and well-being. They can recommend a healthy snack, have water available, link fitness with nutrition, and organize a pre-shift group run ending with a healthy group breakfast to promote camaraderie among the officers (IACP Center for Officer Safety and Wellness, n.d.).

Supervisors need to lead by example by limiting the number of times they go out to eat while on their shift. They can discuss healthy meal options at restaurants and grocery stores, and use lunch breaks to encourage officers to leave their vehicles and eat when possible. This establishes an eating routine and can increase physical activity.

CASE NOTES

Michele Zandman-Frankel, Instructor Certified with the state of New Jersey to Instruct the Nutrition and Fitness Courses at the New Jersey Police Academies, notes, "Having proper nutrition translates to having better performance and directly affects LEO mental health, well-being and confidence. If officers are 100%, they can GIVE 100%. We have instructed recruits at the Monmouth County Police Academy and taught at the New Jersey State Police Academy in Sea Girt. We assisted in the Sayreville Police Department resiliency program to discuss the science of nutrition and infusing that education into the department as well as the South Brunswick Police Department.

"Being that nighttime shift workers have a hard time managing nutrition and sleep, try limiting caffeine, make sure foods are micronutrient dense, establish a bedtime routine, and avoid blue light before bed. Focus less on 'good food' or 'bad food' and more on macro/micronutrients (protein, fats, carb, vitamins, and minerals). Discover the correct balance for your unique physical and mental needs. Focus on fat loss. Eliminate sugary drinks and limit alcohol. Learn what your macronutrient intake should be for your goals and lifestyle. To create a body composition shift, eat an adequate amount of protein, prioritize resistance training, and stay consistent with your plan.

"If your goal is to gain muscle, be in an appropriate caloric surplus distributed correctly amongst your macronutrients. If your goal is fat loss, be in an appropriate caloric deficit. Restricting calories excessively may lead to future binge eating and rebound. Your plan must be sustainable and your goals realistic. Resistance training is insurance against chronic injury and maintaining a healthy body fat percentage. Provide accountability and support systems for eating well by working with a nutritionist. Create accountability teams amongst your fellow officers, friends and family.

"Be proactive in combating obesity by eliminating/limiting overly processed foods, sugary drinks, and alcohol. Convenience stores are usually open 24 hours that have grilled chicken, hardboiled eggs, Greek yogurt, cottage cheese, ready to drink Protein Shakes, lean cold cuts, fruits and veggies. Customize almost any option to be macronutrient-friendly. Veer away from anything deep fried, cheesy, or smothered in oils and mayonnaise. Focus on protein heavy options and scout out the menu ahead of time" *(M. Zandman-Frankel, personal communication, July 15, 2023).*

Employee Assistance Program (EAP)

Employee Assistance Programs (EAPs) are voluntary, confidential programs that optimize an organization's success by helping employees manage challenges negatively affecting their job performance, health, and well-being (U.S. Office of Personnel Management, n.d.). EAPs help organizations prevent and cope with workplace violence, trauma and emergency response situations (Office of Personnel Management, n.d.). EAPS are optional, workplace-based services that provide free, confidential assessments, brief counseling, referrals, and follow-up services to employees who are experiencing personal or work-related issues that impact mental and emotional health such as drug and alcohol misuse, stress, sorrow, and family troubles.

Some EAPs fall short in understanding law enforcement stressors or recommend mental health professionals who do not understand the nuances of the job. Officers are fearful to go to HR or their EAP due to confidentiality issues. They fear that if their supervisor finds out, they might lose their job or have their gun taken away. Although EAPs may work well for other types of careers, they don't work as well for officers. EAPs usually have a list of resources of outside mental health providers and how to access them without guidance as to the type of counseling or therapy and whether they understand police job-related trauma or the stressors related to spouses and partners of officers. I asked LEOS what is getting in the way of their wellness:

- "I have no idea what to expect from my EAP and don't trust them."
- "I have a toxic supervisor. I stay under the radar, but it is impacting my health."
- "Wellness? We eat our young. Period."

A Standardized Approach is Needed

There must be standardized care when an officer accesses services. They require a thorough explanation as to what might happen if they reach out for help. They should be told what to expect if they decide to get treatment. For example, if they call a hotline, they need to know the next steps. If they contact a peer for support, they need to know if the chief is notified. An EAP provider cannot provide effective assistance if they have issues with poor communication and non-confidentiality.

Command staff and supervisors need to establish healthy standards of on- and off-duty conduct because a lack of accountability may bleed into everything from sloughing off reports to sloppy uniforms (Shults, 2019). Agencies can standardize the support they offer and adapt it accordingly to the needs of the officers in the department. There should be a standard approach to maintaining confidentiality and expectations about what could happen if an officer discloses their mental health struggles.

Mental Fitness is Just as Important as Physical Fitness

Although it is possible for a LEO to experience VT, it is just as possible to experience vicarious resilience. This can occur when a traumatic experience spirituality becomes a therapeutic resource and inspires hope in the officer. Vicarious resilience increases self-awareness and self-care practices, the ability to be resourceful, changed life goals, and the ability to remain present while listening to trauma narratives (Killian et al., 2017).

For those who have not experienced vicarious resilience and are struggling with their mental health, organizations can implement evidenced-based interventions to provide enhanced education and support. The occupational task of sprinting after a criminal is a physically demanding task that law enforcement personnel must conduct (Lentine et al., 2021). Just as significant are the mentally demanding tasks. Everyone in the department needs to be trained to identify mental health issues, to look out for one another and recognize indicators and warning signs of chronic stress. Focus on mental fitness!

CASE NOTES

Brandon Meyer, husband, father, Assistant Chief of Police Greensburg, IN Police Department, notes, "I wholeheartedly believe that mental fortitude and wellness are just as important as physical fitness. It's critical for agency heads to be part of the change that reduces stigma within their organization. In times of crisis, understanding that it is okay to reach out for help is only part of the battle. Picking a name from a long list of professionals during that time can be overwhelming.

"Our agency has implemented a voluntary mental wellness health visit once a year as part of our overall wellness program. Our hope is that our officers can find someone during these visits that they trust and feel comfortable with so that they know where to turn in times of crisis. Ideally, we can also use those visits to proactively approach the stressors that lead to bigger issues if left to fester" *(B. Meyer, personal communication, January 12, 2023).*

Officers need organizational assistance to cope with stress and trauma because when they feel such support, they are more likely to use stress intervention programs (Acquadro Maran et al., 2022). When organizations focus on employee health, physical health is maintained with fewer somatic symptoms, and absenteeism is also reduced (Shifrin & Michel, 2021).

How does your agency respond to the mental health needs of its officers?

Mental Health Support–Police Clinical Network Providers

Philosopher Aristotle asserted, "You will never do anything in this world without courage. It is the greatest quality of the mind next to honor." It takes courage and curiosity to get help, especially when feeling resentful and angry. Rather than an in-house psychologist providing direct counseling services, a department can offer a referral network of mental health professionals inside as well as outside the community who are trained in police mental health issues.

Mental health professionals must understand crisis situations facing LEOs. Personal issues can include an officer involved shooting of a human or pet, a LODD, employee misconduct on-duty and off-duty, human error, in custody death, questionable use of force, and an officer killed off duty (Pal et al., 2023). If they don't understand officer stressors, they can do more harm than good.

CASE NOTES

Scott Medlin, author of *Mental Health Fight of the Heroes in Blue: How to mentally survive working as a police officer*, shares six tips:

1. Policing is what you do, it is not who you are;
2. Your thoughts lead to your emotions, which lead to your actions, which lead to your results. Be mindful of your thoughts;
3. Professional assistance is there if you really desire change;
4. You're not tough. You're a person who can be affected;
5. Move! That's right. Move your body. Stay physically active; and
6. Increase your standard as a person. You weren't born to settle for and be defined by the negative *(S. Medlin, personal communication, April 25, 2023).*

Protective Factors

Administration or command can oversee the well-being of the department and focus on protective factors. Regular supervision, specific trauma training, and a culture that validates VT are protective factors (Sutton et al., 2022). Having a good relationship with one's supervisor and peer support based on best practices are protective factors. Interventions can focus on individual characteristics, life circumstances and the work environment:

- **INDIVIDUAL CHARACTERISTICS:** age, personality, coping style, personal trauma history.
- **LIFE CIRCUMSTANCES:** work experience, social support, and spiritual resources.
- **WORK ENVIRONMENT:** role, work setting, exposure to trauma, agency support, workplace cultural styles of expressing problems and getting help.

VT interventions on an organizational level should be tailored interventions to an officer's individual characteristics, setting and type of trauma (Kim, et al., 2021).

> **LAW ENFORCEMENT CONSIDERATION & PERSONAL INSIGHT**
>
> What mental health improvements can be integrated into various levels across your agency?

Peer Support

Internal police peer support programs that focus on operational, organizational, and personal stressors have significantly brought about changes in current police culture (Milliard, 2020). Officers share the same values of sticking with traditional masculinity norms and the issue with confidentiality regarding asking for mental health help. What cuts through that is peer support because they have an easier time talking with fellow officers than they do strangers who are not officers.

Mike Crum, suicide interventionist, Marine Corps veteran, and Violence Prevention Specialist at Fl. Army National Guard, notes, "When thinking about officer wellness and resilience, law enforcement mental health and suicide, we have to ask ourselves, 'If not me, then who?' If we do not stand up to suicide, who will? When an officer is in emotional, physical, or spiritual conflict with themselves, fellow officers should speak up and be the guiding light of hope and resilience to ensure the safety and life of their fellow officers. If not you, then who?" *(M. Crum, personal communication, October 2, 2023).*

Overall, first responder peer support interventions are effective at boosting self-efficacy and willingness to talk with peers about mental health, assessing intention to die by suicide, and promoting treatment-seeking behaviors (Horan et al., 2021). As a rule, peer support personnel are of great value and, irrespective of the police agency's size, peer support is cost effective and beneficial (Kates, 2008).

LAW ENFORCEMENT CONSIDERATION & PERSONAL INSIGHT

Can you let yourself become vulnerable and connect with a trained peer?

Peer support groups offer social and emotional support for officers who are experiencing psychological difficulties and struggling in life due to traumatic experiences at work (Klimley et al., 2018). To combat negative work experiences, studies point to self-care strategies and peer support (Helpingstine et al., 2021). A few ideas departments can do right now to create a culture of self-care while encouraging it at an individual and programmatic level are to urge using vacation time, promote mental health support, talk about self-care in team meetings, encourage taking breaks outside, increase the stability of scheduling shifts, and provide training about vicarious trauma.

Leah Marone, MSW, LCSW notes, "A LEO recruit can find an accountability partner. Someone who values and encourages structure, balance, and time for recovery. Preferably this is a partner who has similar goals and can serve as a source of accountability when it comes to their overall self-care. Friendly competition could be interwoven into this relationship, but overall, consistency is key.

"Scheduling regular check-ins that validate efforts and wins while also uncovering barriers and obstacles is critical, especially for those who are prone to burnout and perpetual exhaustion. Adopting a mindset that supports living proactively rather than reactively requires self-awareness, the ability to maintain boundaries, and create circles of support" *(L. Marone, personal communication, December 19, 2022).*

Who are Peer Supporters?

A peer support person is a trained colleague, who provides day-to-day emotional support for department employees, responds to critical incidents, and recognizes, and when necessary, refers cases to a licensed mental health professionals (IACP, 2016). Peer supporters are chosen based on their personality and years of experience. They typically have access to peer support groups around-the-clock, and they may also include coworkers who have undergone specific training (Klimley et al., 2018).

Why Peer Support?

LEOs may not ask for help because they question the competency of professional helpers outside of the field to recognize their unique demands (Waters et al., 2007). Peer support can enhance officer resilience when they are struggling and act as a buffer by lessening the effects of stressful experiences. Peer support team members have more than just a confidential non judgmental conversation and that the discussion of shared experiences promotes the sense that they are not alone, contributes to enhancing their mental health literacy, encourages not having shame in help seeking, and significantly contributes to reducing stigma (Milliard, 2020).

> **LAW ENFORCEMENT CONSIDERATION & PERSONAL INSIGHT**
>
> What goes through your mind when you think of peer support?

Accountability

Accountability is a responsibility that increases competency and morale and knowing what they need to do and doing it. Being vulnerable, they communicate their problems to those who could provide insight and are answerable on the promises that they make to themself. They can ask:

- In what ways do I hold myself personally accountable to manage stress and trauma?
- Am I going to take ownership of how my behavior impacts my well-being?
- Am I ready to talk about mental health and learn ways to prevent suicide in fellow officers?
- What values do I hold that can help me be more accountable for my actions?
- Am I following through on a commitment to focus on psychological safety and wellness?

Psychological First Aid

Demands facing officers are shown to negatively impact physical and mental health (Clements, 2020). Psychological first aid (PFA) training can be offered as it is associated with significant improvements in confidence, knowledge, perceptions, attitudes, skills, and enhance the capacity to provide this type of aid (Kouvatsou et al., 2022).

Group Educational Briefing

During group educational briefings, no one is asked to tell the story of the incident (Laura, et al., 2016). Rather, they learn about available mental health supports, are taught healthy ways to cope with stress, and are given an opportunity to ask about their reactions and be reassured about their experience.

Service Dogs

To manage organizational challenges, some police organizations are incorporating the use of service dogs to support their officers. Canine support animal exposure is significantly linked to perceived organizational support. Having a wellness program with a service dog that is permanently assigned to a full-time police officer handler influences officer wellness (Quick et al., 2018). After exposure to a service dog, officers report being more likely to request their department's help with mental health.

Although unclear how it occurs, evidence suggests that partnership with a service dog may be related to less PTSD symptom severity (Jensen et al., 2022). Although access to canine support animals in the workplace did not appear to influence overall psychological wellness, these animals may provide temporary stress relief (Curley et al., 2022).

> **LAW ENFORCEMENT CONSIDERATION**
> **& PERSONAL INSIGHT**
>
> Would officers in your department think that it is a good idea to have canine support available?

Holistic Approaches

Police agencies who have implemented holistic proactive approaches to officer's mental health report a decline in the negative impacts of job-related stressors (Craddock & Telesco 2022). Holistic proactive approaches that focus on mental health and well-being are an additional piece of equipment that an officer can carry to remain effective as they protect and serve.

Approaches are mindfulness-based stress reduction (MBSR), eye movement desensitization and reprocessing (EMDR), Reiki and therapeutic touch. Movement is a critical part of healing when it involves focusing on psychological pain and tension and not the actual trauma. Yoga and Qigong are moving meditations to balance mind and body through postures and stretches, controlled breath, and noticing body sensations to achieve a relaxed state.

> **LAW ENFORCEMENT CONSIDERATION
> & PERSONAL INSIGHT**
>
> What holistic strategies (e.g., Tai Chi, yoga, meditation, prayer, aromatherapy, herbal teas) would you try?

Building Trust Through Partnerships

A partnership is a group of organizations with a common interest who work together toward a mutual goal. This collaboration helps to not only reconcile differences with a target population for outreach, but also decrease burnout in LEOs. Strategic partnerships with community organizations can be vital to the success of a police department's initiatives and mission. Forming a partnership that is mutually beneficial can be community-based, government based, or faith based.

We need to promote strong law enforcement-community relationships. For example, law enforcement leaders can partner with the Department of Human Services or community medical centers. Overall, collaborating with community stakeholders and jointly establishing solutions can help to mitigate burnout in police officers. For example, training police and citizens in Playback Theatre transforms the broken narratives of police-community relations into a place of meaning making and enhanced positive attitudes.

CASE NOTES

Dr. Robert Neimeyer, Professor Emeritus at the University of Memphis and currently Director of the Portland Institute for Loss and Transition, is a supporter of Playback Theatre and recognizes the problem of negative police–community relations. He and his colleague Dr. Melissa Smigelsky oversaw the evaluation of the *Performing the Peace* project in addition to his work promoting meaning making in those who are traumatically bereaved. Dr. Neimeyer notes, "Playback Theatre improves police–community relations through promoting individual relationships focused on connection and shared humanity.

"Playback Theatre brought together five police officers and five formerly incarcerated individuals from the same community to share their experiences by compassionately performing, with coaching, critical incidents in one another's life stories. This collaborative approach is a model that police departments can use with recruits to senior leadership. It can move their community from a focus on blame, hostility and mutual antipathy to a shared connection and hope.

"Playback Theatre is a creative form of audience-inspired theater. It provides a space for LEOs and ex-offenders to create an environment of safety and understanding to address relational problems. LEOs and ex-offenders sit side by side on stage and share stories of trauma and loss, and a common hope of transforming the narrative of police community engagement. Collaboratively, an audience member shares their story and then watches actors and musicians bring it to life through speaking and music to inspire healing.

"LEOs face many barriers to reporting distress and seeking help. The emotional outcomes of violence on them is underreported. Findings of the project document that training police and citizens in this method can transform the broken narratives of police-community relations into a place of making meaning of stressful life experiences and increased positive attitudes toward each other. We encourage police departments to reach out to Playback Memphis for guidance in how they can integrate Playback into their organizational learning structure" *(R. Neimeyer, personal communication, August 21, 2023)*.

Mission Statements Maintain Officer Safety and Health

Mission statements explain why the department exists and focus on values that drive its purpose, ways to protect and serve, enforce laws, and safeguard constitutional guarantees. They emphasize public safety and provide protection through leadership. Blue family well-being needs to be included to ensure psychological safety and wellness. Here are a few ideas to incorporate into a mission statement. To increase:

- Wellness in officers and their families while they protect and serve.
- Officer safety while they enforce laws and ordinances.
- An officer's family resilience while building community resilience.

Virtual Reality

Studies show that virtual reality enhances operational police training in high-stress situations. Stressors incorporated into virtual reality training practices include a stranger suddenly walks into a room, a person holds a gun, rocks fall from a building, an injured child cries at a crime scene, a loud scream in an apartment building search, a door loudly closes, smoke from an apartment, a light switches off at a crime scene, and an aggressively barking dog (Zechner et al., 2023).

In Chapter 5, we focused on trauma sensitive mindfulness. A virtual reality (VR)-based mindfulness training can reduce anxiety and depression, and improve sleep quality, emotional regulation, and mood (Ma et al., 2022). Attending an online VR-based mindfulness training should be supervised by a mental health professional if the officer has been traumatized.

Metaverse Virtual World

Although virtual reality is used as a training practice, it can also be used to create a therapeutic alliance between an officer and a mental health practitioner. The Metaverse merges physical reality with digital virtuality, fundamentally changing the way we interact with one another. It allows multisensory interactions where avatars communicate as they teleport to virtual worlds (Mysakidis, 2022).

I was invited to do a presentation for this first-of-its-kind experience at the Wellness in the Metaverse Summit, hosted by Hope4Med, a wellness platform. The attendees were avatars (e.g., first responders, mental health care providers). Officers can consider creating an avatar and learn about mindfulness or receive counseling anonymously. Being that as many as one-third of all first responders experience mental health stigma (Haugen et al., 2017; Wheeler et al., 2021), being an avatar might offer them the confidentiality that they seek.

Speaking Up

I recently served on a conference panel with a police chief and fire captain. After several questions were asked about the stressors of the job, the fire chief shared his personal struggles with mental health. Then, a question was asked of me on VT. Rather than answering, I looked directly at the fire chief. I thanked him for sharing his personal struggles and told him that he might have given someone in attendance the strength to reach out for help and saved someone from dying by suicide. After I acknowledged his bravery, he then looked at the audience who gave him a big round of applause. We must appreciate the impact of those leaders who speak up about their own issues.

THE NEXT STEP

The lesson to take from the studies and viewpoints described in this chapter is this: if departments are not vicarious trauma-responsive, the mental health of officers and their families may suffer. Subsequently, in Chapter 7 we emphasize ways to build family resilience.

REFERENCES

American Psychological Association (2021). *Trauma.* https://www.apa.org/topics/trauma#:~:text=Trauma%20is%20an%20emotional%20response,symptoms%20like%20headaches%20or%20nausea

Acquadro Maran, D., Magnavita, N., & Garbarino, S. (2022). Identifying organizational stressors that could be a source of discomfort in police officers: A thematic review. *International Journal of Environmental Research and Public Health,* 19(6). https://doi:10.3390/ijerph19063720

Bandura, A. (1993). Perceived self-efficacy in cognitive development and functioning. *Educational Psychologist,* 28(2), 117–148. https://educational-innovation.sydney.edu.au/news/pdfs/Bandura%201993.pdf

Bonner, H. S., & Crowe, A. (2022). Mental health programming for law enforcement: a first look at trends and perceptions of effectiveness. *Journal of Crime and Justice,* 45(50), 552–566, https://doi:10.1080/0735648X.2022.2045209

Baek, H., Han, S., & Seepersad, R. (2021). The impact of social support and occupational stress on burnout in the Trinidad and Tobago police service. *Police Quarterly,* 10986111211036007.

Beer, O. W. J., Beaujolais, B., Wolf, K. G., Ibrahim, A., & Letson, M. E. (2022). How children's advocacy centers law enforcement officers cope with work-related stress: Impacts and approaches to self-care. *Policing and Society.* https://doi:10.1080/10439463.2022.2127712

Birch, T. (2004). *Radical Acceptance: Embracing Your Life With the Heart of a Buddha,* Bantam Books.

Blumberg, D. M., Papazoglou, K., & Schlosser, M. D. (2020). Organizational solutions to the moral risks of policing. *International Journal of Environmental Research and Public Health,* 17, 7461, 1–26. https://pdfs.semanticscholar.org/30c2/7fdeb8fd86f12840cd00d025bb967c608462.pdf?_ga=2.196489580.1314610572.1671551109-1566975226.1671551109

Brough, P., Chataway, S., & Biggs, A. (2016). You don't want people knowing you're a copper! A contemporary assessment of police organizational culture. *International Journal of Police Science & Management,* 18(1) 28–36.

Bureau of Justice Assistance (2022). *Public Safety Officer Support Act of 2022,* 136 STAT. 2098, Public Law 117–172, 117th Congress. https://bja.ojp.gov/program/psob/BILLS-117hr6943enr

Bureau of Justice Assistance. (2022a). Mental health training: Strategies for small and rural law enforcement agencies. https://doi:bja.ojp.gov/doc/mental-health-training-strategies.pdf

Clements, A. J., Sharples, A., & Kinman, G. (2020). Identifying well-being challenges and solutions in the police service: a World Café approach.

The Police Journal: Theory, Practice and Principles 94, 81–101. https://doi:10.1177/0032258X19898723

Council on Criminal Justice (2021). CCJ Taskforce on policing. officer wellness. Policy assessment. https://counciloncj.foleon.com/policing/assessing-the-evidence/xiv-officer-wellness/?gclid=EAIaIQobChMInYqd7s_b-wIVh3N-vBB2kCwP8EAAYASAAEgKsfvD_BwE

Craddock, T.B., & Telesco, G. (2022). Predicting psychological outcomes in officers exposed to traumatic events. *Journal of the American Academy of Experts in Traumatic Stress*, Winter-Spring, 24–35.

Curley, T., Campbell, M. A., Doyle, J. N., & Freeze, S. (2022). First responders' perceptions of the presence of support canines in the workplace. *Journal of Police and Criminal Psychology*, 37, 804–812. https://doi.org/10.1007/s11896-021-09477-4

Dicks, N.D., Shoemaker, M.E., DeShaw, K.J., Carper, M.J., Hackney, K.J., & Barry, A.M. (2023). Contributions from incumbent police officer's physical activity and body composition to occupational assessment performance. *Frontiers in Public Health,* 11, 1–7. https://doi: 10.3389/fpubh.2023.1217187

Dombo, E. I., & Sabition, C. A. (2019). Creating trauma-informed schools: A guide for school social workers and educators (SSWAA Workshop Series). Oxford University Press.

Drew, J. M., & Martin, S. (2023). Mental health and wellness initiatives supporting United States law enforcement personnel: The current state-of-play. *Journal of Community Safety & Well-being*, 8(1), S12-22. https://www.journalcswb.ca/index.php/cswb/article/view/298/817

Edmondson, A. C., & Bransby, D. P. (2023). Psychological safety comes of age: observed themes in an established literature. *Annual Review of Organizational Psychology* and Organizational Behavior, 10, 55–78.

Farr-Wharton, B., Xerri, M., Saccon, C., & Brunetto, Y. (2021). Leadership matters to the police: Managing emotional labour through authentic leadership. *Public Money & Management*. https://doi:10.1080/09540962.2021.1940481

Filkins, A., Wallace, H., & Dornbos, N. (2021). The effectiveness of wellness programs within police departments at addressing police officer health.

Frazier M. L., & Tupper C. (2016). Supervisor prosocial motivation, employee thriving, and helping behavior: A trickle-down model of psychological safety. *Group & Organization Management*, 43(4), 561–593. https://doi.org/10.1177/1059601116653911

Hallinan, S., Shiyko, M.,Volpe, R., & Molnar, B.E. (2021). On the back burner: Challenges experienced by change agents addressing vicarious trauma in first response and victim service agencies. *Traumatology*, 27(3), 316-325.

Haugen, P. T., McCrillis, A. M., Smid, G. E., & Nijdam, M. J. (2017). Mental health stigma and barriers to mental health care for first responders: A systematic review and meta-analysis. *Journal of Psychiatric Research*, 94, 218–229.

Helpingstine, C., Kenny, M.C., & Malik, F. (2021). Vicarious traumatization and burnout among service providers for victims of commercial sexual exploitation. *Journal of Child Sexual Abuse*, (30)6, 722-745. https://doi:10.1080/105387 12.2021.1938771

Hilliard, P., & Lopez, D. (2019). *Lead, motivate, engage: How to INSPIRE your team to win at work*. People Performance Publishing.

Horan, K. A., Marks, M., Ruiz, J., Bowers, C., & Cunningham, A. (2021). Here for my peer: The future of first responder mental health. *International Journal of Environmental Research and Public Health*, 18, 11097.

International Association of Chiefs of Police (IACP) (n.d.). Center for officer safety and wellness. Eating Well On-the-Go: How Agencies Can Provide Education and Support to Improve Officer Nutrition and Well-Being. Bureau of Justice Statistics. U.S. Department of Justice. https://www.theiacp.org/sites/default/files/2018-09/eating%20well%20on%20the%20go.pdf

International Association of Chiefs of Police (IACP) (2016). Police Psychological Services section, "peer support guidelines," San Diego, CA: IACP Police Psychological Services Section. https://www.theiacp.org/resources/peer-support-guidelines

Jenkins, S. R., & Baird, S. (2002). Secondary traumatic stress and vicarious trauma: A validational study. *Journal of Traumatic Stress: Official Publication of the International Society for Traumatic Stress Studies*, 15(5), 423–432. https://doi.org/10.1023/A:1020193526843

Jensen, C. L., Rodriguez, K. E., Maclean, E. L., Wahab, A. H. A. W., Sabbaghi, A., & O'haire, M. E. (2022). Characterizing veteran and PTSD service dog teams: Exploring potential mechanisms of symptom change and canine predictors of efficacy. https://doi.org/10.1371/journal.pone.0269186

Kates, A.R. (2008). *CopShock: Surviving Post-traumatic Stress Disorder (PTSD)*, (2 ed.). Holbrook Street Press.

Killian, K., Hernandez-Wolfe, P., Engstrom, D., Gangsei, D. (2017). Development of the Vicarious Resilience Scale (VRS): A measure of positive effects of working with trauma survivors. *Psychological Trauma*, 9(1), 23–31.

Kim, J., Chesworth, B., Franchino-Olsen, H., & Macy, R.J. (2021). A scoping review of vicarious trauma interventions for service providers working with people who have experienced traumatic events. *Trauma, Violence, & Abuse*. https://doi:10.1177/1524838021991310

Klimley, K. E., Hasselt, V. B., & Stripling, A. M. (2018). Post-traumatic stress disorder in police, firefighters, and emergency dispatchers. *Aggression and Violent Behavior*, 43, 33-44. https://doi:10.1016/j.avb.2018.08.005

Kouvatsou, Z., Degermedgoglou, G., Karamagioli, E., & Piloulis, E. (2022). Psychological first aid training of police officers. *Journal of Police and Criminal Psychology.* https://doi.org/10.1007/s11896-022-09523-9

Lambert, E. G., Qureshi, H., & Frank, J. (2021). The good life: Exploring the effects job stress, job involvement, job satisfaction, and organizational commitment on the life satisfaction of police officers. *International Journal of Police Science & Management*, 23(3), 279–292. https://doi.org/10.1177/14613557211016494

Laura, U., Friedhoff, S., Cochran, S., & Pandya, A. (2016). *Preparing for the unimaginable: How chiefs can safeguard officer mental health before and after mass casualty events.* Washington, DC: Office of Community Oriented Policing Services.

Lentine, T., Johnson, Q., Lockie, R., Joyce, J., Orr, R., Dawes, J., & Ronai, P. (2021). Occupational challenges to the development and maintenance of physical fitness within law enforcement officers. *Strength and Conditioning Journal*, 43(6), 115-118. https://doi.org/10.1519/SSC.0000000000000679

Lepold, A., Tanzer, N., Bregenzer, A., & Jimenez, P. (2018). The efficient measurement of job satisfaction: Facet-items versus facet scales. *International Journal of Environmental Research and Public Health*. 15(7), 1362. bit.ly/3PvQXaf

López-Cabarcos, M. Á., López-Carballeira, A., & Ferro-Soto, C. (2023). How to prevent hostile behaviors and emotional exhaustion among law enforcement professionals: The negative spiral of role conflict. *International Journal of Environmental Research and Public Health*, 20(1), 863. https://doi.org/10.3390/ijerph20010863

Luthans, F., Avolio, B. J., Avey, J. B., & Norman, S. M. (2007). Positive psychological capital: Measurement and relationship with performance and satisfaction. *Personnel Psychology*, 60, 541–572.

Ma, J. Zhao, D., Xu, N., & Yang, J. (2022). The effectiveness of immersive virtual reality (VR) based mindfulness training on improvement mental-health in adults: A narrative systematic review. *EXPLORE*, 1-9. https://doi.org/10.1016/j.explore.2022.08.001

Milliard, B. (2020). Utilization and impact of peer-support programs on police officers' mental health. *Frontiers in Psychology* (11), 1686. https://doi: 10.3389/fpsyg.2020.01686

Moran, R. J., & Asquith, N. L. (2020). Understanding the vicarious trauma and emotional labour of criminological research. *Methodological Innovations*, 13(2). https://doi:10.1177/2059799120926085

Morabito, M. S., Pattavina, A., & Williams, L. M. (2021). Vicarious trauma, secondary traumatic stress or burnout?: An exploratory study of the effects of investigating sexual assault cases on detectives. *Policing: An International Journal*, 44(1), 77-92.https://doi.org/10.1108/PIJPSM-07-2020-0123

Morton, L., Cogan, N., Kolacz, J., Calderwood, C., Nikolic, M., Bacon, T., Pathe, E., Williams, D., & Porges, S. W. (2022). A new measure of feeling safe: Developing psychometric properties of the Neuroception of Psychological Safety Scale (NPSS). *Psychological Trauma: Theory, Research, Practice, and Policy.* https://doi.org/10.1037/tra0001313

Mysakidis, S. (2022). Metaverse. *Encyclopedia*, 2(1), 486-497. https://doi.org/10.3390/encyclopedia2010031

Newman A., Donohue R., & Eva N. (2017). Psychological safety: A systematic review of the literature. *Human Resource Management Review*, 27(3), 521–535. https://doi.org/10.1016/j.hrmr.2017.01.001

Newell, C.J., Ricciardelli, R., Czarnuch, S.M., & Martin, K. (2022). Police staff and mental health: barriers and recommendations for improving help-seeking. *Police Practice and Research*, 23(1), 111-124. https://doi:10.1080/15614263.2021.1979398

Office of Personnel Management (n.d.). What is an employee assistance program? *Work life.* OPM.gov. rebrand.ly/y2p2lii

Pal, J., Carter, K., Kowalczyk, E., & Townsend, C. (2023). Strategic communications for law enforcement executives. Washington, DC: Office of Community Oriented Policing Services. https://rb.gy/doq7b

Pearlman, L. A., & Mac Ian, P. S. (1995). Vicarious traumatization: An empirical study of the effects of trauma work on trauma therapists. *Professional Psychology: Research and Practice*, 26(6), 558–565. https://doi.org/10.1037/0735-7028.26.6.558

Porges, S. W. (2022). *Polyvagal theory: a science of safety. Frontiers in integrative neuroscience*, 16, 27.

President's Task Force on 21st Century Policing. (2015). *Final report of the president's task force on 21st century policing.* Washington, DC: Office of Community Oriented Policing Services. https://cops.usdoj.gov/pdf/taskforce/taskforce_finalreport.pdf

Purba, A., & Demou, E. (2019). The relationship between organisational stressors and mental wellbeing within police officers: a systematic review. *BMC Public Health*, 19, 1286. https://doi.org/10.1186/s12889-019-7609-0

Quick, K. M., & Piza, E. L. (2022). Police officers' best friend?: An exploratory analysis of the effect of service dogs on perceived organizational support in policing. *The Police Journal*, 95(1), 127–151. https://rb.gy/aduuz

Santamaria, N., Gerdtz, M., Kapp, S., Wilson, L., & Gefen, A. (2018). A randomized controlled trial of the clinical effectiveness of multi-layer silicone foam dressings for the prevention of pressure injuries in high-risk aged care residents: The Border III Trial. *International Wound Journal*, 15(3), 482-490. https://doi: 10.1111/iwj.12891

Shifrin, N. V. & Michel, J. S. (2022). Flexible work arrangements and employee health: A meta-analytic review. *Work & Stress*, 36(1), 60-85. https://doi: 10.1080/02678373.2021.1936287

Shults, J. F. (2019). *8 reasons you may need to leave your department.* https://www.police1.com/police-jobs-and-careers/articles/8-reasons-you-may-need-to-leave-your-department-SwZgD0Uw4f5fCsVo/

Sullivan, C. M., Goodman, L. A., Virden, T., Strom, J., & Ramirez, R. (2018). Evaluation of the effects of receiving trauma-informed practices on domestic violence shelter residents. *American Journal of Orthopsychiatry*, 88(5), 563.

Sutton, L., Rowe, S., Hammerton, G., & Billings, J. (2022). The contribution of organisational factors to vicarious trauma in mental health professionals: a systematic review and narrative synthesis. *European Journal of PsychoTraumatology*, 13(1). https://doi:10.1080/20008198.2021.2022278

Taylor, B. G., Liu, W., & Mumford, E. A. (2022). A national study of the availability of law enforcement agency wellness programming for officers: A latent class analysis. *International Journal of Police Science and Management*, 24(2), 175–189.

U.S. Department of Justice (2019). *Law enforcement best practices: Lessons learned from the field.* Washington, DC: Office of Community Oriented Policing Services. https://cops.usdoj.gov/RIC/Publications/cops-w0875-pub.pdf

U.S. Office of Personnel Management (n.d.). *Employee Assistance Programs.* rb.gy/msxqd

Waters, J. A., & Ussery, W. (2007). Police stress: history, contributing factors, symptoms, and interventions. *Policing: An International Journal*, 30(2), 169-188. https://doi.org/10.1108/13639510710753199

Wheeler, C., Fisher, A., Jamiel, A., Lynn, T. J., & Hill, W. T. (2021). Stigmatizing attitudes toward police officers seeking Psychological Services. *Journal of Police and Criminal Psychology*, 36, 1–7.

Wild, J., Greenberg, N., Moulds, M. L., Sharp, M-L., Fear, N., Harvey, S., Wessely, S., & Bryant, R. A. (2020). Pre-incident training to build resilience in first responders: Recommendations on what to and what not to do. *Psychiatry* (83)2, 128-142. https://doi: 10.1080/00332747.2020.1750215

Witters, D. & Agrawal, S. (2022). The best management secrets for impacting employee mental health. Gallup. Workplace. https://rb.gy/5ikv1

Zechner, O., Kleygrewe, L., Jaspaert, E., Schrom-Feiertag, H., Hutter, R. I. V., & Tscheligi, M. (2023). Enhancing operational police training in high stress situations with virtual reality: Experiences, tools and guidelines. *Multimodal Technologies and Interaction*, 7(2), 14. https://doi.org/10.3390/mti7020014

7 | LAW ENFORCEMENT FAMILY SUPPORT: SPOUSES, PARTNERS, PARENTS, AND CHILDREN

OBJECTIVES

After reading and considering the content of this chapter, the reader should be able to:

- Examine ways to build family resilience.
- Select ways to go from work-family conflict to work-family synergy.

In My Experience & Lessons Learned

JASON PALAMARA

After the experience of the young victim, a teenage girl who was murdered, I felt hyperarousal symptoms such as being easily startled and sleep difficulties. She remained a constant in my mind.

It was not easy to manage my emotions. I was traveling nationally and internationally on a consistent basis and was getting sick a lot. When I was home, I felt as though I was elsewhere. I constantly thought of the young victim, how her life was taken, and the gruesome details. I would often review the crime scene and autopsy photos—images forever burned in my memory.

The victim became a part of me. I became cynical. My anger and irritability often got the best of me. I made poor decisions as I managed my experience with excessive drinking. I was experiencing behavior and relationship issues such as problems separating work from my personal life, not having enough time with my family, feeling disconnected from them, and having conflicts with my wife. When able to sleep, nightmares of losing my loved ones would wake me. Many times, I was forcefully woken crying about the loss of someone close to me. I would wipe my face, descend once again to my pillow, and fall back to sleep. I didn't connect what was happening at home to the trauma at work.

My beliefs about my world were reflective of my experience and interpretations. Over time, I became more overprotective of my family—a common hypervigilance indicative of a career in law-enforcement. I sat in public places with a view of the door. I needed to be aware of the exits in the event something happened. I didn't want to feel like I was powerless to respond, especially if I was with my family. When I shared special moments with family and close friends, I thought about how I would remember that moment in the future when they were no longer alive. I thought about death and danger in the simplest of experiences.

As I advanced in my career, I spent more time at work and less time with my family. I had a multitude of interviews conducted, hundreds of reports read and written, and evidence collected and reviewed. I chose not to go home when I was able to, which caused relationship problems. It is convenient but unrealistic to say that you should never bring your work home. Although you do not have to talk about your job at home, it often affects how you act and who you have become while at home. My boundaries were shot.

My wife handled all that came with raising our children and their growing up without their dad around. Parties were attended alone and plans most often changed or were canceled at the last minute because I decided to make that end of tour arrest. As I soared in my profession, I chipped away at much more. Performing my best at work came with consequences. I was unaware that this was happening until many years later.

Truly effective change didn't happen for me until I embraced stretching myself inside, so I could stretch myself outside. It was painful and unfamiliar at first, but worth the effort. I didn't have anyone who shared this perspective when I joined the police department. I want to be that person for you. You can choose to put this book down and go it alone or decide to stretch, be curious, and keep reading. You have a general understanding of what is healthy to eat, and the benefits of stretching and exercising for overall well-being. Do you have the same familiarity when thinking about being mentally healthy at work and at home?

As LEOs, we are data driven, organized, and detail focused. A perpetrator commits a crime and there is an immediate solution—arrest or summons. We obtain this immediate solution or answer to a problem and conduct our days "by the book." The problem begins when we expect or look for life outside of work to operate by the same standards. What we do today may benefit us more in the long term than in the immediate short term. Although admittedly easy in theory, it is very difficult in practice.

I recently shared with Barbara a photo of my daughter when she was about five years old, sitting on an NYPD Mounted Unit horse during Precinct Family Day. I am in uniform standing next to her, sporting a smile from ear to ear. I have a tight grip on the back of her pants so she wouldn't fall off. She is smiling with a slight tilt of her head as if to say, "I got this, dad."

I kept that grip as she navigated her teenage years, sometimes a bit too tight. Precinct Family Days are opportunities to include the ones you love in what you do. To build family resilience, your children need a clear image of where you are and what you are doing when you are not with them. They can grow up with you, and with a greater understanding and appreciation for what you do. I still feel a bit of sadness when I look at that photo. I can't help but think back on what family life was like then and the difficult years that followed.

No one said, "Hey kid, just be careful you don't work yourself out of a marriage and your kids' life" or "here is what you should look out for and best ways to ensure you grow both on the job while building a strong family life." Stretch your ideas on what you think this job is and what you can make it become. It is possible to be a rock star at work and have a healthy home life. I learned ways to make more time for my family, be present and engaged. Everything fell into place when I had self-awareness. It wasn't until I learned new ways to open the doors I had closed, that my life and the ones that shared in it saw things begin to change.

It was my fortieth birthday party. My daughter took the mic as I stood looking stoic, knowing that at any moment I would shed tears. Unscripted, she passionately spoke of our relationship that was tested through some difficult years when she was learning to be a woman, and I was learning how to be a better dad. She spoke about the meaning of our relationship, how it made her who she was, and thanked me for never giving up listening to her or being there for her. I become emotional every time I watch the video of her speech, as I realize that I am never going to get back lost years and missed opportunities to watch her grow now that she was no longer my little girl.

It is never too late to begin again or to change course. Change begins with you. You are fully responsible for where you are in life. Be the change you want to see in your life and in your relationships. Watch what happens. Although my children like me now—at least I believe they do—for years as I worked on various cases they may have said otherwise. On most occasions, I left before my family woke and returned after they were asleep. At most, we got a piece of the weekend together when I wasn't a zombie due to a lack of sleep.

A good aspect of the law enforcement profession is having the knowledge to protect my family. I'd rather know what would keep most up at night than not. The unhealthy side of this coin is how overprotective I was of my children and those I loved. At times, being a good cop caused me to damage our relationships. When my children needed me the most, as they navigated difficult times, I was fighting crime or absent sitting next to them. I was at home, yet still far away. I wondered if I had done irreparable damage to them and our relationship. My mother once told me, "Never stop talking to them." It proved to be some of the best advice I could have ever received.

We can make a positive change and walk a different path when we are intentional about it and ask the right questions. Those internal conversations are important. I never questioned spending my time around the same community group at work and then doing the same when off the clock. My wife would joke with me that all my friends were cops. An important lesson that I have learned after years in law enforcement is that it is okay to have a tribe outside of the ones at work.

I recommend that you do the same if you want a healthy career, family, and state of mind. Although I have friends from childhood, and those I have met throughout life, my core contacts were cops or fellow Veterans from my Navy years, which didn't allow me to stretch my potential. Although some of my best friends are cops, they should not have made up my entire network. I needed to include those who helped me create a curiosity to explore what a better me could look like.

The time between the second and third days of an NYPD detective's work week is known as the "turn-around," the six hours between the end of your second shift and the beginning of your third. When the local bar is still open at 2AM, within walking distance of the station house, it is easy to employ unhealthy management tactics. To imagine the cycle, what begins with drinking with fellow officers at the bar, over time, extends to your home. Families become shut out of our world. What is already an unhealthy work-life balance begins taking on more of the qualities of an abusive relationship.

There was always talk inside the department about making schedules more flexible. Units work different schedules for different reasons. Some units continually change, while others have steady day or night tours. When your schedule is never the same, it impacts your well-being. Some cops enjoy this complexity because it helps to facilitate their equally complex lives. I was one of them for a long while.

Some may say, "we are a paramilitary organization and if you don't like the schedule, you can choose another profession." I retort, "we are killing ourselves, and everyone is still wondering why." Is this a one and done fix-it solution? Absolutely not. Let us start by addressing it as a problem. Making schedules more flexible has been statistically proven to improve areas of an officer's life.

Administrators can continue to dig their heals in and maintain the status quo, or decide to work to improve an officer's life. If we can utilize detectives to solve murders that have gone cold for decades, we can figure out what is healthier for the officer and their family than what is currently being done. Grueling schedules and unhealthy habits leave little to no time in between the "work" and the "life" parts for us to find our center. Being human is what should be visualized as our core, and the coating around this core is being a LEO. When we take that LEO coating off, we are left with what truly makes us who we are. The back and forth between both worlds is what makes the LEO profession unique. When substances are used to numb the negative effects of this back and forth, it creates a dangerous environment for us, our family, and our world.

If the normal sleep deprivation wasn't taxing enough, each job brought with it its own demands. Whether I was in the middle of an active scene where a victim had been shot, a situation where I was consoling a bereaved family member, looking for a perpetrator or a missing child, or buried under a pile of paperwork, I was still thinking about my family. Plans with my spouse would change. My wife would have to attend the event alone because I was stuck at work "sitting with a hospitalized prisoner." Thus, a day in the life of a cop. That day would be less meaningful without their partner.

For years, my partner was Det. Evelyn Gutierrez, a trailblazer through her career. She brought insight into our investigations and made me a better detective. She helped me grow far beyond my work in the police department. In the next chapter, Women in Policing, Evelyn shares her experience as a female LEO and the stressors she faced.

My Story & Evidence-Based Practices

BARBARA RUBEL

"Everyone needs a house to live in, but a supportive family is what builds a home."

—**Anthony Liccione**

We are a sight to see, and people are staring. I am five years old and excited to start my first day of kindergarten, I'm wearing my favorite blue skirt and brand new shoes. My father, in his police sergeant's uniform, is holding my hand, his stoic expression a polar opposite to my giddy one. The school crossing guard is giving my dad the side eye as she holds out her flag for us to cross. Other parents and kids stare at us. I feel proud that my dad is walking me to school. Only with hindsight did I realize that not only was it odd for a father to walk their kid to school then, but especially a police sergeant father.

At dinner that night, I ask my parents why everyone was staring. My mother winks at my father and says, "Because your father has blonde hair, blue eyes and is handsome as the day is long." They both laugh and tell me that if anyone asks, I'm to say that I'm a prisoner who is allowed to attend school when not in jail. I feel the thrill of excitement at being included in this new fun game and can't wait to try it out on someone at school the next day.

During the 1960s, my family went to The Police Recreation Center in the Catskill Mountains, NY. They called it The Police Camp. Families caught frogs at the edge of the lake, swam and took out the rowboats, making circles around the small body of water. We brought the frogs back to the hotel and kept them in the bathtub until housekeeping complained. As the years passed, younger officers lost interest in going to The Police Camp, and so it closed its doors.

A few months ago, Jason and I were invited to be on a podcast. I noticed a small statue behind Jason's desk of an officer holding a flag standing next to a child who had his arm wrapped around the officer's arm. It was a miniature of the statue that had lived at The Police Camp, and the fond memories of being with other blue families rushed back.

The Blue Family

Family Resilience

Family resilience refers to the ability of a family to manage loss, suffer disruption, and find solutions to their problems in a healthy way such as shared beliefs, ability to make meaning of their life's work and having a hopeful outlook (Walsh, 2020). Family resilience is the strength that enables them to effectively cope, individually and as a group, with difficult life circumstances and grow from their experiences. Family resilience focuses on characteristics that increases the ability to adapt to the difficulties of *living blue*. Although resilient LEOs are the foundation of the department, we all know it is the family that helps them stay mentally healthy.

CASE NOTES

Nicholas Greco IV, M.S., B.C.E.T.S., C.A.T.S.M., F.A.A.E.T.S., president and founder of C3 Education and Research, and law enforcement trainer, notes, "On your days off, you actually take off and spend time with your family, friends, and outside interests. No work, no shop talk! It's also a good time to communicate with your spouse or partner and have a focused, connected, and meaningful conversation each day. You and your significant other need to decide what and how much you will talk about. Some partners want to know all the details, others want just the Cliff Notes/basic cable version. Some couples will need no words as they sit and cuddle together on the couch and watch TV. Regardless, you need to let your loved one in your life in your world. Here are some tips for officers and their families to reduce stress and build resilience:

- **TALK.** Yes, it's that simple. Talk with those you trust. Start with a good friend or your spouse or partner and involve them. You can't carry the weight all by yourself and you don't have to.
- **ACCEPT YOUR LIMITATIONS.** You are not invincible; you, just like every other human can and will make mistakes. You need to rest, recharge and center yourself.
- **MEDITATE.** Even taking two minutes of quiet time can make a big difference in helping you to stop and take a step back. Other options include yoga and deep breathing too (e.g., inhale for five seconds, exhale for five seconds and repeat a few times).
- **EXERCISE.** Lift weights, do push-ups, run outdoors or on a treadmill, hit the heavy bag, practice yoga, go for a walk—just do something active. Get out there and burn off some steam in a healthy way. If you don't have the time, make time, and take a brisk twenty-minute walk. Even five minutes walking outside could be beneficial.
- **SLEEP.** Easier said than done, but sleep is restorative and promotes both physical and mental health. Ideally, you should try to get 7-9 hours of sleep a night.
- **HYDRATE.** Cut back on high caffeine power drinks and weight gaining sodas. Water is an optimal choice. Flavor it with sliced fruit, cucumbers, or even some non-caffeinated drink additives. Just read the labels.
- **THE POWER OF PETS.** Research has consistently shown that the mere act of petting an animal can reduce stress levels, blood pressure, and help a person's mood.

- **RECONNECT.** Take time to spend with your family and reconnect with them. They need you as much as you need them to get through this.
- **TAKE BREAKS FROM THE NEWS.** Turn off the TV, put down the phone, disconnect from the world to avoid negative news. Set aside times when you will check the news, but don't constantly check throughout the day as this can raise stress levels. Only go to reliable sources.
- **TALK TO SOMEONE.** If you are unable to talk with friends or family or simply want to seek out greater peace in your life, make an appointment with a trained therapist" *(N. Greco, personal communication, January 28, 2023).*

Helping Blue Families Flourish

Family was important to my parents, which made me flourish. Flourishing refers to being fulfilled, putting character strengths into practice, and finding meaning in life. My parents and I often played the game Scrabble. I created words from the letters on each wooden tile. Usually my words were "dog," "mom," or "car". My parents were in a whole other playing field. Their words were "badge" or "arrest". One time, my father's tiles spelled out, "handcuffs." He acted as though he won the lottery. He took us out to Chinese food that night to celebrate his two-syllable word.

Although education and religion are paths to flourishing, so are work and family (VanderWeele, 2017). Psychologist Martin Seligman coined the phrase, flourishing, as living a good life by finding fulfillment, accomplishing meaningful and worthwhile tasks, and connecting with others at a deeper level (Seligman, 2011). Although personal resources and resilience enhance well-being, flourishing is a state of complete well-being (Lee at al., 2021). It impacts the interaction between the family and work domain (Du et al., 2018).

Flourishing involves happiness, life satisfaction, physical and mental health, meaning of life, life's purpose, character and virtue, and social relationships (VanderWeele, 2017). Flourishing begins with developing a feeling of self-respect and a calm inner gladness to be the person you are (Schiraldi, 2022). It is to feel good while effectively functioning and knowing that life is going well (Huppert & So, 2013). Ordinarily, families flourish through lifestyle behaviors, daily healthy habits, and when agencies care about creating synergy between work and family.

> **LAW ENFORCEMENT CONSIDERATION & PERSONAL INSIGHT**
>
> In what way does your family resilience and connection promote flourishing?

Work-Family Conflicts

Work-family conflict describes the incompatibility between pressure experienced at work and family life and that conflict centers on how work interferes with family and how family interferes with work (Amstad et al., 2011). Issues with mental health and job pressure are strong predictors of work-family conflict (Beutell et al., 2008; Beutell & Gopalan, 2021). Increased stress of having a spouse with a mental or physical health problem causes employees in various fields to have higher work–family conflict (Fettro & Nomaguchi, 2018). Family problems rooted in clinical research point to finances, intimacy and sex, child rearing, not spending enough time together due to shift work and long hours, religion, household tasks and communication.

> **CASE NOTES**

Emily Nash, MA, MFT, family coach, law enforcement wellness specialist, and sergeant's wife, notes, "Identify the tools you have established for *Living Blue*. Text if you are running late or if there is an officer involved shooting, so your partner knows you're safe. Eat together. Have date nights. It's ok to spend time together in silence. Make it a point to integrate healthy coping skills into family fun. Sign up to do a run together. Take an art class, try yoga at the park, go shooting together, get out in nature, and enjoy game night. There will be times when your partner needs space and that is ok. You can show you're there by making sure they have healthy things to eat and stay hydrated, make their coffee and any other simple tasks.

"Address behaviors that are negatively affecting your family. Pay attention to clues like overindulging, not following through with tasks, avoidance, disinterest in activities and other changes from healthy patterns. Lovingly express your concern and what you have noticed. That opens a dialog about what you can do together to bring homeostasis back to the family. That may mean asking for outside help to establish a new system at home. Build your resilience together and establish a home where they feel defended and protected mentally and emotionally" *(E. Nash, personal communication, October 8, 2023).*

Sleep deprivation and insomnia can take a toll on the family. LEOs can recognize their chronotype, which is usually split between eveningness and morningness in relation to their spouse/partner's chronotype. A lark chronotype has energy levels that peak in the morning with their energy decreasing the rest of the day. An owl's energy level peaks in the late evening, increasing the rest of the day. A hummingbird chronotype has energy levels that peak at mid-morning with an early evening slump. A heron's chronotype has energy levels that peak at mid-morning and mid-evening with an afternoon slump. Although a chronotype regulates sleep and wake periods, sleep deprivation could impact a LEO's energy, no matter if they refer to themselves as an early bird or a night owl.

> **LAW ENFORCEMENT CONSIDERATION & PERSONAL INSIGHT**
>
> Whether you have a problem sleeping or a sleep shift disorder, would your family say that it is time to talk to someone about it?

Officers may work on the holidays or have a second job. Long hours may leave little time for family events. They may miss their child's sports activities, and they feel guilty about their lack of presence. It is hard to set a goal to be there for family when they feel as though they are not even present for themselves. Hypervigilance, fatigue, disrupted plans, ambiguous loss, limited family time and social support, on-the-job injuries or illnesses, family violence, and secondary trauma impact the family (Cox et al., 2022).

Families struggle as they find solutions to the constant stressors related to role overload for the non-police parent, not enough family time, or socializing, lack of routines, and crossover stress that is transferred to family members (Cox, 2022). Disruption to family and social lives causes negative emotions (e.g., anger, resentment, guilty) for prioritizing work over family (Davies, 2022).

It is difficult for officers to change their mindset at the end of their shift. Although they believe that they are protecting their family from stress, decompressing before coming home by occasionally fraternizing with colleagues can inadvertently be translated by the spouse, who doesn't understand the need to de-stress, as avoidance or not prioritizing their homelife, if not communicated beforehand (Bellon & Krawczyn, 2022).

Work-Family Synergy

Carl Rogers (1995), a psychologist who created the humanistic theory of personality development said, "The good life is a process, not a state of being. It is a direction, not a destination." Synergy is about a connection between work and family and the ability to communicate and collaborate about well-being whether at work or at home.

Positive energy flows between an officer and their spouse and family creating a strong connection and increasing wellness on and off the job. When positive things happen in the family, it enhances the quality of life at work and vice versa (Greenhaus et al., 2006). When an officer eats healthily at home and gets eight hours sleep, their job is positively impacted. By the same token, when they are satisfied with their job and feel supported in their role, their family life is positively impacted.

CASE NOTES

Tiffany Atalla, a Licensed Marriage and Family Therapist, Director of Clinical Development and Training – First Responder Wellness, notes, "For Blue relationships to thrive, speak positivity into your marriage and about your marriage to others (no criticism, judgment, reactive discussions). Create time and space where both people are calm and willing to resolve conflict or debrief past situations. As you explore suggestions, dare to dream together. No dream dashers. Have daily check-ins. Steer away from asking 'How was your day,' and rather ask, 'What is something interesting that happened today?' Have weekly check ins. Ask, 'What is one thing I can do for you or for us this week?'

"Create decompression plans together. Talk with your partner about what helps you decompress quickly to be present for the family again. Recognize that your spouse needs to know when their time to throttle down their responsibilities running the home will be or when they can transition from being the primary parent. They may decompress in ways different from yours. Keep your sense of humor and have sex. Schedule dates before picking up OT. Take turns planning them. Create teamwork. Make trades. For example, sometimes a chart, chore swap is helpful. Just because you have been the 'trash boss' for years does not mean that you like it or that you are unwilling to trade chores. Rather than asking your partner to complete a 'Honey Do List,' create a 'We Do List.' Post the household jobs and then cross them off to show how well you both work united.

"Plan vacations from work and responsibilities. Outsource assistance or care when needed. Manage shift work stress, mandatories, and schedules that interfere with planning special days by compensating with other events or holidays. For example, if a child's birthday is on a shift day, plan a family celebration at the station with a cake the day of and plan a surprise dinner two days ahead of time. It takes preparation and intention; however, blue families can be experts at making it work" *(T. Atalla, personal communication, January 21, 2023).*

Healthy Work and Family Life

Resiliency programs need to stem from within the department or through peer networks to build positive coping skills (Stogner et al., 2020). The same holds true for spousal resiliency programs—they need to be developed from within the department and with spousal feedback. Police agencies can implement blue family friendly, evidenced-based mental health programming. Mental and physical well-being programs can reduce instances of alcohol abuse, thoughts of suicide, negative perception of others, excessive force complaints, relationship conflict, and officer turnover (Craddock & Telesco 2022).

First-line supervisors need to recognize the value of interventions, such as family outreach and support services. Programs for families can focus on the issues that impact the entire family such as negative media coverage, ambushes on police and calls to defund the police. When designing work-family policies, managers need to remain flexible as they consider the family context and the complexity of each employee's family system to accommodate more family situations and customize policies according to their family background (Fan et al., 2022). What happens in the work environment could extend to the home environment and influence the work-family relationship (Bonab et al., 2013).

Mental wellness and family training should be addressed at the academy and continued throughout an officer's career. To help police perform their family roles and reduce work-life conflict, management strategies can include voluntarily part-time, compressed workweeks, flexible time, and family leave. Being that a LEO may be struggling with their physical and mental health, supervisory support for work and for family/personal issues should be explored (Beutell, 2010).

Family-friendly practices and policies could increase officer well-being and family well-being. Departments can offer family-friendly work schedules; have an on-duty fitness workout facility; have cookouts and bowling outings with other blue families; build an on-duty restorative resting room; have "lunch and learn" sessions on sleep deprivation and nutrition; and provide training activities for spouses and children.

Being that secondary trauma can worsen existing difficulties in communication and emotional intimacy in couples, understanding the impact of trauma on them may lead to greater resources to help support them when an officer is directly exposed to work-related trauma (Landers et al., 2019). Agencies can focus on shared values, positive attitude, and compatible goals between work and family. Programs that promote synergy between family and work motivate officers and provide them with skills to avoid emotional exhaustion and to cope with a risky work environment (López-Cabarcos et al., 2023). For example, police agencies can sponsor events for squads where families can get together.

When an officer feels that police work is significant and purposeful, they make meaning of their role, which leads them to achieve their work goals, stimulating personal growth, learning and development (Bakker, et al., 2017). Organizations and policymakers can promote practices that help employees manage roles at home and at work because when they develop successful behaviors in one role (e.g., at work), benefits spill over to the other role (e.g., at home), (Strong, 2023).

When individuals and organizations enhance and sustain work-family synergy, there is an increase in job satisfaction and well-being (Nicholas et al., 2021). When LEOs have a positive experience with their family, those pleasant emotions can be involuntarily transferred to their work (López-Cabarcos et al., 2023). The positive transfer of resources from the family setting can improve a police officer's performance, increase job satisfaction and supportive behaviors (Lin et al., 2021).

> **LAW ENFORCEMENT CONSIDERATION & PERSONAL INSIGHT**
>
> How can your department enhance synergy between work and family?

Strategies for Couples

Several LEOs have shared their strategies that helped them reestablish a connection with their spouse/partner:

- "I pray every evening with my wife and kids."
- "We set up a monthly potluck dinner with other blue families."
- "We read the same book on true crimes and discuss it."
- "We started equally distributing responsibilities, so resentment does not set in."

> **LAW ENFORCEMENT CONSIDERATION & PERSONAL INSIGHT**
>
> On a scale from 1 to 5 (1 very unsatisfied – 5 very satisfied), how would you rate your family relationships?

Communication

"What do you need from me in order for you to give me what I need?" A simple statement that can help couples communicate their needs. The most frequent issue between unhappy couples is their inability to communicate. Every issue between maladjusted couples has its origins in their lack of understanding of their own feelings, thoughts, and personality features. (Pirmoradi et al., 2023). Here are a few communication tips:

- Do not interrupt when listening to a traumatic story.
- Check in with one another and take turns sharing thoughts and feelings.
- To avoid blame and have them understand your perspective, be mindful when using "you" statements instead of "I" statements.
- After the conversation, consider debriefing to make sure that both of you are okay.

CASE NOTES

Sarah Guenette, a trainer in the public safety field, notes, "If the first responder walks in after a shift and says, 'I can't talk right now, I need some time' this needs to be acceptable to the partner without further probing or nagging. Alternately, the first responder partner needs to understand that they need to return to their partner and have a conversation. These are the sort of parameters that are ideally established ahead of time, not in the moment" *(S. Guenette, personal communication, March 31, 2023).*

Marriage Counseling

According to the Harris Poll (2022) although more than half of U.S. adults think that seeking out help from a mental health professional is a sign of strength, 32% don't know where to find it. Many are finding it online through telehealth specialists. Telehealth is the use of electronic information and telecommunication technologies to provide long-distance clinical health care and health-related education (Human Resources & Services Administration, 2022).

CASE NOTES

Barbara Bigalke, founder of the Center for Suicide Awareness, notes, "LEOs will often not tell their spouse about their job because they are protecting them from what they see, have lived through it once, and feel that there is no need to retell it. There is a lack of communication which overflows to other areas in their personal lives. Spouses may feel as if their spouse is not present or as though their mind is somewhere else. The vicious cycle is that the LEO then fears their spouse will leave due to lack of communication. Breakdown of communication is a common stumbling block" *(B. Bigalke, personal communication, January 12, 2023).*

Whether online or in person counseling, marriage and family therapists, specifically trained in helping couples, must be well versed in police issues and ensure complete confidentiality, or it might not work. Although marriage counseling might be beneficial, departments can consider a spousal support program that hosts family events and training.

Do We Need Marriage Counseling?

Here's a handy tool for you and your spouse/partner to review possible outcomes of marriage counseling or therapy. These thought-provoking statements can help you to reestablish a connection and help you see where you both are stuck. Check off the statements that are important to you. Have your spouse/partner do the same. Then compare your answers and explore why your relationship is worth saving.

Counseling and Therapy Outcomes	Officer	Spouse/ Partner
I want to feel more connected to you.		
I want to make our relationship a priority.		
I want to understand you better.		
I no longer want to walk on eggshells when I am around you.		

162

Counseling and Therapy Outcomes	Officer	Spouse/ Partner
We can possibly make our arguments more productive.		
We can learn ways to set better boundaries.		
I want to learn how to show you that I appreciate you.		
I hurt you and want you to realize how sorry I am.		
I need us to stop being defensive so we can hear what we are saying.		

Mental Health Resources

Although a LEO could benefit from counseling or therapy, many do not seek treatment due to stigma in the police culture (Casas and Benuto, 2022). Although wellness programs are available, they experience higher rates of mental health concerns than the general population (Carleton et al., 2020). If they are not ready for counseling or a wellness program, they can start by leaning on their spouse or another significant person as an informal way to get help.

A study found that 74% of public safety personnel in a Canadian sample of 2,975 would first seek care from their spouse, which suggests wanting more informal mental health services than more formal, clinical services (Carleton et al., 2019). Relationships between officers and their spouses, partners, parents, children, and family members are a common thread woven through the requests for counseling either by the officer or a family member dealing with work-family conflicts. LEOs have noted that improved mental health resources for their families would be valuable (Newell et al., 2022).

Diane Poole Heller, Ph.D., a therapist and leading expert in adult attachment theory believes that trauma is a break in the relational field. If a person was raised in a less-than-ideal setting, significant attachment bonds were not formed or were unreliable, and to protect themselves, they developed coping strategies that were brought over into their adult relationships. Officers can consider exploring how their childhood abuse, neglect, or household dysfunction may be influencing their relationship with their spouse or partner.

During the past few years, police families were impacted by demonstrations, difficult deployments, backlash from the public, and being doxed, where their private information would be searched for and then published on the Internet (National Policing Institute and COPS Office 2022). Agencies are recognizing ways to help those *living blue*, manage stress and flourish. A hopeful future direction draws on emerging evidence that police agencies are focusing on blue families. When blue families are resilient, everyone benefits.

THE NEXT STEP

In this chapter we focused on flourishing, work-family conflict and building family resilience. Meet us in the next chapter, where we shine a spotlight on women in policing.

REFERENCES

Amstad, F.T., Meier, L.L., Fasel, U., Elfering, A., & Semmer, N. K. (2011). A meta-analysis of work-family conflict and various outcomes with a special emphasis on cross-domain versus matching-domain relations. *Journal of Occupational Health Psychology*, 16(2), 151–169. https://doi.org/10.1037/a0022170

Bakker, A.B., & Demerouti, E. (2017). Job demands-resources theory: Taking stock and looking forward. *Journal of Occupational Health Psychology*, 22, 273–285.

Bellon, S., & Krawczyn, J. (2022). Chapter 5. Relationships: A "Make It or Break It" Suicidal Factor, In O. Johnson, K. Papazoglou, J. Violanti, J. Pascarella (Eds.), *Practical considerations for preventing police suicide: Stop officer suicide*, 91-112. Springer. https://doi.org/10.1007/978-3-030-83974-1_5

Beutell, N.J., & Gopalan, N. (2021). Pathways to work-family synergy: resources, affect and wellbeing. *Journal of Family Studies*, 27(4), 556-572. https://doi: 10.1080/13229400.2019.1656664

Beutell, N.J., & Wittig-Berman, U. (2008). Work-family conflict and work-family synergy for generation X, baby boomers, and matures: Generational differences, predictors, and satisfaction outcomes. *Journal of Managerial Psychology*, 23(5), 507-523. https://doi.org/10.1108/02683940810884513

Beutell, N. (2010). The causes and consequences of work-family synergy: An empirical study in the United States. *International Journal of Management*, 27 https://www.researchgate.net/publication/259467246_The_Causes_and_Consequences_of_Work-Family_Synergy_An_Empirical_Study_in_the_United_States

Bonab, M.B., Ebrahimpour, D., & Ghorbani, A. (2013). Quality of work life and family functioning in faculty members of Islamic Azad university. *Life Science Journal*, 10 (Suppl. S2), 105–113.

Carleton, R.N., Afifi, T.O., Taillieu, T., Turner, S., Krakauer, R., Anderson, G.S., McCreary, D., Ricciardelli, R., Cramm, H. A., Groll, D., & McCreary, D.R. (2019). Exposures to potentially traumatic events among public safety personnel in Canada. *Canadian Journal of Behavioural Science*, 51(1), 37–52.

Carleton, R. N., Afifi, T. O., Turner, S., Taillieu, T., Vaughan, A. D., Anderson, G. S., Ricciardelli, R., MacPhee, R. S., Cramm, H. A., Czarnuch, S., Hozempa, K., & Camp, R. D. (2020). Mental health training, attitudes toward support, and screening positive for mental disorders. *Cognitive Behaviour Therapy*, 49(1), 55–73. https://doi.org/10.1080/16506073.2019.1575900

Casas, J. B., & Benuto, L. T. (2022). Breaking the silence: A qualitative analysis of trauma narratives submitted online by first responders. *Psychological Trauma: Theory, Research, Practice, and Policy*, 14(2), 190–198. https://doi.org/10.1037/tra0001072

Cox, M., Norris, D., Cramm, H., Richmond, R., & Anderson, G.S. (2022). Public safety personnel family resilience: A narrative review. *International Journal of Environmental Research and Public Health*, 19(9), 5224. https://doi.org/10.3390/ijerph19095224

Craddock, T.B., & Telesco, G. (2022). Predicting psychological outcomes in officers exposed to traumatic events. *Journal of the American Academy of Experts in Traumatic Stress*, Winter-Spring, 24-35.

Du, D., Derks, D., & Bakker, A. B. (2018). Supplemental material for daily spill-over from family to work: A test of the work–home resources model. *Journal of Occupational Health Psychology*, 23(2), 237–247. https://doi.org/10.1037/ocp0000073.supp

Fan, Y., & Lin, Q. (2022). Putting families at the center: The role of family system in employee work-family conflict and voice behavior. *Journal of Business and Psychology*. https://doi.org/10.1007/s10869-022-09828-w

Fettro, M. N., & Nomaguchi, K. (2018). Spousal problems and family-to-work conflict among employed US adults. *Journal of Family Economic Issues*, 39, 277–296.

Greenhaus, J.H., & Powell, G.N. (2006). When work and family are Allies: A theory of work-family enrichment. *Academy of Management Review*, 3, 72–92.

The Harris Poll (2022). Public perception of mental health and suicide prevention survey results September 2022. https://suicidepreventionnow.org/static/executive-summary-2022-9c5a59e0f8016f1803570b11cfd3cb29.pdf

Heller, D. (2023). *The heart of healing in relationships*. https://artofhealingrelationships.com/?oprid=12837&ref=1134876

Human Resources & Services Administration (2022). *What is telehealth?* https://www.hrsa.gov/rural-health/topics/telehealth/what-is-telehealth

Huppert, F.A., & So, T.T.C. (2013). Flourishing across Europe: Application of a new conceptual framework for defining well-being. *Social Indicators Research*, 110(3), 837–861. https://doi. org/10.1007/s11205-011-9966-7

Landers, A.L., Dimitropoulos, G., Mendenhall, T.J., Kennedy, A., & Zemanek, L. (2019). Backing the blue: Trauma in law enforcement spouses and couples. family relations. *Interdisciplinary Journal of Applied Family Science*. https://doi.org/10.1111/fare.12393

Lee, M. T., Weziak-Bialowolska, D., Mooney, K. D., Lerner, P. J., McNeely, E., & VanderWeele, T. J. (2021). Self-assessed importance of domains of flourishing: demographics and correlations with well-being. *Journal of Positive Psychology*. https://doi.org/10.1080/17439760.2020. 1716050

Liccione, A. (n.d.). Goodreads. https://www.goodreads.com/quotes/837847-everyone-needs-a-house-to-live-in-but-a-supportive

Lin, S.H.J., Chang, C.H.D., Lee, H.W., & Johnson, R.E. (2021). Positive family events facilitate effective leader behaviors at work: A within-individual investigation of family-work enrichment. *Journal of Applied Psychology*, 106, 1412–1434.

López-Cabarcos, M.Á., López-Carballeira, A., & Ferro-Soto, C. (2023). How to prevent hostile behaviors and emotional exhaustion among law enforcement professionals: The negative spiral of role conflict. *International Journal of Environmental Research and Public Health*, 20(1), 863. https://doi.org/10.3390/ijerph20010863

National Policing Institute and COPS Office (2022). *21st Century protest response: promoting democracy and advancing community and officer safety*. Washington, DC: Office of Community Oriented Policing Services.

Newell, C.J., Ricciardelli, R., Czarnuch, S.M., & Martin, K. (2022). Police staff and mental health: barriers and recommendations for improving help-seeking. *Police Practice and Research*, 23(1), 111-124. https://doi:10.1080/15614263.2021.1979398

Pirmoradi, S., Amini, N., Keykhosrovani, M., & Shafiabadi, A. (2023). Effectiveness of solution-focused brief therapy on marital commitment and marital burnout among couples with marital conflicts: A randomized trial. *Journal of Midwifery and Reproductive Health*, 11(1), 3614-3622. https://doi: 10.22038/jmrh.2022.65120.1899

Rogers, C. (1995). *On becoming a person: A therapist's view of psychotherapy*. Houghton Mifflin Company.

Schiraldi, G. (2022). *Moving forward after adverse childhood experiences: How to move from suffering to flourishing*. https://www.pacesconnection.com/Blog/Moving-Forward-After-Adverse-Childhood-Experiences-How-To-Move-From-Suffering-To-Flourishing

Seligman, M. E. P. (2011). *Flourish: A Visionary New Understanding of Happiness and Well-being*. Atria Books.

Stogner, J., Miller, B.L., & McLean, K. (2020). Police stress, mental health, and resiliency during the COVID-19 pandemic. *American Journal of Criminal Justice*, 45, 718–730. https://doi.org/10.1007/s12103-020-09548-y

Strong, C. (2023). Human flourishing through behavior change, 85-96. In M. Las Heras, M. Grau Grau, Y. Rofcanin (Eds), *Human Flourishing: A Multidisciplinary Perspective on Neuroscience, Health, Organizations and Arts*, Springer https://library.oapen.org/bitstream/handle/20.500.12657/59341/1/978-3-031-09786-7.pdf

VanderWeele, T. J. (2017). On the promotion of human flourishing. *Proceedings of the National Academy of Sciences of the United States of America*, 114(31), 8148–8156.

Walsh, F. (2020). Loss and resilience in the time of COVID-19: Meaning making, hope, and transcendence. *Family Process*, 59(3), 98-911. https://doi: 10.1111/famp.12588

8 | WOMEN IN POLICING

OBJECTIVES

After reading and considering the content of this chapter, the reader should be able to:

- Describe stressors policewomen encounter throughout their career.
- Examine practices to alleviate some of the stress experienced by policewomen.

In My Experience & Lessons Learned

JASON PALAMARA

February 16, 2014, was my first day at my new office on Gold Street in downtown Brooklyn. I had a lot less time on the job compared to the twenty years or more most in the unit had. As soon as I walked into the building and entered the office, located on the first floor of 300 Gold Street, I realized why it was called "Cold Case." Stepping into the office was like stepping onto the set of "That Seventies Show." I thought, maybe the people working there liked to feel like they were back in the time when the crimes they were investigating were committed or maybe they just liked the old school look.

I was greeted by Det. Evelyn Gutierrez, the only female detective in the unit. While still a detective in the Special Victims Unit, Evelyn assisted the case detectives on the infamous Baby Hope case and was ultimately invited to join the unit. Evelyn became my partner. We worked on investigating and solving some of the city's most notorious unsolved homicides. We adapted quickly when speaking with a witness or in an interrogation based on how the individual reacted to engaging with one or the other of us. If she was a better fit to interview a suspect, I would step aside, and she would take the lead and vice versa. We had balance.

I interviewed my partner, Det. Evelyn Gutierrez for this chapter. We have come full circle. I have had both female and male partners throughout my career. At times, I was in units with both at the same time. I never had an issue with a female partner which provided a unique angle in certain situations that would otherwise be lost if with another male. I always felt a bit overprotective. However, with Evelyn, never once did I question whether or not she would have my back if we found ourselves in a fight.

There were times that I witnessed Evelyn on the receiving end of a supervisor's wrath that was not the same as with some male colleagues. Never once did she complain that something was unfair, or she was being targeted. These situations seemed to make her stronger and more determined to push ahead. In our conversations, I asked her to share some of the obstacles she faced and any advice she has for female LEOs. Detective Evelyn Gutierrez took me under her wing. I am honored today to consider her part of my family. Years later, I would retire proud of the work we would leave in our wake.

Meet Evelyn Gutierrez

My role as a woman in NYPD was special to me. I had to compete with men and some bad ass women. I never wanted to play the role that said, I should get anything in my career because I was a Hispanic female or seen as weak because I was a woman. I was an equal. My job was to protect and serve just like everyone else who took that oath. If I ever received preferential treatment, it was because I was being rewarded for doing my job, not just for being a woman in the NYPD. It was one of the most amazing challenges in my life.

When I first became a police officer, my brother was also on the job. The pressure that I could never disrespect, dishonor or embarrass him, was real. I come from a strict upbringing. My parents settled in NYC in the early 1960's from Puerto Rico. It's in our culture to have respect and pride in who we are and what we do. My dad is a U.S. Army Korean War Veteran, which is where my brother and I have that LEO gene. It meant the world to make my family proud. As the only female, it meant that I had to compete and prove that I was one of the guys-but keep my femininity. I am an alpha female, but most importantly, I felt respected enough to fit in. I had to fill the shoes of other female Cold Case detectives that came before me. It was an honor to be a part of this.

I worked with men and women on patrol, in the squad, Special Victims, then in Cold Case. I received the same treatment from my bosses and peers as everyone else as far as workload and incentives. In my role as a female detective, I was sympathetic, compassionate, and treated others with respect. Police contact with people usually is not under pleasant circumstances. As officers, we need to bring a caring heart to everything we do. Although I could never understand why someone would commit a heinous crime, I let the many I spoke to that had, know that doing a bad thing does not always make them a bad person. I gained their confidence, through my behavior whether they were peers, victims, or perps.

Most times, acting as a mom or big sister to my partners, I wanted to take care of them and the public. It became overwhelming having a family at home, at work, and the people of the city of New York. I had to remain strong mentally because I know that people just need people. No matter your profession or role, we are human and need to show one another that we are loved and cared for. I love investigating cases, bringing closure to families, helping them, which was always my goal. When it came to my work family, I looked forward to that every day of my career. I loved being around my peers. They wanted the same things I wanted and shared the same passion and drive. We were there for each other.

My advice to female LEOs is to never forget your family. They will be your sanity from what you deal with at work. While in special victims, I raised two teenage daughters. I often heard stories from teenage victims about their lived horror. I went home and told my daughters stories and asked them to have conversations with me about whatever was on their mind. Nothing they said or questions they asked surprised me. There are those in our profession who say never tell your family what you dealt with at work. Once you sign out, turn the job off and deal with your family. Well, if it wasn't for my family, I wouldn't be able to function. Our job does not treat us right when it comes to mental fatigue.

How many times do you have to hear the same story, the same cries for help from your victims and their families, or hear a perp say things like, "because she deserved it?" It is unhealthy keeping all of that inside. In our profession, we need an outlet. Talk to someone you trust. I chose my peers. Talking to your partner, an academy buddy, your spouse, siblings, adult children- yes, I said children, can make a huge positive impact on your mental well-being. Don't tell them every little detail. Explain it in smaller terms.

Most of your family and friends will find your job interesting, others may give you critical feedback. Most importantly, you spoke about it. If I am mentally fatigued because my work is overwhelming, and I just want to talk to let out the stress of the cases or organizational stressors, I should be able to have a conversation, so I can feel better, and not be worried about getting in trouble as a result. Single LEOs, be careful who you choose to have in your life. Most men or women either don't respect what you do or find who you are and what you do to be intimidating. It has been my biggest struggle. Personally, I don't trust people. I think the job did that to me. Maybe it was from what I saw daily. I chose my job first. I am that girl who married the job.

My Story & Evidence-Based Practices

BARBARA RUBEL

"The research on women in policing, and on women in the male-dominated fields more broadly, consistently shows the need for female role models and mentoring to attract and retain women candidates."

—Rineer et al., 2023

Honoring the Trailblazers

After serving in the Women's Army Corps (WAC) during WWII, my mother attended Cortland State Teachers College on the G.I. Bill. After graduating with a bachelor's degree in teaching, she spoke to a friend about finding a job as a teacher. Her friend was going to take the exam to be a policewoman and advised my mother to take it as well. In 1948, the first civil service exam for policewomen was given. Only a couple of years later, my mother and her friend took the exam. Although her friend failed, my mother passed and went into the police academy where she was not allowed to train with men. Thus became the beginning of 30 years on the force. When my mother retired on October 9, 1980, we celebrated all that she had accomplished.

Times have changed since my mother became a policewoman when she had to wear a skirt. It wasn't until 1970 when Police Commissioner Murphy assigned the first group of women to patrol. In 1973, the Bureau of Policewomen was abolished and the first gender-neutral civil service exam for police officers was held. That year, policewomen and patrolmen were renamed "police officer."

Advancing to the Next Level

Not many women were in authority when my mother became a policewoman in the early 1950s. In 1974, her friend, Gertrude Schimmel, was appointed as the first female Inspector. In 1976, Captain Vittoria Renzullo was appointed as the first Precinct Commander. In 1977, women were assigned to the nine Homicide Units at the time. In 1978, the Department increased the number of female detectives.

My mother invited her friends, Gertrude Schimmel and Felicia Shpritzer, to our home to celebrate Gertrude's appointment as the first female Deputy Chief. As the women sat around the kitchen table talking, with me listening in, my chin perched on my hands as my elbow rested on the table, Felicia told the story of what she had accomplished 17 years before Gertrude's appointment to Chief.

In 1961, Felicia sued to allow women the right to take the sergeant's exam. As a result of her lawsuit, 126 policewomen took the sergeant's exam for the first time in 1964. Gertrude told me how upset she and Felicia were with my mother in 1964 because she refused to take the sergeant's exam. My mother did not take the exam because my father, a police sergeant, told her that they "already have one sergeant in the family." She made the decision to not take the test and advance up the ranks. I was astonished that this independent and strong woman listened to him.

Felicia and Gertrude become the first female sergeants and they sued again. In 1967, they both became the first female lieutenants. Then in 1971, Gertrude became the first female police captain and the first female deputy inspector, a year later.

LAW ENFORCEMENT CONSIDERATION & PERSONAL INSIGHT

What stressors are women faced with when entering a career in law enforcement?

I was honored to be the general session closing speaker at The Mid-Atlantic Association of Women in Law Enforcement (MAAWLE), and the opening speaker at the Midwest Summit for Women in Law Enforcement. Conferences like these focus on women serving in Law Enforcement and highlight their success. For example, a study on policewomen found that resilience training is effective in increasing their resilience, job satisfaction, and psychological well-being and in reducing their occupational stress (Chitra et al., 2021). Nationally, women make up less than 13% of full-time police officers.

In 2018, The National Institute of Justice (NIJ) hosted a Research Summit on Women in Policing. Among the 100 attendees were police leaders, researchers, and professional organizations. The 30×30 Initiative goal is the representation of women in police recruit classes to 30% by 2030. The attendees made several recommendations: support mentoring, create flexible, family-friendly policies, enforce harassment policies, find advocates, re-examine physical fitness standards, publish issue briefs on relevant research, create research, learn from research in other fields, prioritize the issue, invest in partnerships, reframe conversations about women in policing, and commit to long-term work (U.S. Department of Justice, 2019).

The attendees focused on key research questions that were divided into five themes: Charting a Course, Culture, Performance, Recruitment and Retention, and Promotion (U.S. Department of Justice, 2019).

1. **CHARTING A COURSE:** how the experiences of women in policing has changed in the past 30 years, barriers, race, ethnicity, gender, diversity, creating cultural changes, improving data collection,

men's perspectives on women in policing, and advancing women in policing.

2. **CULTURE:** changing policing cultures to better integrate into the department, a toxic policing culture, reducing harassment, how academies can better serve women, and changing language to lessen discrimination.

3. **PERFORMANCE:** needing a metrics to measure the extent to which women in policing thrive, how they are impacting organizations, whether they perform differently than men, citizen complaints and the use of force in comparison to men.

4. **RECRUITMENT AND RETENTION:** why women decided not to become officers, making the profession enticing and an interesting career option for girls, postnatal nursing policies, and why women leave policing.

5. **PROMOTION:** the representation of women across ranks, promotion rates, discrimination, and increasing number of women in leadership.

Recruiting Women in Policing

Studies have found that to reduce the perception of work-life conflict, recruitment materials ought to emphasize work-life balance and family-friendly policies because it is frequently referred to as an obstacle for women in considering a career in law enforcement (Yu, 201; Cambareri & Kuhns, 2018).

> **LAW ENFORCEMENT CONSIDERATION & PERSONAL INSIGHT**
>
> If you were creating a video to recruit women, would you include community-oriented behaviors or show high-speed driving, the use of firearms, a K-9 officer, and a SWAT team?

Taniguchi et al. (2023) studied recruiting women in policing and recommends that recruiting material,

- Has women-focused messaging in videos to improve motivation, relevance, and positive perceptions of the advertisement for women.
- Highlights officer support and wellness initiatives to ensure officer well-being.

174

- Includes complete and diversity-focused job descriptions focusing on improving perceptions of organizations.
- Contains simple additions to descriptions highlighting agency initiatives related to diversity and work-life balance.
- Appears on an agency's website, being that it is the predominant way individuals seek out information about an agency.
- Focuses on community-service aspects of policing based messaging rather than longer-term career benefits.

CASE NOTES

Sergeant Donna Brown (Retired), award winning author, *Behind and Beyond the Badge: Stories from the Village of First Responders with Cops, Firefighters, Dispatchers, Forensics, and Victim Advocates,* notes, "When I was hired in 1979, I was one of only five women at my department. A year or two prior, a woman sued my city as they did not hire women as police officers. We were not totally welcomed with open arms by the rank and file or by the citizens of our city. The prevailing thought had been that women could not physically do the job and were therefore a liability.

"Being one of the first came with the pressure that everyone was watching, and every action/reaction was under a microscope and openly criticized. We constantly had to prove ourselves worthy of wearing the uniform. With the hiring of a new and more progressive police chief, more women were hired.

"As time went on, women began earning new assignments as detectives or in other specialty units and began being promoted on merit not 'just because.' After several years in our Criminal Investigations Bureau supervising various units, I was chosen by our chief to supervise our Homicide Unit and did so for ten years.

"To my knowledge, I am the only woman to have done so at my old department and, even though I know there must be others, I've never met another Detective Sergeant supervising or that has supervised a Homicide Unit. I strongly believe that the personnel of any law enforcement agency should reflect the community they serve. While I have seen great strides with women in the law enforcement profession, there is still room for improvement" *(D. Brown, personal communication, April 26, 2023).*

175

Women in Law Enforcement Face Unique Stressors

Policewomen are often neglected in most of the research of police stress as studies predominately look at policemen (Chitra et al., 2021). We need to pay attention to female officers given their rates of psychological distress (Drew & Martin, 2023). Besides operational and organizational stressors, interpersonal stressors include lack of support from colleagues, gender discrimination, sexual harassment, interpersonal conflict, and lack of confidentiality (Thompson et al., 2006). Policewomen manage family commitments while they manage working alone at night, overtime, negative comments from the public, increased assignments, and working on holidays. (Kavith & Gayathri, 2018).

CASE NOTES

April Switala, Police Sergeant, Bloomfield Township Police Department, Michigan, mental health trainer/advocate, notes, "The strength that we perceive in our physical self with the armor and badge that we shield it with is an illusion. The trauma and stress that we subject our minds to throughout our career can overwhelm that shield. We must armor and care for our whole self; body and mind" *(A. Switala, personal communication, March 16, 2023).*

In 2016, a study by Violanti and colleagues found that policewomen experience a 37% higher occurrence of lack of support from their supervisor compared to male officers. In 2022, a national survey was collected by the Nebraska Association of Women in Police. Of 114 anonymous responses, top issues identified were lack of fitting equipment or uniforms (61%); supportive women mentors (59%); women's health policies (55%); and representation in training staff (54%). Other responses were sexual harassment at work (45%); and mental health & self-care for women (40%).

While 43% reported that women's issues have made them contemplate leaving their agency, 40.7% reported that women's issues have made them consider leaving law enforcement entirely. When asked if their agency had policies that addressed women's issues (e.g., maternity leave, lactation standards), 49% responded yes, 37% responded no, and 14% responded that they did not know (The Nebraska Association of Women in Police, 2022).

Lori Aagard, North Precinct Captain, Seattle Police Department, notes, "Be proud and confident of who you are and don't change to try and fit in. We all have our strengths, so use and develop those in your career. Be kind and consistent. Maintain healthy habits and remember your family outside of work is more important than the job" *(L. Aagard, personal communication, September 30, 2023).*

Managing the Stress

Female officers are significantly more likely to use positive coping strategies compared to male officers (Bonner & Brimhall, 2022). Studies show that when policewomen accessed wellness services, particularly, peer support and mental health professionals, they were more likely than male colleagues to find them effective. The challenge will be to ensure that female officers, who might be most in need of support, have access to services and actively engage with them (Drew & Martin, 2023).

Practices that can alleviate some of the stress that policewomen experience are mentoring and sponsorship by law enforcement leaders to career tracks; creating flexible, family-friendly policies (e.g., parental leave, non-rotating shifts); improving and enforcing harassment policies; enlisting police chiefs, male officers, and civic leaders in the promotion of gender parity; re-examining physical fitness standards for officers; supporting women in police academy training; and learning from research in other fields (Starheim, 2019). Agencies can offer non-rotating shifts for predictable childcare services, partner with the YMCA to offer programs at reduced rates, and work with childcare groups that allow early drop-offs and late pickups (Elkins, 2022).

Several female LEOs have shared their insight:

- "I am surprised that I made it through the academy, which is not female friendly."
- "If you want to recruit more women, the department should consider having a daycare provision."
- "We need fixed shift schedules. Period."
- "Post-natal nursing was a big problem for me."

- "We are usually excluded from masculine bonding events."
- "We are not in what is known as the 'old boys club.'"
- "There is a double standard that has to be addressed."
- "It's a male dominated system, so we need male leaders to have our back."
- "It's deep rooted. I don't think I will ever be promoted."
- "I was concerned that my complaint would remain confidential because I was a woman."
- "Filing the sexual harassment claim made me stronger."
- "We need a state-wide network of women mentors."
- "Supervisors need to boost the confidence of female officers, so they take on positions of leadership."
- "Women must apply for leadership roles. The more apply, the more become leaders."

CASE NOTES

Chief Vera Bumpers, Metro Police Department, Houston, TX notes, "Women LEOs are a positive impact in the profession and community. They are intentional about making a difference and building sustainable bridges" *(V. Bumpers, personal communication, February 21, 2023).*

Although there is no quick fix to attract and retain women in law enforcement, incentives can focus on flexibility to increase a department's womanpower.

THE NEXT STEP

In the previous chapters, we focused on police well-being, stress, ACEs and Polyvagal Theory, burnout, maladaptive coping, moral injury, vicarious trauma, and blue families, while this chapter covered women in policing. None of the stressors of the job compare to a line of duty death (LODD). Therefore, in Chapter 9, we discuss LODD, death notification, and ways to support the bereaved blue family.

REFERENCES

Bonner, H. S., & Brimhall, A. (2022). Gender Differences in Law Enforcement Officer Stress and Coping Strategies. *Police Quarterly*, 25(1), 59–89. https://tinyurl.com/349r7s22

Cambareri, J. F. & Kuhns, J. B. (2018). Perceptions and perceived challenges associated with a hypothetical career in law enforcement: differences among male and female college students. *Police Quarterly* 21(3), 335–357

Chitra, T., & Karunanidhi, S. (2021). The impact of resilience training on occupational stress, resilience, job satisfaction, and psychological well-being of female police officers. *Journal of Police and Criminal Psychology*, 36, 8–23.

Drew, J. M., & Martin, S. (2023). Mental health and wellness initiatives supporting United States law enforcement personnel: The current state-of-play. *Journal of Community Safety & Well-being*, 8(1), S12-22. https://www.journalcswb.ca/index.php/cswb/article/view/298/817

Elkins, L. C. (2022). Increasing your department's womanpower: *Tips for Recruitment and Retention*, 15(4). https://cops.usdoj.gov/html/dispatch/04-2022/womanpower.html

Kavitha, G., & Gayathri, S. (2018). A study on stress among women police constables. *International Journal of Pure and Applied Mathematics*, 119(18), 3875-3886.

The Nebraska Association of Women Police (2022). *Concerns of US Women Police. International Association of Women Police (IAWP)*. http://dx.doi.org/10.2139/ssrn.4432124

Rineer, J. R., Taniguchi, T. A., Aagaard, B., Brinton, J., Duhart-Clarke, S. E., Presler-Jur, P., & Wire, S. (2023). How do law enforcement agencies recruit diverse applicants? *International Journal of Police Science & Management*, 0(0). https://doi.org/10.1177/14613557231185661

Starheim, R. P. (2019). *Women in Policing: Breaking Barriers and Blazing a Path*, 1-33. National Institute of Justice. https://tinyurl.com/msdjyp9w

Taniguchi, T., Rineer, J.R., Hoogesteyn, K., Wire, S., Mangum, L. (2023). Recruiting women into policing. *Policing: A Journal of Policy and Practice*, 17, https://doi.org/10.1093/police/paad049

Thompson, B. M., Kirk, A., & Brown, D. (2006). Sources of stress in policewomen: A three-factor model. *International Journal of Stress Management*. 13, 309-328.

U.S. Department of Justice (2019). National Institute of Justice Special Report. *Women in Policing: Breaking Barriers and Blazing a Path*, 1-33. https://tinyurl.com/bdhttmm4

Violanti, J. M., Fekedulegn, D., Hartley, T. A., Charles, L. E., Andrew, M. E., … & Burchfiel, C. M. (2016). Highly rated and most frequent stressors among police officers: Gender differences. *American Journal of Criminal Justice*, 41(4), 645-662.

Yu, H. H. (2019). Work-Life Balance: An exploratory analysis of family-friendly policies for reducing turnover intentions among women in U.S. federal law enforcement. *International Journal of Public Administration* 42(4), 345–357.

9 | END OF WATCH

DEFINITIONS

DEATH PACKET - a packet containing an officer's personal information given to the next of kin if they die in the line of duty.

LINE OF DUTY DEATH (LODD) - when an officer is killed or died while performing their duties.

OBJECTIVES

After reading and considering the content of this chapter, the reader should be able to:

- Explain eight characteristics of a death notification after a LODD.
- Review ways to support bereaved individuals.

In My Experience & Lessons Learned

JASON PALAMARA

I had a rare weekend at home and we were celebrating my daughter's birthday with our family. Sunday, March 13, 2011, started out as a happy occasion but quickly changed. I learned of an officer who had died in the line of duty. I sat with my family as we watched a video compilation my brother Anthony had made for my daughter's birthday. We were laughing and shedding tears of joy as we saw how much she had grown. We left the TV on after the video and suddenly the news broadcast a developing story. I recognized the area the reporter was referencing as my own command. Within seconds, my phone was on fire. Word spread rapidly that Officer Alain Schaberger had died in the line of duty. His information was being shared along with that of the perpetrator. Police Officer Alain K. Schaberger was killed while effecting an arrest for a domestic incident.

A career criminal pushed him over a Brooklyn stoop ending his life. Alain was a ten-year veteran of the New York City Police Department and assigned to the 84th Precinct in Downtown Brooklyn at the time of his death. Besides a LEO, Alain was a U.S. Navy Veteran. Grief seems to be magnified when you have a connection to the person. I knew Alain and was assigned to the same precinct's detective squad when he was killed. But there was someone else I knew well—the individual who killed him. Over the years, I had arrested him multiple times.

Today, my wife describes me as having been completely disconnected and a shell of myself as the day unfolded. I felt what I have felt many times before—an immense anxiousness to rush back to work. The desire to join the fight coursed through my veins, although there was no fight to join. Before the gravity of what had happened could set in, the news broadcast the death of another officer that had occurred just a mile from my home. A police officer from a neighboring department had mistakenly killed Nassau County Police Officer Geoffrey Breitkoph, while both were responding to the same job. There was no refuge from the shock of these events as the joy I had felt only moments before was stolen.

Although I knew Alain and didn't know Geoffrey, it didn't matter. They both wore the same uniform that I did. The LEO tribe is a special one. We know what dangers await us every time we clock in for duty, and can vividly relate and place ourselves in the shoes of our fallen brothers and sisters. We have been there and done that. I knew Alain. I knew the perp who took his life. I had put handcuffs on the very same hands that took Alain's life. I was a mile from where Geoffrey died on a day that was supposed to be full of happiness.

My heart broke for my brothers in blue. I was in shock, sad, and angry. I asked myself how it was possible that this career criminal who was provided with so many chances, squandered every one of them to ultimately take the life of a hero who would have assuredly given his life for him if called to do so. I will never have an answer to this question. Unfortunately, this would not be the last officer killed in the line of duty.

In many departments, those in the role of chief lead next steps when there is a line of duty death (LODD). No matter our rank, we all have an opportunity to be leaders. In moments like this, everyone looks to the chief for guidance. NYPD Patrol Guide procedure 202-35 reads that the chief will *act as a representative of the Chief of Department and assume command of incident if highest ranking member of the service on the scene.*

Regardless of rank, supervisors feel the roller-coaster of emotions like those they are called to lead. From this position, all communications are relayed to headquarters, other units, and personnel involved. What is exhibited by command staff and supervisors in the chaos, or in the day to day, is adopted by everyone that follows. The acceptance and understanding of those that are struggling by those in authority, if commonplace, fosters and cultivates a healthier department.

Mental health struggles and, more specifically suicide, do not discriminate based off rank. I have experienced the loss of my fellow LEOs from the rank of police officer, detective, sergeant, as well as Chief. When we lose a brother or sister in the line of duty and are feeling the crushing weight of pain, we collectively, as a blue culture, need to create an environment that allows for each of us to be vulnerable in our grief. When we find ourselves struggling in silence, we must tap into our greater collective knowing that we are not on an island alone. Leadership's response to our struggles is paramount. It should not be taboo to ask for help or fear that our struggles will travel up the rank ladder. When our blue culture changes to allow for this kind of response, we will see our suicide numbers decline.

A line of duty funeral is like no other. A sea of pristine dress uniforms with their white gloves and patent leather shoes invades the hometown of every LEO who has died in a solemn display of respect to honor the life of service and ultimate sacrifice made for their fellow human. "There is no greater love then to lay down one's life for one's friends" (Holy Bible (2015). New Living Translation. John 15:13. Tyndale House Publishers). Uniforms from departments both nationally and internationally adorn the funeral precession route. While officers stand at attention, the flashing of lights from hundreds of highway cops come into view as the hum of their motorcycles grows louder. Metal police barricades line the sidewalk so the public can observe-interlocked as the cops in attendance are in mourning.

For a few hours, spectators pay respect to a stranger that has given their life to keep them safe. The ceremonial unit and the bands steady drumbeat, which seem to be in cadence with your heartbeat, follow behind, marching in lockstep as they bring the fallen officer peacefully lying in a black hearse to the house of worship. Too many times I have stood imagining it was my family in the black vans slowly following my casket. Silence seems to fall on the city that never sleeps. You can hear a pin drop.

Through our collective grief we console one another. We laugh and connect with fellow cops we have not seen for some time; we commonly reference it as a reunion of sorts. We will stand no matter the weather or duration for the honor of rendering one final salute wishing we could turn back time. We wish we had been in the fight with the fallen to have battled alongside them.

Our fallen comrade leaves the house of worship with the detail that delivered them there. Customary in the NYPD, is a final drive by the officer's residence before arriving at their final resting place. As the officer and everyone in attendance leaves the house of worship, helicopters approach in the distance. With each rotation of their blades, they pass overhead at low altitude as though hovering in place. They depart with a gap in their formation to symbolize the officer that had paid the ultimate sacrifice. Once it is over, we bury it deep.

In the NYPD, when you put in a call for help over the radio, the response you get from fellow officers is the size of some small departments. When you are working, you know what support you have that is only seconds away. Too often, we forget this when we are fighting our silent battle. We struggle as we collectively grieve for a lost colleague. If we come out in force during our workday (prevention) and following a death (postvention), then how about we do the same while we all have the chance to make a difference (intervention)? The other side of the coin is that, individually, we recognize that our brothers and sisters are *living blue* like we are and are just waiting to respond to your call.

When an officer is killed in the line of duty, there is a convergence on their family by an outpouring of support from the department and often additional support from the community. When Alain was killed, the precinct muster room was filled with more food than we could eat.

I remember the days and months following the attacks of September 11th, 2001, and how much support and care the city gave us. Never lasting, it sure is nice when it's there. When a command suffers the loss of an officer, the neighboring ones lend their officers to assist in and cover operations to allow the officers of the affected command to attend the services. I have seen much change by way of internal support provided to those affected in these instances.

Responses such as Critical Incident Stress Management, Peer Support, and Therapy Dogs are commonplace following a LODD or death of an officer by other means. If this is not happening in your department, it should happen. Officers from units inside of the Health & Wellness Section are assigned to the bereaved spouse of the fallen to attend to their needs. Often outside organizations like the Stephen Siller, Tunnel to Towers foundation assist in paying off the remaining mortgages left for a spouse.

When a family member loses their LEO, they are reminded of how big their blue family is. Police Commissioner James O'Neill (Ret.), funeral for Det. Brian Simonsen (EOW: 2/12/19), notes, "So, the next time you see the lights and you hear the sirens, take a moment to think about who answers those calls for help."

I often think of death. Although I thought this would wane as the distance from my time in service increased, it hasn't. I would rather have every detail about what could happen. From this knowledge and from personal experience with loss, I have prepared for my death. I have developed the process of always thinking about the day the person I am spending my time with will no longer be with me or when they will lose me. I snapshot the moment in my mind. I squeeze every bit of joy I can from it while giving as much love to the person as I can, knowing that at some point it will be but a memory. At first, this was hard to deal with and what would often keep me up at night.

Be aware of the precious time you share with those you care about. Try not to allow thoughts to paralyze and rob you from being mindfully present with them. Don't take special moments for granted. Don't focus your thoughts elsewhere. If what you are doing is taking you away both physically and mentally from who you are doing it for—your family, maybe it's time to think differently. As your LEO brother, I don't have to know you to tell you that I am genuinely proud of you. You are reading this book because you are, at the very least, curious. Keep this curiosity, because your life depends on it.

In always thinking of the worst-case scenario, I have learned to best prepare for it. More specifically, ensuring the ones I love most are taken care of when they no longer have me to take care of them. I want to live the life God intended me to live. The reality is, my last day is ultimately not my choice.

For the longest time, I did not have the proper amount of life insurance that would enable my wife and children to not have to worry about finances in the event of my death. It is important to do this sooner than later as the older you get, the more expensive it can be. It is just as important to learn from an expert what is best for you and your family. I made sure that my financials, including banks, account numbers, and contact information, was included in my death plan. This plan was to asist my family in the event of my death.

While writing this chapter, I am reminded of a death that deeply impacted me, as it reminded me of my family and what it would be like to lose my daughter. It was early morning and my squad partner, Det. Billy Bush (Ret.), and I were called to a DOA "Dead On Arrival" job in an apartment complex in Brooklyn. We were assigned to investigate an overdose case.

Upon arrival to what was a college dorm, we walked past all the uniformed officers and building staff anxiously awaiting our arrival. We were met by the building's superintendent who took us to the apartment where he had first noticed a foul smell emanating from within. After he gained entry, he discovered the deceased in a back bedroom and called the police.

One of the tasks on a job such as this is to identify the victim. An eighteen-year-old college student was lying on her bed with a laptop open as if she had died doing her schoolwork. Another young life cut short. I wanted to drop everything and call my daughter to make sure she was okay. This case and others like it made me question how well I was being as a dad. Was I doing enough to protect my children from ending up like this?

After we left, I had the responsibility of informing the girl's father, who was a local judge, as to what had happened to his little girl. Seeing anyone, any parent, any family member break down upon receiving such news is difficult. However, seeing someone I have experienced at a high level of authority seemed to cut a bit deeper. There is no authority that is insulated from the magnitude of pain of this kind of loss. We are all vulnerable to the painful experience of loss. What happened to this child was the result of a deadly mixture of substances with prescribed medication. What initially looked like a suicide was an accident.

Death notifications are difficult and become a part of the bereaved individual's loss narrative. The notifier is the messenger of words no human ever wants to hear. As we met the father on the steps in front of his home, I informed him that his teenage daughter was gone. His cry echoed through the street. The shock and weight of our words caused him to buckle to the ground. We helped him up, hugged him for what seemed like eternity, and left him with his family to mourn. Sometimes the best words are those unsaid and replaced by a tight embrace. I went home that night and held my daughter a little tighter.

When we leave this life, and our loved ones, our conversations will cease. In the books that I read, I underline what moves me, impacts me or teaches me to grow. One day, my children will pick up this book, *Living Blue*. My hope is that they will be able to converse with me through my written words and that I will be able to continue to teach them long after I am gone. Perhaps they might even highlight words on a page, like their dad.

My Story & Evidence-Based Practices

BARBARA RUBEL

"Self-awareness is a supreme gift, a treasure as precious as life. This is what makes us human. But it comes with a costly price: the wound of mortality. Our existence is forever shadowed by the knowledge that we will grow, blossom, and, inevitably, diminish and die."

—Irvin D. Yalom

My first understanding of a line of duty death (LODD), was when my mother was faced with the risk of being feloniously killed. It was either the late 1960s or early 1970s when the fear hit me hard as I was getting ready to go to school. My mother asked my father if she should go to work that day being that a group, declared by the FBI as a communist organization, wanted to kill a NYC policewoman.

I stood frozen in disbelief and fear. I prayed that my father would tell her to stay home. But he said, matter-of-factly, "Go to work. Do your job." He was a sergeant after all. She was a policewoman. I was a child *living blue*. I went to school that day and told my teacher, "My mother may be killed today," and was told not to worry. As if those simple words could help at all. Anxiety gripped me throughout the day and was alleviated only after my mother was safely home at the end of the day. We never talked about the group wanting to kill a policewoman ever again.

> **LAW ENFORCEMENT CONSIDERATION**
> **& PERSONAL INSIGHT**
>
> What is it like for you working in an anti-cop climate?

Line of Duty Death

The emphasis of this chapter is to provide agencies with points to consider when developing policies for Death Notification after a LODD and to direct the agency in providing support to those who are bereaved. A LODD is defined as officers dying due to felonious or accidental incidents or suicide.

> **CASE NOTES**
>
> Dianne Bernhard, C.O.P.S. Executive Director, Retired Deputy Chief of Columbia (MO) Police Department, notes, "When a line-of-duty death occurs, a lot of agencies become very protective of the surviving family members of their fallen brother or sister. The surviving co-workers, whether they were at the scene or not, need support as well. I know firsthand how real survivor's guilt is. What could have been done differently? What if I had been there? The 'what ifs' can consume a person in the aftermath of any critical incident.
>
> "One thing I know for sure is how difficult it is to care for others when you aren't caring for yourself, especially when it comes to grief. As a surviving co-worker myself, it can be easy to push down the feelings or turn

to unhealthy coping mechanisms. As the Executive Director of C.O.P.S., I'm proud to see the law enforcement community turning a page on that mindset and putting wellness at the forefront. Starting that conversation is the first step. The C.O.P.S. organization is here to listen and give guidance for all the steps that will follow" *(D. Bernhard, personal communication, December 5, 2022).*

To be a LODD, the death (e.g., heart attack, COVID-19, stroke, vascular rupture, cancer) is a result of service; one can see a cause-and-effect relationship that connects duty to injury (Supporting Heroes, 2022). Officers may have been ambushed, killed during an arrest, a domestic disturbance, while on foot pursuit, or at a traffic stop. The names of the federal, state, tribal, and local LEOs who have died in the line of duty are engraved on the walls of the National Law Enforcement Officers Memorial and dedicated during a candlelight vigil held on the National Mall in Washington, D.C. (NLEOMF, 2023).

Felonious Death

An officer is feloniously killed by an offender if they are mortally wounded and die while doing their job. Deaths can be related to ambushes, investigative/enforcement activity, unprovoked attacks, and response to disorderly/ disturbance calls. Firearms are used in most felonious deaths. In 2023, LODDs were from COVID-19, duty-related illness, 9/11 related illness, aircraft accident, assault, automobile crash, COVID-19, drowning, duty-related fall, fire, gunfire, heart attack, motorcycle crash, and vehicular assault (Officer Down Memorial Page, 2023).

Those with more experience had a higher risk of being feloniously killed than those with less than one year of experience, and officers were much more likely to be killed in incidents where they didn't fire their weapon (Mercado, 2020). Two common patterns in felonious LODD are highest frequency, ages 30–39, and experience, 0–4 years (Tucker-Gail et al., 2022).

Accidental Death

When an officer dies due to an accident while doing their job, the death is an "accidentally killed" LODD. Also, they can die in the line of duty from natural causes, COVID-19, heart attacks, and conditions related to 9/11.

Heart Attack

Police officers have significantly higher levels of cardiovascular disease such as angina, pectoris acute myocardial infarction, and cerebrovascular disease, than those employed in other occupations (Han et al., 2017; Keeler et al., 2021). Deaths due to a heart attack are prevalent due to strong association between stressors of police work that impact physical and psychological health (Reingle Gonzelez et al., 2019; Violanti et al., 2020).

Operational demands such as exposure to death, violence, trauma, shift work, poor quality of sleep, and difficult associations with the public as well as organizational demands such as bureaucratic frustrations, poor leadership and management, heavy workloads, and lack of social support (Acquadro Maran et al., 2018; Purba & Demou, 2019) impact their cardiovascular health (Gendron et al., 2018; Violanti et al., 2017). Furthermore, their cardiovascular risks can be reduced through wellness programs that focus on cardiovascular education and intervention (Violanti et al., 2020; MacMillan et al., 2017; Saffari et al., 2020).

Fallen K9s

As a child, I had a German shepherd police dog, the breed that is the number one most popular police working dog. When Patches died, it was the only time in my life I saw my father cry. Today, I have a hard time viewing social media posts of police canines who need to be put down at the end of their life and watch them walk through a line of officers standing outside the vet's office or when a K9 is killed in the line of duty. K9s have died in the line of duty from gunfire, heatstroke, car crashes, stabbings, animal- or fire-related injury, struck by a vehicle and vehicular assault (Officer Down Memorial Page, 2022).

Although there are few studies on police dogs who die a LODD, Barberi and colleagues (2019) looked at a database of 96 police dogs that died in the line of duty in the U.S. between 2011 and 2015. They found that more police dog deaths were reported in 2014 and 2015, during summer months, with half clustering in the Southern region of the U.S. Police dogs who died were mostly younger and recently employed by the policing agency. The most frequent cause of death was heat exhaustion, followed by gunfire and automobiles.

Death Notification

A death notification is an official communication of the death of a loved one conducted mostly by a doctor, nurse, or a LEO (De Leo et al., 2020). When an officer dies, dispatch is notified, first aid or emergency medical services respond, and the deceased is identified. The officer or supervisor ensures that the scene is secured, witnesses are identified, and officers directly involved are relieved due to the traumatic situation. The death notification team usually includes a police chief, the primary notifier, police chaplain, and sometimes a crisis team member. Delivering a death notification is a stressful assignment with absence of training and inadequate aftercare (Hofmann et al., 2022).

As a hospice bereavement coordinator, I ran a support group for family members. At times, they would describe their experience of getting a call from a hospice nurse telling them that their loved one had died. I also facilitated a suicide loss support group. Frequently, members would discuss being notified by officers. In my homicide group, members would share what it was like for an Emergency Department physician to deliver the bad news.

Whether death was expected or not, if a death notifier is a nervous wreck or lacked empathy, their disposition could impact grief. No matter the type of death, group members complained about a notifier appearing nervous or as though they just wanted to get it over with and leave. During the group, bereaved members shared how the words and demeanor of the notifiers influenced their grief and have become a part of their loss narrative. Being that notification symbolizes a defining moment between the life that was and the life that will be without a loved one, notifiers must have adequate preparation to positively influence the quality of the communication and the outcomes it creates (De Leo et al., 2020). Death notification must be a compassionate response.

Being Prepared

When delivering bad news, the notifier takes into consideration health characteristics of the person being told of the death. For example, advanced age, ill health, or psychological vulnerability can complicate the notification process (De Leo et al., 2022). In 2001, I developed a death notification acronym, PREPARED, which identified eight characteristics to alleviate the stress associated with delivering bad news. These strategies may be completed in any order or at the same time.

- **PERSONAL:** express emotion in a relaxed way, be aware of your body language and have direct eye contact.
- **RESPONSIBILITY:** have control over the situation and know what morally needs to be done.
- **EDUCATE:** inform them of the facts, clarify the details of what happened, and instruct them on what to do next.
- **PRACTICAL:** be flexible while being clear, straightforward, and actively engaged depending upon the situation.
- **ALLIANCE:** show that the spiritual relationship continues after death and convey that the connection between the bereaved family and the police force remains.
- **REALISTIC:** accept what happened while focusing on the certainty that the officer is "really dead".
- **EMPATHETIC:** show genuine concern and be sensitive to the family member's feelings as you share the experience of what they are going through.
- **DIRECT:** be straightforward in answering all questions about what happened, and what will immediately occur in the aftermath.

After a LODD, the department is in mourning with customary expressions of grief (e.g., draped badges). LEOs may not have a sense of safety. They need to feel connected to one another and maintain a sense of hope. Grief is a process that could ebb and flow throughout their lifetime. Supervisors can consider having one-on-one check-ins and mention how they too are struggling with grief and how they are managing their reactions.

Emergency Notification Packet–Important Papers

As a bereavement specialist with hospice, I met with patients and their families to review personal records and discuss end-of-life practices. We talked about their beliefs and values regarding terminal illness and dying, advance directives, quality-of-life concerns, their living will, and durable power of attorney for health care. My experience has proved that although it is difficult to talk about death, we must prepare important papers, so we don't burden our family with not knowing what to do, who to call, or with not knowing our wishes.

Don't head out before reading what is usually called the "emergency notification packet." Information in the packet is completed by an officer when they are hired. Emergency notification forms ensure that the Chief and liaisons know what the deceased officer wants done if they should die. Some departments update the packet during an annual employee evaluation, but others update it at the semi-annual firearms qualification. The Administration often keeps the documents in the packet up to date, realizing that relationships change such as an ex-spouse's address and telephone number and the ages of children.

The documents include the officer's religion, marital status, name and addresses of spouse and children, type of funeral services preferred, names and telephone numbers of a religious contact, a lawyer and financial advisor, social security, LODD benefit information, and location of the will, safety deposit box and key. The documents include insurance benefits such as life insurance, Veterans' insurance, funeral insurance, and mortgage insurance. Also included are real estate property deeds, mortgage documents, loan notes, vehicle titles and registrations, and membership certificates.

Financial accounts and beneficiaries include checking and savings, investment/brokerage accounts, IRAs, stocks, bonds, annuities, credit and debit card accounts and passwords. The packet includes who is spoken to, whether next of kin has a mental or physical problem, and preferences for relaying the bad news. Although it is customary that the Chief provides the notification, the officer may want their partner to deliver the bad news. However, they may not be trained to say the right words or are emotionally distraught.

LEOs should continually update their emergency notification packet and consider all that needs to be done after their death. Loved ones need to contact representatives from social security, life insurance, banking, and credit agencies. They need to update voter registration, cancel the driver's license, close credit cards and email accounts, delete social media accounts, and complete and contact the three credit bureaus to notify them of the death. They must retitle any assets and need access to bank accounts. Officers need to think about that individual who may have to take care of their business during this overwhelming and emotional time.

Death Notifiers

Death notifiers are compassionate and empathetic individuals who gather the information needed from the notification packet. They identify legal next of kin and whether they have a medical problem, are suffering from a mental health challenge, or have a disability. If that is the case, they may decide to bring a third person who is a medical/mental health professional, or an interpreter at the time of notification. Two people in authority, the police chief or their designee, and police chaplain, should do the death notification of the legal next of kin.

Having more than two people might be overpowering at a time of initial grief. However, a third person from the crisis team such as a social worker or officer's partner can be present for additional assistance (e.g., to arrange babysitting services). They can remain in the vehicle and step out if needed. There can be two vehicles. The second vehicle is available in case a family member needs to be transported to the hospital or if they need a ride to view the body.

Place of Notification

The death notification can take place at the family residence or place of work. If the notification is at the home, ask if you can come inside and sit down. Ask if anyone else is in the residence. When a chief and chaplain arrive, the family member already has a suspicion that something terrible has happened. They may have received a call from a friend who told them what they have seen on social media. As you confirm what they have heard, shed light on the details of what happened. Tell them that you have bad news.

Ask about any children and their ages living at the residence and if they want their children to be present. Do not use a child as an interpreter if there is a language barrier. If the notification team goes to a person's work, do not tell their boss what happened. Only state that you need to speak to the employee. Ask for a private room, if available. If the bereaved does not live in the area, the department liaison should request assistance from law enforcement agencies in appropriate jurisdictions for in-person notification. Be available by phone during the notification in case the officer providing the assistance to the survivor has any questions.

Delivering Bad News

After introducing yourself and the person with you, you can keep the statement simple or more elaborate. Consider:

- "We have some sad news."
- "We have to deliver bad news."
- "We have to share some bad news."
- "We are so sorry to have to deliver some bad news."
- "We are sorry that we have some very bad news to give you."

Choose a brief or longer statement. Avoid abstract euphemisms such as "We have lost him." Make sure you mention the deceased officer's name and that they died. You can say, "…is dead" or "has died." Breathe and make room for silence. Then tell them briefly what happened that caused the LODD. Keep it short. Be prepared for a response ranging from complete silence, lunging at you, screaming, breaking something, or running to another room. Speak slowly. As they ask questions, assure them that it was their loved one who died and how you know that to be the fact. Share details of what happened, the location of their loved one, the process for viewing, and autopsy information.

> **LAW ENFORCEMENT CONSIDERATION & PERSONAL INSIGHT**
>
> Notice what happens in your body when you focus on this difficult topic. What healthy strategies could help you to manage your thoughts and feelings?

Before You Leave

If the body is at the hospital, tell them that you will let the hospital supervisor, usually someone from the department, know that the notification has been made, and that the family is on their way to view their loved one. Mention the deceased person's name. Use words "dead" or "died" and not "passed away." Tell them how sorry you are for their loss. Never leave a bereaved family member alone. Wait until someone comes to be with them. Write down information that they need. You have become a part of the first phase of the notification. Keep in mind that the next phase includes referral to supportive networks or bereavement services that assist them in the immediate aftermath, but also in the long term (De Leo 2022a).

After You Leave

After a death notifier leaves, what was said could remain a part of the bereaved person's loss narrative. Everyone in the room was on an emotional rollercoaster. Although notifiers can get off the ride and take time to debrief, the bereaved person is left in the aftermath. As the jolted family members try to hold back their screams, they stay on the ride with sweaty palms and heart beating, barely holding on. Reflect on that emotional rollercoaster ride. Although you are off the ride, your mind might bring you right back to it at any point in time. Check in with the other death notifiers with you. Review what went well and what you could have done differently. Focus on immediate thoughts and emotions, and check in with your body.

> **LAW ENFORCEMENT CONSIDERATION & PERSONAL INSIGHT**
>
> If you must deliver bad news, you will probably need to connect with a chosen safe person. Who would that be?

Funeral Planning and the Memorial Service

As noted earlier, the emergency notification packet includes everything the family and the department needs to know when planning a funeral such as:

- Will there be a last call?

- Will there be a mourning shroud on badges and department buildings?
- Will the flag fly at half-staff?
- Will the officer have a final call honor guard?
- What mortuary or crematorium is being used?
- Where is the cemetery?
- Who are the officiants or eulogists?
- What are the names of the pall bearers ?
- Is there a preferred charity for contributions?
- What are the preferred music selections for the service?
- What photos will be shown near the casket?
- Will the casket be draped in a flag?
- Who will be presented with the flag?
- Will there be a 21-gun salute or playing of "Taps"?
- Will there be a fly over?
- Where should personal letters of condolence be sent?

Take into consideration the viewing, scheduling services, media involvement, number of attendees, seating and letting the community know what happened.

Release of Officers Name

Although many departments use their official Facebook page to include telephone numbers, links to their website and photos of community activities, they can use their page to announce a LODD. Agency policy outlines when the LEO's name is released to the media. A 100 to 150-word announcement can be pinned to the top of the post along with a photo of the deceased and a black band around the department logo (Friese, 2020).

Honoring Those Who Died

In 1962, President Kennedy declared that Peace Officers Memorial Day be observed on May 15th. Over 50 years later, communities continue to celebrate National Police Week, which always falls in observance of May 15 to honor those who died a LODD. Although there are annual candlelight vigils, departments can fly a flag at half-staff, create a memorial or donate to support families of fallen LEOs.

Palette of Grief® Reactions after a LODD

A LODD affects peers, the department, family and friends, and the wider police community. Those affected could experience grief based on their relationship and psychological proximity. The Palette of Grief® becomes a metaphor for a blending of reactions after a LODD (Rubel, 2019). The Palette of Grief includes emotional, physical, behavioral, cognitive, and religious/spiritual reactions.

Emotional reactions can include shock, anger, helplessness, or sadness. Cognitive reactions can include trouble concentrating, disorientation, and having unwanted pictures of the death in their head. Behaviorally, they could become quiet or self-destructive. Physically, they can experience nausea or muscle tension, be easily startled, feel exhausted or faint. Spiritual grief reactions can range from finding comfort through prayer to being angry at God.

Supporting Family Members and Co-Workers

Liaisons

Police departments have procedures in place for a LODD that include protocol, expectations, and duties of those involved, including but not limited to, the Chief and department liaisons. A liaison includes a family support liaison, usually a lieutenant from peer support services. They are the facilitator between the family and the department regarding funeral arrangements and offer direction on paperwork and inform the family of investigative updates and court proceedings.

- **A FUNERAL LIAISON** can focus on ceremonies and memorials.
- **A BENEFITS LIAISON** can focus on paperwork, including LODD benefits, social security, veterans' benefits, and life insurance.
- **A HOSPITAL LIAISON** works with hospital personnel to ensure a private waiting room for survivors, that an area is set up for media, and that a uniformed officer guards the body. They also prepare survivors as to what to expect when they view their loved one's body.

Police Mental Health Professionals

In 1994, a bereaved father attended my suicide loss survivor support group. As the facilitator, I asked members to introduce themselves and share their relationship to the person who had died. A husband and wife sat next to each other. She said that her daughter had recently died. Her husband, appearing stiff, formally said, "I am here to support my wife."

After the meeting, he met me in the hall. He told me that he was a police officer and was sorry to learn of my dad's suicide. He and his wife attended several meetings. He never said a word, other than, "I am here to support my wife." After the group, he would meet me in the hall. Although he felt comfortable speaking to me, I also advised him to speak with a compassionate peer or police chaplain.

> **LAW ENFORCEMENT CONSIDERATION & PERSONAL INSIGHT**
>
> If you would consider attending a peer-led bereavement support group, what must be taken into consideration before you show up?

THE NEXT STEP

In this chapter we identified characteristics of a death notification and ways to support bereaved individuals. When death is sudden it can be hard to manage the whirlwind of emotions. This is especially true after a suicide. In Chapter 10, the focus is on LEO suicide.

REFERENCES

Acquadro Maran, D., Zedda, M., & Varetto, A. (2018). Physical practice and wellness courses reduce distress and improve wellbeing in police officers. *International Journal of Environmental Research and Public Health*, 15(4), 578. http://dx.doi.org/10.3390/ijerph15040578

Barberi, D., Gibbs, J.C., & Schally, J.L. (2019). K9s killed in the line of duty. *Contemporary Justice Review*, 22(1), 86-100. https//:doi:10.1080/10282580.2019.1576128

De Leo, D., Zammarrelli, J., Giannotti, A.V., Donna, S., Bertini, S., ...Anile, C. (2020). Notification of unexpected, violent and traumatic death. A systematic review. *Frontiers in Psychology*, 11, 2229, 1-16. https://tinyurl.com/mtmnjd7u

De Leo, D., Congregalli, B., Guarino, A., Zammarrelli, J., Valle, A., ...Cipolletta, S. (2022). Communicating unexpected and violent death: The experiences of police officers and health care professionals. *International Journal of Environmental Research and Public Health*, 19(17), 1-14. https://doi.org/10.3390/ijerph191711030

De Leo, D., Guarino, A., Congregalli, B., Zammarrelli, J., Valle, A., Paoloni, S., & Cipolletta, S. (2022a). Receiving notification of unexpected and violent death. *International Journal of Environmental Research and Public Health*, 19(17), 1-15. https://tinyurl.com/yxrzs2sd

Department of Justice (2022). Federal Bureau of Investigation. *FBI's law enforcement officers killed and assaulted data collection.*

Friese, G. (2020). Using Facebook to announce an LODD. *Police1.* https://tinyurl.com/2tr9yypa

Gendron, P., Lajoie, C., Laurencelle, L., & Trudeau, F. (2019). Cardiovascular health profile among Québec male and female police officers. *Archives of Environmental & Occupational Health*, 74(6), 331-340. https://doi:10.1080/19338244.2018.1472063

Han, M., Park, S., Park, J.H., Hwang, S., & Kim, I. (2017). Do police officers and firefighters have a higher risk of disease than other public officers? *BMJ Open* https://tinyurl.com/4msjf2de

Hofmann, L., Glaesmer, H., Przyrembel, M., & Wagner, B. (2022). The delivery of death notifications, associated stress and use of aftercare in police officers: a mixed-method approach. *Police Practice and Research*, 23(5), 584-599.

Holy Bible (2015). New Living Translation. John 15:13. Tyndale House Publishers.

Keeler, J.M., Fleenor, B.S., Clasey, J.L., Stromberg, A., & Abel, M.G. (2021). Predictors of arterial stiffness in law enforcement officers. *International Journal of Environmental Research and Public Health*, 18, 10190. https://doi.org/10.3390/ijerph181910190

MacMillan, F., Karamacoska, D., El Masri, A., McBride, K.A., Steiner, G.Z. Cook, A., ...George, E.S. (2017). A systematic review of health promotion intervention studies in the police force: study characteristics, intervention design and impacts on health. *Occupational and Environmental Medicine*, 74, 913-923.

Mercado, G. (2020). *Law Enforcement Officers as Victims of Felonious Killings and Assaults*. Doctoral dissertation. Nova Southeastern University. NSUWorks, Abraham S. Fischler College of Education. https://nsuworks.nova.edu/fse_etd/262.

National Law Enforcement Officers Memorial (2023). *Fallen law enforcement officers from across the country to be honored during 35th annual candlelight vigil on May 13 in Washington, D.C.*, Newsroom. https://nleomf.org/fallen-le-officers-honored-during-35-candlelight-vigil-may-13/

Officer Down Memorial Page. *Honoring officers killed in 2023.* https://www.odmp.org/search/year?year=2023

Officer Down Memorial Page (2023). https://www.odmp.org/

Purba, A., & Demou, E. (2019). The relationship between organisational stressors and mental wellbeing within police officers: a systematic review. *BMC Public Health* 19, 1286. https://doi.org/10.1186/s12889-019-7609-0

Reingle Gonzalez, J.M., Jetelina, K.K., Bishopp, S.A., Livingston, M.D., Perez, R.A., & Gabriel, K.P. (2019). The feasibility of using real-time, objective measurements of physiological stress among law enforcement officers in Dallas, Texas. *Policing: An International Journal*, 42(4), 701-710. https://doi.org/10.1108/PIJPSM-12-2018-0184

Rubel, B. (2019). *Loss, grief, and bereavement: Helping individuals cope.* (4th ed.). SC Publishing, Western Schools.

Saffari, M., Sanaeinasab, H., Jafarzadeh, H., Sepandi, M., O'Garo, K.N., ...Pakpour, A.H. (2020). Educational intervention based on the health belief model to modify risk factors of cardiovascular disease in police officers in Iran. *Journal of Preventative Medicine and Public Health*, 53(4), 275-284. https//:doi:10.3961/jpmph.20.095

Supporting Heroes (2022). Line *of Duty Death Criteria.* https://www.supportingheroes.org/about/lodd_criteria/

Tucker-Gail, K., Eckerley, A., Selman, D. L., Lilley, D., & Stewart, M. C. (2022). Felonious line-of-duty officer deaths (1995–2015): The impact of tenure and age revisited. *International Journal of Police Science & Management*, 24(1), 3-14. https://tinyurl.com/2depe6kd

Violanti, J.M., Fekedulegn, D., Shi, M., & Andrew, M.E. (2020). Hidden danger: A 22-years analysis of law enforcement deaths associated with duty-related illnesses (1997–2018). *Policing: An International Journal*, ISSN: 1363-951X

Yalom, I.D. (2009). *Staring at the Sun: Overcoming the Terror of Death.* Jossey-Bass.

10 | LAW ENFORCEMENT OFFICER SUICIDE

National Suicide Prevention Lifeline 988

DEFINITIONS

SUICIDE - when self-directed injurious behavior with an intent to die causes a death as a result of the behavior.

PREVENTION - goal is to stop people from becoming suicidal.

INTERVENTION - goal is to reduce the likelihood of suicide by individuals deemed suicidal.

POSTVENTION - goal is to encourage healing by mitigating negative effects of suicide exposure.

OBJECTIVES

After reading and considering the content of this chapter, the reader should be able to:

- Review how thwarted belongingness, perceived burdensomeness, and hopelessness, are warning signs of suicide.
- Discuss how an officer's beliefs and attitudes are barriers to their getting help for suicidal thoughts.

In My Experience & Lessons Learned

JASON PALAMARA

When I learn of a fellow LEO who has died by suicide I feel an immense sense of grief. Each of us has walked a similar path only a LEO could understand. Each of us has endured struggles, pains, frustrations, and self-doubts only a LEO could understand.

My own journey could have just as easily led me to the same tragic outcome—deciding that I didn't want to see another tomorrow—as my LEO brother or sister who decided to take their own life. I share my experiences with you in the hope that if you ever find yourself in such a dark place, you pause long enough to decide that one more tomorrow is worth exploring. And trust that there are fellow LEOs out there who are ready to serve and protect you.

A friend and fellow officer was not in a good place. After a few troubling conversations and text exchanges, I told him that he needed more guidance to manage the trauma of the job than I was able to provide. I expressed my worry and asked him if he would be okay talking with a friend of mine, a department chaplain. "Absolutely not. My job will be over," was his reply. I reached out to the monsignor. I would rather him hate me and still be alive, than the unthinkable alternative. For a long time, he refused to speak to me. A few years later, I received a call from him. "Can I come over?" I looked forward to seeing him.

After greeting him at my home, he told me that I was one of the few friends he had shut out, and who had accepted him back once he was ready—without hesitation. We spent the day catching up, reflecting on how we both were in a better place. It was tough for me at the time not knowing what to do for someone that was my brother who I feared would kill himself. I shared this with him, and he acknowledged that it must have been difficult and thanked me for inviting him back into my life.

Happiness had now replaced feelings of confusion and hurt. He had been in pain and feared that seeking help would negatively affect his job. Often these situations turn out much worse. I am saddened when a member of law enforcement or a first responder dies by suicide. There is a brotherhood and sisterhood, a tribe, which is shared within these professions.

You do not have to know the individual personally to experience the pain of a loss by suicide. My lead NYPD academy instructor had died by suicide many years after I graduated. She was a confident, strong woman who displayed no outward signs of a personal struggle. Her death was a shock. Every recruit in my company had a good relationship with her while under her command. Learning about a fellow LEO who has taken their life always hits hard, but having a personal connection with the individual adds a unique layer to the sense of loss.

When I learn about a first responder taking their life I always want to know "why." Though the reasons are never the same, as a former first responder I know I have experienced some of the same darkness that is common with the profession. As a Cold Case Homicide detective in my last years with the department, I investigated murders that hadn't been worked on by anyone in years.

When approaching an investigation, it is ill advised to rely solely on what an investigator had done previously without conducting your own investigation. You wouldn't use the same approach for each case or view one the same as the next. Just like investigating a cold case, you identify the pieces of the puzzle all over again, and begin putting it together in your own way.

An officer's suicide will render us all detectives, asking the same questions we do when investigating a Cold Case murder—and the most painful question is not "why" but "what." What could we have done to prevent this? And to live the life of a first responder, we are uniquely positioned to understand the events that lead to this tragic loss of life. A different approach is needed than simply providing self-service resources.

Let's look at an arguably oversimplified path of a LEO, and then I'll propose a simple change we can all make today that may indeed save lives.

Most LEOs enter the profession at eighteen years of age, before the integral stages of their ability to create a healthy self-image are fully developed. Too often, an officer's sense of self quickly becomes exclusively "law enforcement." When an individual's self-image is solely defined by one thing, and that definition is challenged—by an officer's superiors, the community, the country, our family, even retirement—it places the officer in a potentially dangerous state. Without the emotional fortitude to seek self-worth from a variety of sources, an individual can feel powerless to improve a situation where their identity is questioned. The decision to end one's life—and one's singular source of identity as a law enforcement officer—may become the one thing the officer feels they have any control over when their pain becomes too great.

I propose a radical alternative to this oversimplified path. And it's a radically simple one—let's help the officer develop a healthy sense of self that is broader than merely "law enforcement officer," and teach them the skills necessary to navigate the challenges to self every human being, whether law enforcement or not, will experience in their lives. We already know, all too well, the pains an officer will experience throughout their career. And we already know the medicine too many of our brothers and sisters look to for managing those pains. We already know the tragic outcomes that inevitably follow managing the pain with alcohol, with isolation, with abuse of self and loved ones. We have all of the pieces of the puzzle—all of the evidence—we need to work towards ending LEO suicide. So, let's solve it.

We are fools to think that when an officer feels their only sense of control of their pains is suicide, when their entire sense of identity is in a state of self-doubt, that at that critical moment we should expect an officer to be capable and willing to ask for help. We have collectively failed them by this time, and had been failing them for a long while leading up to this officer's critical moment. We expect them to ask for help when they believe they need it, instead of providing the skills they need in order to successfully navigate a career in law enforcement. Our LEOs deserve better.

I know that I would have benefited from a personal officer support plan that began on my first day in the academy. In addition to the training I received in self-defense, crisis management, and on how to de-escalate situations within the community I was assigned to police, and in forensic investigative techniques—all of which allowed me to be successful at the "law enforcement" part of my self-image—I would have benefited from emotional and mental health training, on learning how to recognize signs of personal distress and personal harm risk factors. This is the foundation of stress inoculation training. And I would have benefited from seeing the department prioritize a non-judgmental and non-punitive acceptance of LEOs asking for help. I imagine an academy in which I was assigned a personal peer or counselor who would have helped me co-manage my law enforcement journey through retirement. And through that, I imagine the suicide rate among LEOs would likely not be as high.

In many departments and organizations across the first responder community, there are signs that our first responders are getting better. I witnessed some of this healthier approach while in the New York City Police Department and their peer-support program. I can only hope we continue to advocate for this across the country, and once and for all see our LEOs decide to explore what feeling better looks like.

The decision to end one's life becomes the one thing an officer feels they have control over. It is a sense of control that has been lost in a world unfamiliar to what they once knew. We are mistaken to think that at this critical point we should expect an officer to be willing to ask for help. When feeling that the only option is to simply disappear, this "*ask*" may be way too late.

I want to propose that collectively the conversation shift from asking us to seek help when we need it, to a more adaptive approach in attempting to turn the tide of what is an increasing problem in police departments. This has already begun in many departments and organizations across the first responder community. I was witness to this approach while in the NYC Police Department.

Here is what I propose. Like a math equation, there may be different formulas that give you the same answer. The formula allows a person to develop skills before they need them that will help them navigate to a cooler calm when they are in emotional distress. This is the foundation of stress inoculation. While they may share the same inputs (job stress, violence, risk to life), a first responder's processing of those inputs is unique.

They deserve and would benefit from a plan that begins in the academy with their emotional and mental health prioritized and co-managed by a personal peer or counselor assigned to them on their journey through to retirement. Throughout their career, they should receive education on signs, risk factors, and where to get help in and outside of the department. It is inefficient to tell officers to ask for help when they need it and believe that our work is done. If that worked, there likely would not be as many suicides by LEOs as there are each year.

When an officer dies by suicide, what follows by way of a long-standing tradition to honor and celebrate them is different: no department wide notification to send to officers to stand in dress uniform at attention at the funeral, no media coverage, or shared public morning of the loss of a hero. Where we would not want to glorify the act chosen, for an officer who dies by suicide, as a society, we owe something more. It is said that we should not remember how one dies, rather how they lived. I suggest this is a good place to start.

My Story & Evidence-Based Practices

BARBARA RUBEL

"Out of suffering have emerged the strongest souls; the most massive characters are seared with scars."

—Kahlil Gibran

My father died by suicide after serving 21 years on the police force. When I received the news, I was in the hospital awaiting the birth of my triplets. It was a strange confluence of one of the best and worst times of my life. I wanted to bury him with his sergeant stripes. But it was too late to find the patch. Ordered by my doctors to be on complete bedrest, I couldn't go to the funeral and say a proper goodbye.

For over 30 years, I have been involved in postvention. In 1994, I created and facilitated a monthly suicide-loss support group, *(SOLAS) Sharing Our Loss After Suicide.* I was the Administrator for the American Foundation for Suicide Prevention, NJ Affiliate. I worked at the Suicide Prevention, Behavioral Health Care Department at the University of Medicine and Dentistry of NJ, (UMDNJ), and was an Open to Hope forum moderator for suicide loss survivors. I wrote *But I Didn't Say Goodbye: Helping families after suicide,* (3rd ed.). I was a contributing writer for several resources that focused on suicide, and served on committees for the American Association of Suicidology. I was on the National Advisory Group, WV Council for the Prevention of Suicide. I was a virtual grief specialist, offering support for suicide loss survivors around the world. All of this was my way of making meaning of my father's suicide and helping others who have been through the same thing.

Suicide is a Public Health Problem

Suicide is a public health problem that must be addressed. Law enforcement training for suicide prevention must be updated by department leaders using a public health strategy. This calls for upgrading both the content and delivery. If they concentrate specifically on the daily stressors and risk factors that LEOs face, they can stop dangerous behaviors. Suicide is when self-directed injurious behavior with an intent to die causes a death because of the behavior (National Institute of Mental Health, n.d)

Whereas suicidal ideation is where a person thinks about death, whether they have a plan or intent, a suicide attempt means self-harming behaviors associated with some intention to die (Turecki & Brent, 2016).

In 2021, 48,183 people died by suicide, which means 1 death every 11 minutes (CDC, 2023). In 2022, the provisional data indicates approximately 49,449 deaths (CDC, 2023a). Suicide is highest in middle-aged (45-64) white men. On average, there are 130 suicides per day and firearms, the first-ranked method, account for almost half of all suicide deaths (AFSP, n.d.). The second-ranked method is by suffocation/hanging and the third-ranked method is by poisoning (Violence Policy Center, 2018).

Suicide rates among officers are higher than the U.S. general working population (Violanti, 2022). Rates may be high due to increased alcohol use, withdrawing from those who could provide support, or acting reckless. Military veterans and first responders are the most affected groups with the rise of suicide (CDC, 2021). More officers die by suicide than in other LODDs (Heyman et al., 2018).

Inconsistent Data Collection

Due to inconsistent data collection practices, the exact number of LEO suicides is unknown (Dixon, 2021). Badge of Life (n.d.) posted a statement on their website about the unclear data surrounding suicides, the assumptions as to why officers and federal agents die by suicide, and what is needed is research using accepted methods to identify and scientifically analyze the variables in each situation to gain more insight.

CASE NOTES

John Kelly, Law Enforcement Life Coach, Retired Sergeant, 30 Year Veteran of Broward County Sheriff's Office, notes, "I just know that getting ahead of this problem means putting the work in on the front end, identifying the areas in our lives that place us at risk and then doing something proactively to prevent the slide from turning into an avalanche" *(J. Kelly, personal communication, January 12, 2023).*

Suicide and Adverse Childhood Experiences (ACEs)

An expanding body of research suggests that childhood trauma and even one adverse childhood experience increases suicide ideation and attempts (Dube et al., 2001; Thompson et al., 2019). A study of Veterans who recently contemplated suicide found that Adverse Childhood Experiences (ACEs) are more predictive of suicide ideation than serving in a combat zone or having a traumatic brain injury (Blosnich et al., 2017).

As noted in chapter 2, ACEs are abuse, neglect, or household dysfunction before the age of 18. We are impacted by our early experiences. We can focus on ACEs to recognize the effects of childhood experiences that have never been addressed. We can get education about how childhood trauma impacts current relationships and the job, and learn healthy coping skills and improve adaptive functioning.

ACEs can get in the way of how an officer tolerates and manages distress. This is especially true if they have not developed skills, such as emotional regulation or interpersonal support. Their personality traits may interfere with their getting treatment. They need to remember that it takes strength to get help to manage the stressors in their life.

> **LAW ENFORCEMENT CONSIDERATION & PERSONAL INSIGHT**
>
> Today, what is motivating you to get help for your childhood trauma or to remain in treatment?

Thwarted Belongingness and Perceived Burdensomeness

Thomas Joiner's interpersonal psychological theory of suicide suggests that thwarted belongingness and perceived burdensomeness can lead to suicide ideation (Calati et al., 2022). Thwarted belongingness applies to being lonely and socially isolated (Podlogar et al., 2017), where a person perceives a lack of meaningful connections with those around them (Pennings et al., 2017, p. 539).

Perceived burdensomeness is when a person feels useless or difficult as to be a burden on those around them (Podlogar et al., 2017, p. 337) and "does not contribute to the group and is a liability to the group's well-being and safety" (Pennings et al., 2017, p. 539). Perceived burdensomeness is a determinant of suicidality in Veterans (Bell et al., 2018). Perhaps my father, a WWII veteran and police sergeant, killed himself because of perceived burdensomeness and felt like a burden to his family, especially at the point in my life when I was about to give birth to triplets.

Hopelessness, and Cognitive Distortions

Hopelessness

Those with PTSD and depression have a greater rate of dying by suicide (Gradus et al., 2010). Although departments focus on PTSD, they also need to focus on trauma-related stress, insomnia, depression, and hopelessness. They need to realize that an officer's personal accomplishments are a protective factor, and they can increase self-confidence and self-efficacy regarding work-related issues by offering educational support to reduce stress and specialized psychological support to lessen feelings of hopelessness (Civilotti et al., 2022).

CASE NOTES

Patrick J. Fitzgibbons, Retired Law Enforcement, notes, "Keep going. No matter how dark it gets. I have been in dark places and there is light if you open your mind and let it in" *(P.J. Fitzgibbons, personal communication, January 12, 2023).*

Depression and burnout are significant predictors of hopelessness. Feelings of hopelessness can be caused by financial issues, health problems and negative incidents that have impacted one's self-esteem (Civilotti et al., 2022). Hopelessness closes the ability to think about the future and can feel like loss of hope and desperation. It is important to listen to what is not being said as much as what is being said, when we focus on an officer's experience of hopelessness.

> **LAW ENFORCEMENT CONSIDERATION & PERSONAL INSIGHT**
>
> On a scale from 1 to 5 (1 no need – 5 must need), does your department need a mandated training on strategies to mitigate depression?

Cognitive Distortions

Although there are triggers for suicidal thoughts, officers considering suicide may be dealing with cognitive distortions. These are erroneous, unreasonable, or excessive methods of thinking and believed to be a major factor in the emergence and persistence of many mental disorders (Morrison et al., 2022). They may cut themself off from others. They think that they are a bad person, a failure, they don't belong, or are a burden. Here are 10 questions to ask a LEO about the conclusions they draw about themselves due to thinking errors:

1. Are they blaming themself unnecessarily?
2. Are they assuming the worst of the situation?
3. Are they thinking about what happened in an extreme way?
4. Are they focusing more on their failures rather than their successes?
5. Do they apply negative labels when describing themself?
6. Although what happened was not their fault, are they personalizing it?
7. Do they minimize a positive thought and emphasize a negative thought?
8. Are they drawing conclusions without any evidence to back them up?
9. Are the conclusions that they draw from what happened not telling the whole story?
10. Are they too embarrassed to tell anyone what they are thinking?

Cognitive distortions are faulty patterns of thinking that can impact behavior in a negative way. At times, thoughts may not match up with reality.

Risk Factors for Non-Protective Service Occupations

Officers experience higher rates of trauma exposure and current PTSD than the general population (Soomro et al., 2019). Suicide risk factors for non-protective service occupations are interpersonal conflicts, traumatic incidents such as child abuse, a colleague's death, work schedules, agency functioning, management styles, administrative burden, work-related barriers to help-seeking, stigma associated with mental illness, and fear of negative consequences (Bureau of Justice Assistance (n.d.). Triggers for suicidal thoughts are non-ending depression, ACEs, substance misuse, relationship issues, physical health, financial problems, and criminal, or legal problems, such as being under investigation.

Risk Factors for Suicide in Police Officers

Suicide risk factors in police officers include being a middle-aged white male; being single, divorced, or widowed; suffering from depression, anxiety, and hopelessness; erratic shift schedules on family relationships; having alcohol use and abuse issues; being directly or indirectly exposed to violence; and being exposed to suicide and death (Zimmerman et al., 2023).

Besides pre-employment factors, the profession is subjected to a continual rise in the number of officers that die by suicide and future pre-employment efforts must consider a methodology that can identify and assess the associated suicidal risk factors in candidates (Johnson et al., 2022). Police suicide is complicated by unhealthy ways to cope, lack of adequate support and exposure to distressing events, available lethal means, and culturally acceptable alcohol use (Violanti, 2022). Also, LEOs may think other officers won't trust them if they don't drink around them.

CASE NOTES

Ernest Stevens, a retired police officer; main subject of Emmy Award winning HBO Documentary, *Ernie and Joe: Crisis Cops*; co-author, *Mental Health & De-escalation: A guide for law enforcement professionals*; and Deputy Division Director, Law Enforcement - The Council of State Governments Justice Center, notes, "The issue of police suicides has affected me tremendously. I have attended eight officer suicides from my own department. I have been a police officer for 28 years in a large city. It does not matter if your town is big or small, everyone has mental health. For some officers, their mental health is good, for others it may be a difficult time. Everyone is in a different place on their journey. Why don't law enforcement officers get help? Stigma.

"The labels that are given to individuals with a mental health diagnosis can be crippling. Stereotyping is the elephant in the room that no one wants to talk about. Let's shrink the size of the mental health crisis in America and put the focus on law enforcement. Is there a mental health crisis in law enforcement? The answer is a resounding yes. We, law enforcement officers, are killing ourselves at a greater rate than dying in the line of duty.

"Who would have thought that the most dangerous part of our job would be ourselves? Why is it so difficult for an officer to ask for help? Why is it so difficult to be vulnerable? Why do the numbers of law enforcement officers' suicides continue to rise each year? Police leadership has a huge responsibility to ensure the safety of their officers. Officers are equipped with body armor, de-escalation techniques, and weaponry, but what is leadership doing about an officer's mental well-being? Are resources available? How do officers navigate the barriers of stigma and being labeled as weak or inadequate?" *(E. Stevens, personal communication, March 15, 2023).*

Insomnia is Associated with Thoughts of Suicide

A study on police found that extended work schedules, shift work, occupational stress, and exposure to dangerous and traumatic events are negatively impacting sleep and recommend employing sleep hygiene promotion programs (Garbarino et al., 2019).

CASE NOTES

Nick Paproski, Director of External Affairs at Connecticut Association of Paramedics and EMTs, notes, "Whether the trauma we experience causes poor sleep or poor sleep from shift causes us to struggle to process trauma, is ultimately immaterial. No matter the cause, poor sleep worsens outcomes for all major mental and emotional disorders. Fixing sleep should therefore always be a primary objective for any wellness or mental health treatment plan" *(N. Paproski, personal communication, January 31, 2023).*

The National Wellness Survey for Public Safety Personnel Summary Report (2022) found that for sworn law enforcement, there was a strong association between lack of sleep/sleep issues and depression. If an officer tosses-and-turns all night, that will impact how they feel all day. Exposure to trauma at work increases the probability of experiencing traumatic stress, which impacts sleep quality and mental health.

CASE NOTES

Dr. Valerie Wolfe has spent the last 35 years helping people with a variety of health and mood problems. She has worked with veterans, active duty military, police officers, fireman, and elite athletes, to improve their sleep and performance. She has advised people around the world on how to improve their lives and reach their goals using best practice strategies.

Dr Wolfe notes, "Good sleep helps law enforcement officers perform at their best and facilitates the healing, growth and repair of the body after stress. When they sleep, their bodies transition through 3 main stages often referred to as light sleep, deep/delta wave sleep and REM (rapid eye movement) sleep. Light sleep takes up about 50% of our time spent sleeping and allows humans to rest without burning a lot of calories. Under normal/ non-threatening situations deep sleep (which facilitates healing) and REM sleep (which helps us with memory and creativity) take up approximately 25% each of our time spent asleep. Each cycle of light - deep - REM lasts about 90 minutes and we tend to have 4-6 of these cycles during the night.

"During deep/delta wave sleep our bodies heal. However, it can be difficult to wake quickly from a deep sleep and perform tasks without errors. It is very common for law enforcement officers to unconsciously limit their deep sleep during the night to be able to wake quickly and respond effectively to a crisis. Unfortunately, not getting adequate deep sleep stresses their body and increases the risk of developing heart disease, hypertension, glucose intolerance, unintended weight gain or weight loss and cognitive decline.

"During REM sleep or 'paradoxical sleep' a LEO's heart rate, respiration, and brain wave activity increases. Their body and brain waves during REM are very similar to someone who is awake and doing tasks. During REM, their brains integrate new information with old information. A benefit of REM is that they can create new solutions to problems by integrating new ideas in a non-standard way, thus creating the ah-ha or lightbulb moment. During REM, they process trauma and trim away neurological pathways no longer needed. To perform at their best, LEOs need to have adequate REM and delta wave sleep.

"Delta wave sleep occurs mostly during the beginning of the sleep session and REM elongates as the sleep session continues. Elongating light sleep beyond the 50% mark helps conserve resources, but too much light sleep tends to cause sleep inertia (feeling foggy headed, achy) and over time, can negatively effect their mood and body. Strategies to improve sleep include:

- Have a consistent wake up time, using fatigue to fall asleep quickly and sleep through the night.
- Avoid naps - but if you do take a nap or sleep in on the weekends, compensate by going to bed a little bit later than usual. It is better to be slightly sleep deprived, than to catch up and negatively affect your sleep architecture.
- Make sleep space dark, cool, quiet and safe; helping your body and brain to relax by avoiding bright light near bedtime.
- Avoiding stressful phone calls and violent TV shows.
- Do some gentle stretching or yoga before going to bed.

"For LEOs, it is helpful to have cues for their unconscious that indicate that they are safe to well versus needing to be on alert. For example, while sleeping at the station they could use different bed clothes, have different blankets, smells, sounds and routines to cue their brain when it should be safe to enter and enjoy deep sleep. If they experience a traumatic event, it is important to review the experience and problem solve/have a plan for next time, even if the plan is to simply let the incident go and move on with life.

"If they do not process stressful events, they tend to linger in working memory, which can inhibit both delta wave and REM sleep. LEOs can perform well for short periods of time when sleep deprived by triggering their sympathetic nervous system or stress response. However, if they don't have good sleep architecture, over time they will fatigue their bodies, become less adept at doing their jobs/learning/being flexible and hasten the onset of both medical and mood disorders" *(V. Wolfe, personal communication, August 27, 2023).*

Sleep deprivation (insomnia), can be caused by shiftwork, failing to get enough sleep, which causes problems learning new concepts, to be forgetful and a depressed mood (Agrawal et al., 2022). Common sleep disorders in officers (e.g., obstructive sleep apnea, insomnia, excessive sleepiness, falling asleep while driving at least once a month), lead to adverse health, performance, and safety outcomes (Rajaratnam et al., 2011). These disorders correlate with heart disease, high blood pressure, cognitive impairment, safety violations attributed to fatigue, administrative errors, car accidents, and uncontrolled anger toward a suspect (Rajaratnam et al., 2011). They need educational programs about sleep and be provided annual screenings for sleep disorders while shift schedules maximize off-duty time allowing for recovery (Kennedy-Hanson, 2020).

LAW ENFORCEMENT CONSIDERATION & PERSONAL INSIGHT

On a scale from 1 to 5 (1 very poor – 10 excellent), how would you rate your quality of sleep?

Predict And Manage Suicide Risk Factors

The FATAL 10

Many are quick to say that PTSD and the "job" are the leading issues that result in suicide. However, it is often the lack of attention and proper coping skills around exposure to stress and trauma that can result in issues with relationships and using substances (Johnson, 2022). The *Ruderman White Paper Update on Mental Health and Suicide of First Responders*, notes that police officers are more likely to die by suicide than in the line of duty (Nissim et al., 2022). The white paper analyzed why an increase in first responder mental health and suicide prevention programs has not been effective. The Blue Wall Institute data from 2017 to 2019 found that 15% of cases of suicides noted PTSD and anxiety and 32% of cases noted depression or being depressed and despondent in the months, weeks, and days preceding the suicide (Johnson, 2020).

The Fatal 10 of Law Enforcement Suicide, coined by Dr. Olivia Johnson, helps to predict and manage suicide risk factors and attempts among police officers, and identifies and addresses red flags and questionable behavior before negative outcomes occur (Johnson, O., 2022). Dr. Johnson's data from nearly 700 cases of law enforcement and correctional officer suicides (e.g., active, sworn, retired and former officers) found ten major themes as contributors to suicide, known as the FATAL 10:

1. Interpersonal Relationship Issues;
2. Substance Abuse & Addiction;
3. Cumulative Trauma & Stress;
4. Sleep Disturbance;
5. Mental Health Concerns;
6. Medical Issues;
7. Firearm Access;
8. Under Investigation;
9. Pending/Nearing Retirement; and
10. Other Major Life Events/Situations.

CASE NOTES

Dr. Olivia Johnson, a nationally recognized suicidology investigator who focuses on law enforcement suicide notes, "Suicide is not a new phenomenon to law enforcement or first responder populations, but many believe it is. Sadly, this same belief keeps us repeating the same things over and over without changing the outcome. If we want to stop or at least reduce deaths by suicide, we must stop with all the slogans, mantras, and feel-good phrases and do the real work. The real work includes making a comprehensive, strategic plan around conducting research and collecting data. We must then take what we learn and apply it to the populations in a timely, logical, and understood method" *(O. Johnson, personal communication, March 1, 2023).*

Barriers to Getting Help

The deteriorating relationship with the public is eating away at departments and impacting the mental health of its officers. Captain Tammy Norton (2022) maintains that departments can't ignore staff that come to work with alcohol on their breath or display depressive behavior. These departments need to focus on it being okay to seek help.

CASE NOTES

Deputy Chief Michelle Small, Deputy Chief/K9 Handler/Trainer/ Instructor at City of Bath, Maine, notes, "I have lost friends and colleagues to suicide. It is an area that command staff can never lose sight of. We must increase our knowledge and awareness and make sure that our officers and support staff know we are here for them always. I try and make it a point to build close relationships with my officers so that they never feel embarrassed or judged for what life brings their way. We are family. It is important for them to know I have struggled as all of us at one point in our lives have.

"We must provide services and resources for them but first and foremost we must connect with them. Being a servant leader means being there always for those we serve. We lead together through not just the easy bright moments but even more importantly through those difficult dark times. We must be cognizant of our own well-being so that we are the best version of ourselves to take care of our people not if, but when that time comes, because it will come and they should never feel alone" *(M. Small, personal communication, February 4, 2023).*

Barriers are fear of the consequences for seeking help, unclear confidentiality laws, policies or misinformation, limited resources, and a culture that avoids addressing mental wellness or emotional problems of any kind (IACP, 2014). According to the Harris Poll (2022) barriers that prevent those thinking about suicide from seeking help are feeling like nothing will help (70%), lack of hope (66%), not knowing how to get help (56%), and embarrassment (59%).

Shauna "Doc" Springer, Ph.D. notes, "Suicide is the threat in the blind spot of many of our first responders. A first responder can be in so much pain, and in such an altered state of mind, that he or she has no conscious awareness of how dangerously suicidal he or she has become. First responders are intensively trained to focus on external threats and socialized to act like invulnerable 'heroes.'

"As a result, it becomes difficult for many of them to perceive how deeply dangerous the internal voice of despair can become. Sometimes what masquerades as 'heroism' on the job is actually the manifestation of a death wish—a desire to flip the script of a death-by-cop suicide plan. For these reasons, first responders benefit from being connected to trusted experts who understand the threats in their blind spots" *(S. Springer, personal communication, April 21, 2023).*

Beliefs and Attitudes

A U.S. national survey of adults found certain beliefs and attitudes about mental health and suicide are changing: 94% believe that at least sometimes suicide can be prevented; 75% say that most people who die by suicide usually show some signs beforehand; 96% would take action to prevent suicide if someone close to them was thinking about suicide; 66% believe they don't have enough knowledge to tell if someone is thinking about suicide; and 80% are open to learning how they can do more to help someone in need (the Harris Poll, 2022). Several officers shared their beliefs with me:

- "Fear of repercussions in disclosing my problem, are you kidding me. I would be branded as weak. That is not happening."
- "We must learn how to help our brothers. I'm taking QPR with a couple of the guys. No one ever told me about this stuff."
- "I can see how uncomfortable my brothers are when I start to talk about my mental health. We go out for a drink, talk football, and so that pretty much fixes the problem."
- "I never trusted him because he never drank with us. I wouldn't share my issues with him if he wasn't drinking. He never told me that he

was going through something. I thought he was doing fine. Now he's dead."

- "I didn't know where to access mental health care and I surely wasn't going to ask one of the guys."
- "I don't think that we have mental health information in our work benefits package. But I never looked."
- "Ensure confidentiality. I don't want anyone to know I have issues. You can use this but don't use my name in your book."

Recommendations for Agencies

Police Executive Research Forum (2019) developed 10 recommendations for agencies that provide a path for preventing suicides: 1. data collection; 2. psychological autopsies; 3. routine mental health checks; 4. leadership from the top; 5. gun removal policy; 6. confidential support programs and training; 7. easy-to-access confidential well-being tools; 8. regional partnerships; 9. family support; and 10. communications plan.

Mental Health Professionals Who Understand LEOS

Mental health professionals may not understand the stressors of LEOs, be vetted or culturally competent to recognize their numerous cultures, ethnicities, religions, genders, and sexual orientations (IACP, 2023). Agencies must seek out mental health professionals who understand the culture, the stressors, and have the therapeutic skill to work with LEOs. These professionals need to be aware of best practices to screen for chronic suicidal ideation, intent, and planning, which are risk factors for attempts and suicide. LEOs with a persistent suicidal state may not respond well to typical crisis management strategies and need trained professionals in evidence-based, suicide-specific care related to officers, or a treatment plan won't work.

Awareness Campaigns

Although they may resist getting help, they won't resist talking to someone if it will make them feel stronger. Most officers don't have a clue as to who to reach out to. An awareness campaign about who to call and what to do might help.

Peer-to-Peer Programs

Peer-to-peer programs can prevent intentional self-directed violence. There are trained peers who are part of the police community that can help them manage their suicidal thoughts.

Team Culture to Recognize the Stressors

Start at the academy teaching recruits how to build resilience and use stress management skills, so they are ready for the organizational police structure that will impact their health. Acquadro Maran et al. (2022) found that team culture can fight the stigma of seeking support by focusing on specific stress prevention, treatment, and initiatives. The organizational police structure can encourage focusing on the incidences of stressful circumstances and undesirable behaviors that weaken well-being at work (Lopez-Cabarcos et al., 2022).

Stressors related to suicide are lack of organizational support, trauma, shift work, stigma related to asking for help, and difficulties fitting in with the police culture, can cause relationship issues and increased alcohol use (Violanti et al., 2019). Focus on major causes of stress, attitudes about the external work environment and how an officer perceives danger, distrust of citizens, and cynicism toward their complaints (Paoline & Gau, 2023). Also, don't lose sight of the fact that we can't blame the job for an officer's suicide. Risk factors and red flags may be present way before they put on their uniform.

CASE NOTES

Alexander Castellanos, Police Captain, Miami, FL, notes, "Leaders must be more aggressive in their involvement with officers who experience traumatic events. After experiencing a traumatic event or an officer is experiencing mental health issues, departments nationwide must implement policies that mandate officers be removed from the frontlines and the day-to-day work-related stress until a proper evaluation is conducted, and the officers have been given sufficient time to recover emotionally. This is rarely done anywhere. Usually, the officer is sent to psychological services and placed back into regular service soon after.

"Equally important is for the officers to be cognizant of their physical and mental health. Too often officers are more concerned with making money and career advancement that they neglect their own mental and physical well-being. Individual officers must maintain a regular exercise regimen and engage in hobbies to improve mental and physical health. There is no way around this. Physical decay leads to mental instability and depression.

"The mentality across the board should be 'work to live, not live to work.' If the standard practice across the board, at least during a traumatic event, i.e., officer-involved shooting which results in death of either the subject or the officer, is for a mandatory removal to receive counseling, training and evaluation, then there wouldn't be such a big deal to be removed from the frontline to receive the adequate treatment, etc." *(A. Castellanos, personal communication, January 18, 2023).*

Suicide Prevention & Response Independent Review Committee Recommendations

Suicide Prevention & Response Independent Review Committee (SPRIRC) (2022) recommendations for the military can be applied toward policing and result in large reductions in suicide:

- Separate training should be developed by different audiences and for intended effect.
- Self-injury, self-harm and suicide prevention training can be delivered in small groups with those of similar ranks.
- Modernize content, delivery, and dosage of prevention education and skill building across the career cycle.
- Centralize responsibility for core prevention activities.
- Require mental health professionals to work with any LEO under investigation.
- Minimize shift changes.
- Address excessive alcohol use and the risks it poses in existing training requirements.
- Eliminate legal and bureaucratic barriers to efficient hiring and onboarding processes.
- Expedite the hiring process for behavioral health professionals.

- Select the right people for the right positions based on demonstrated leadership skills and abilities.

Upstream Strategies

Upstream is defined as going in the direction opposite to the flow of a stream (Merriam-Webster, n.d.). We need to encourage conversations about chronic stress way upstream before a LEO has died by suicide. If you are implementing a self-injury prevention, self-harm prevention, or suicide prevention protocol, start with the recruits and teach them about resilience that they will need to tap into when they are faced with the horrors of the job. Also, teach them how ACEs may possibly impact the way that they manage organizational stress, shift work, critical incidents, relationship problems and alcohol use; all of which is associated with suicide ideation in LEOs.

Upstream in relation to self-injury or self-harm prevention, focuses on going towards the beginning—upstream prevention. While command staff and supervisors approach suicide prevention, intervention, and postvention (IACP, 2014, p. 27), they can move the bar to an upstream approach to focus on reducing risk factors and enhancing protective processes that prevent suicide ideation way before an officer is suicidal. Focus on pre-employment testing to identify those who show signs of mental health or substance abuse challenges before they are hired (Rouse et al., 2015).

Prevention can take place, upstream, confidentially, rather than during or after a crisis. Upstream prevention emphasizes issues that impact LEOs way before they become suicidal at the beginning of their career. Upstream prevention recognizes that helping a recruit identify protective factors will reduce risk factors later in their career and into retirement. Furthermore, it understands many of the early precursors such as ACEs.

CASE NOTES

Colonel Rob Campbell, 27-years Army (Retired), author, coach, speaker and trainer, notes, "What I can offer is this: get up stream. Many organizations are trying to address suicide well downstream, at a point where it is too late. Fishing trips, axe throwing, and even behavioral health assistance offered covertly are all great services, but they occur too late, far downstream where problems have metastasized. The focus then, is placed on those suffering and not on the conditions 'upstream' which caused the suffering or on being able to identify the behaviors and or events 'upstream' which may cause an officer to spiral toward self-harm.

"If I and my leaders invested in our people—if we knew them on a deeper level, cared for them, became their champion, and took a vested interest in their growth, they would respond appropriately when the mission finally came or when faced with tempting decisions to misbehave or treat another person poorly. If we invested in them and created a psychologically safe environment, they may be more apt to speak up when hurting. I was convinced that if we knew each other on a deeper level we would be able to see the signs that something was wrong long before the thought of suicide entered a person's head, well upstream" *(R. Campbell, personal communication, December 15, 2022).*

Gatekeeper Training, Brief Interventions and Therapies

Resilience training, suicide brief interventions, therapies and gatekeeper training are in place to possibly prevent suicide.

- **GATEKEEPER TRAINING:** ASK About Suicide to Save a Life; Applied Suicide Intervention Skills Training (ASIST); Connect Suicide Prevention/Intervention Training; Question. Persuade. Refer. - QPR for Law Enforcement; and Yellow Ribbon. Gatekeeper training teaches individuals how to identify warning signs and assist those who are thinking about suicide in getting help. Being that gatekeeper training programs depend on referrals to mental health services, which are frequently nonexistent, understaffed, and/or untrained about suicide risk, strategies are required to provide primary mental health first aid and suicide-focused therapy to community gatekeepers (Quinnett, 2023).
- **BRIEF LAW ENFORCEMENT INTERVENTIONS:** National Suicide Awareness for Law Enforcement Officers (SAFLEO); In Harms Way: A Law Enforcement Suicide Prevention Toolkit; Preventing LEO Suicide: Interactive CD-ROM can be ordered through NCJRS; The Pain Behind the Badge: police suicide prevention webinars;

Comprehensive Framework for Law Enforcement Suicide Prevention; and National POLICE Suicide Foundation.

⬚ **THERAPIES:** Cognitive Behavior for Suicide Prevention (CBT-SP/CT-SP); Attachment Based Family Therapy (ABFT); Collaborative Assessment and Management of Suicidality (CAMS); Dialectical Behavioral Therapy (DBT); Prolonged Grief Therapy.

Safe and Effective Messaging

Although the commonly used phrase is "committed suicide," died by suicide, died of suicide, and died from suicide are phrases that more accurately describe suicide (Rubel, 2020). These phrases respect the deceased and the suicide-loss survivor (e.g., family, friends, fellow officers, community members). The terminology is consistent with how individuals describe types of death (e.g., died of cancer, died by accident) and don't carry the stigma of criminality.

Avoid using language that implies that suicide is inevitable. Although Krishnan et al. (2022) maintains that suicide has been thought to be near epidemic levels in law enforcement populations, this is not the case. Perhaps officers talk about suicide as an epidemic because many of their brothers and sisters have taken their own life, the number of suicides is increasing, and there often seems to be a prevalence of social media postings of LEOs killing themself.

Calling suicide an epidemic or offering statistics without any recommendations for prevention are two instances of messaging that could make suicide appear like an impossible problem to solve (National Action Alliance for Suicide Prevention, 2023). Instead, say that suicide is increasing or rising among officers. Rather than saying that an officer was suicidal, say that they were thinking of suicide, or they were experiencing suicidal thoughts. They are not their mental health diagnosis. Don't say that they are bipolar or a drug addict. Their addiction does not define them. For example, they are addicted to drugs, not a drug addict.

As a suicide loss survivor, I am impacted by how media reports suicide. When I was writing my thesis for my master's degree in community health with a concentration in thanatology, I chose media reporting of suicide because the way suicide is covered has an impact on suicide loss survivors.

Dramatizing or glorifying suicide or describing it as a common response to hardship in the media is associated with an increase in suicide. Responsible reporting reduces the risk of a person taking their own life. When agencies share the news of an officer's suicide, they should follow the recommendations for reporting on suicide at https://reportingonsuicide.org/

Limiting Access to Means of Suicide

Those who own firearms need tailored self-injury or self-harm prevention interventions because of their proximity to lethal means and the cultural and legal factors that exist around gun ownership (Garverich et al., 2023). When my father retired, he returned his service weapon. A few years later, my mother, also a LEO, retired and kept her weapon. As my father got older, he experienced deteriorating discs in his back, was in pain, and used her weapon to end his life. His triplet grandsons were born three weeks later.

I am often asked if my father would not have ended his life if he reached out for help or didn't have access to my mother's weapon. He concealed his motives, otherwise my mother would have removed her weapon from the home. Although he was not suffering from depression, he was paralyzed by pain. As a WWII veteran and police sergeant, he was a strong man who became weak and could not adjust to living in that condition.

"Lethal means safety" means putting time and space between having thoughts of suicide and objects (e.g., firearms, medications). Perhaps during my father's at-risk period, if he didn't have access to a weapon, he would not have killed himself. Conceivably, if he did not have a weapon at home, he may have chosen another means. Having tunnel vision, he could not see another way of ending his pain. I think that my father would not have said a word about his mental health if it meant removing the weapon from his home.

Perhaps departments focusing on prevention can advise officers that taking away their firearm is only temporary, so they don't fear permanent weapon seizure, and that it is more about having distance between them and a firearm during an at-risk period (Stanley et al., 2020). Better yet, fix the problem before they contemplate using their weapon to end their life.

The Israeli Defense Forces created a system where soldiers must leave their firearms at work, so they do not have a weapon at home. Runyan et al. (2017) surveyed LEOs and firearm retailers about their willingness to offer voluntary, temporary storage for suicidal individuals and found that 77% of LEOs and 67% of firearm retailers were willing to provide voluntary, temporary storage for firearm owners concerned about their mental health. Reducing access to highly lethal methods, such as a gun, can help people survive periods of acute suicidal risk (Barber and Miller, 2014). Surveys indicate that legal liability fears are a chilling issue for firearm retailers and law enforcement (Gibbons et al., 2020).

Psychological Autopsy

Agencies gather and use data to guide efforts to prevent suicide. Being that officers have complex behavioral health problems that can lead to suicide, agencies are addressing prevention needs and planning accordingly. They are using data from psychological autopsies and the personal and general suicide data collected by the FBI. Psychological autopsy (PA) explores the emotional, cognitive, social, and spiritual state of a person prior to their death. Unlike a physical autopsy, a body is not physically examined.

PA is performed by talking to those closest to the officer. Did the suicide occur within days of disciplinary action, a demotion, or having to appear in court? A death analysis or investigation identifies their intention when they killed themself. PA can guide an agency prevention program and clarify the manner of death.

Psychological Autopsy Investigator certification™ is available through the American Association of Suicidology (AAS). Although it is a best practice postmortem data collection procedure, PA wasn't performed after my father's suicide. If a PA had been done, his medical records would have been looked at along with investigators talking to my family. The data could have been useful for police suicide prevention purposes, especially for suicide risks after retirement. This research approach of reconstructing contributing factors can help an agency understand why an active or a retired LEO, like my father, died by suicide.

CASE NOTES

Olivia Johnson, president and founder of Blue Wall Institute, notes, "The Law Enforcement Suicide Mortality Database (LE-SMD) does not just produce a 'number,' but rather, a psychological autopsy that takes an in-depth look at every suicide among these populations in a whole new way. Every death is first verified and validated through the use of autopsy, toxicology reports, police reports, social media accounts, agency acknowledgment, and family interviews. This information helps us to better understand the 'why' behind the death, the reasons leading to the death, and in-turn, inoculation training to prevent such deaths and other negative outcomes in the future" *(O. Johnson, personal communication, March 1, 2023).*

The National Law Enforcement Suicide Mortality Database

The National Law Enforcement Suicide Mortality Database™ [LE-SMD] was developed to fill a gap in reporting of suicides, non-fatal attempts, and drug overdose deaths. The database houses data from 2017 to the present day. Their mission is:

1. To provide a confidential reporting system for anyone to report a law enforcement or corrections officer suicide, attempt, overdose, or suspected cause of death to be suicide or overdose;
2. To provide researchers, academics, clinicians, and other qualified professionals access to confidentially verified data regarding law enforcement and corrections officer suicide deaths and non-fatal suicide attempts; and
3. That the research produced from the data to have a direct impact on the field and show measurable reduction in suicide deaths among first responders and the reduction of attempts (The National Law Enforcement Suicide Mortality Database, n.d.).

The Law Enforcement Suicide Data Collection ACT (LESDCA)

A postvention approach involving collecting national statistics can guide agency prevention programs. The Law Enforcement Suicide Data Collection Act (LESDCA) directed the FBI to create a data collection program to monitor officer suicide of current and retired officers. LEOs are considered current or a former officer, criminal investigator, corrections officer, line of duty officer or 911 dispatch operator (Congress.gov, 2020). This program improves the ability to establish suicide data collection. The Attorney General establishes data on current or former LEOs who attempt or die by suicide. Submissions by a law enforcement agency are voluntary unless specific related legislation mandates that an agency reports the data. The Federal Bureau of Investigation (2022) collects:

- **PERSONAL DATA:** age at time of incident, demographics, race, total law enforcement work experience, position status at time of incident, military veteran and branch of service, marital status and number of children.
- **GENERAL DATA:** incident location, type of location, manner of attempt/suicide, murder/suicide or attempted murder/ suicide, number of victims, type of victims.
- **OTHER DATA ELEMENTS COLLECTED:** circumstances, incident information, factors known prior to incident, potential factors made known prior to incident, potential factors documented within the employing agency.

The FBI Uniform Crime Reporting Program manages the data collection with no identifiable officer information to ensure confidentiality. After an attempt or suicide, the law enforcement agency submits the information about the officer and the data resides on the Law Enforcement Enterprise Portal (LEEP). The purpose is to compile national statistics. Agencies authorized to use the program are law enforcement, corrections, telecommunications, and legal system (prosecutors and adjudicators). To spread awareness of police suicide prevention, departments can post on social media, participate in awareness walks, or let LEOs know that supervisors will listen and support them (Law Enforcement Officers Relief Fund, 2022).

Postvention

Fifty years ago, Ed Shneidman coined the term postvention, which refers to supporting those individuals affected by a suicide. "Whereas the goal of prevention is to stop people from becoming suicidal, and the goal of intervention is to reduce the likelihood of suicide by individuals deemed suicidal, postvention mitigates the harmful effects of suicide" (Rubel, 2020). Postvention involves prior planning before a suicide.

Postvention is a strategy that includes any activity following a suicide that encourages healing by mitigating negative effects of suicide exposure. It can lessen complicated grief and suicide contagion among those affected by the death. Postvention needs to be included in a suicide prevention policy. Supervisors must have clear post-event protocols in place being those closest to them are profoundly impacted. Leadership should not rely on an informal, unwritten policy given the potentially harmful aftermath in this close-knit occupation (Violanti et al., 2021). They need to focus on supporting everyone in the department, including families.

CASE NOTES

Jill A. Harrington, DSW, creator and lead editor, *Superhero Grief*, notes, "Suicide loss survivors can be shrouded in the darkest of grief. Tapping into their heroic spirit, police leaders can help shed a light of hope for the bereaved by learning how to compassionately companion survivors through this darkness with information, education, and support. Knowing that they are not alone, that there are heroes all around them, even in the darkest of times, to help set them on a path to rise from the ashes of suicide grief" *(J.A. Harrington, personal communication, July 9, 2023).*

Exposure and Survivors of Suicide Loss

Those who lost a significant person to suicide or who are exposed to suicide are suicide loss survivors (e.g., family member, friend, coworker, neighbor, first responder). They are described as bereaved by suicide, survivor of suicide, and suicide survivor. Based on the 916,115 suicides from 1995 through 2019, there were more than 5.4 million survivors of suicide loss in the United States, or 1 in every 60 Americans. Support must be tailored to the impact that the death had on a suicide-loss survivor's life based on the exposure (Andriessen et al., 2019). Grief reactions include shock, denial, anger, and relief. Other reactions include shame, stigma, and a quest to find the answer to why the person died by suicide (Maple et al., 2017).

Occupational exposure to suicide is related to significant emotional trauma and poor mental health (Aldrich & Cerel, 2020; Lyra et al., 2021), especially for those with multiple exposure to suicide (Nelson et al., 2020). Exposure impacts everyone differently from sadness and social isolation to prolonged grief. Grief intensity will depend upon one's level of closeness. Individuals who may feel impacted can be categorized as suicide exposed, suicide affected, suicide bereaved short-term or suicide long-term (Cerel et al., 2014).

- **SUICIDE EXPOSED** individuals are those who either heard about or witnessed the suicide (e.g., acquaintance, clergy) who usually have minimal grief reactions.
- **SUICIDE AFFECTED** individuals are exposed to a suicide (e.g., police officer, helping professional) who might have mild ongoing grief reactions.
- **SUICIDE BEREAVED SHORT-TERM** is a subset of the suicide affected individuals who were attached to the person who died (e.g., friend, coworker). They usually adapt and move through their grief over time.
- **SUICIDE BEREAVED LONG-TERM** are a subset with the suicide short-term group (e.g., family member, close friend). They may experience trauma symptoms or prolonged grief, which can last more than a year.

Bereavement Protocol

Preferred supports that facilitate post-traumatic growth for suicide loss survivors are providing information, practical assistance, non-judgmental support, peer support, professional counseling, and suggesting ways to honor a person's memory (McGill et al., 2023). Structured bereavement protocol after a suicide can include the following recommendations:

- Information available on managing a suicide loss.
- Designated representative to provide notifications and updates.
- Protocols on wearing a mourning badge, flag at half-mast, and funeral.
- Training peers who volunteer bereavement support.
- Recommending specialized psychotherapy (e.g., Prolonged Grief Disorder Therapy).
- Attending a suicide-loss survivor support group.
- Getting involved in organizations dedicated to prevention.

If you have ever deeply listened to an officer struggling with thoughts of suicide, you will hear them talk about wanting to die, ending their pain, feeling hopeless, lonely, incompetent, being trapped, or a burden and liability to others. Although we understand warning signs and red flags, suicide remains a public health issue. Suicide is complex.

We need to focus on preventing suicide among law enforcement professionals as a group. Mental health professionals need to identify risk factors and protective factors before officers are suicidal and look at the evidence-based studies that inform and empower them. They should consider taking advanced, interactive training based on established core competencies to effectively assess and manage suicidal risk. Trainings are available at the American Association of Suicidology.

CASE NOTES

Dr. Dan Reidenberg, Psy.D, internationally recognized expert, speaker and author on suicide prevention and mental health, notes, "While suicide is coming out of the shadows, it is still shrouded in misperception and shame. This is magnified for those in the law enforcement profession where the belief is that those who serve and protect the public are strong, stoic, and impenetrable, thus leaving them at greater risk of death by suicide, one surpassing death by other parts of their job. When societal anger turns against law enforcement, departmental obstacles make it difficult to come forward, access to lethal means are available, exposure to trauma is repeated (including suicides), interpersonal relationships are challenged and internal pain becomes overwhelming, we must step in to help protect those behind the badge. Preventing tragedies among our law enforcement is needed, necessary and possible. When we accept that pain hurts, even among the strongest who serve our communities, and we officer compassion and access to care, we can save lives" *(D. Reidenberg, personal communication, October 2, 2023).*

THE NEXT STEP

Being that Chapter 9 focused on LODD and Chapter 10 focused on suicide, Chapter 11 looks at the Palette of Grief® and ways to manage traumatic loss in law enforcement.

REFERENCES

Acquadro Maran, D., Magnavita, N., & Garbarino, S. (2022). Identifying organizational stressors that could be a source of discomfort in police officers. *International Journal of Environmental Research and Public Health*, 19(6). https://doi:10.3390/ijerph19063720

Agrawal, S., Kumar, V., Singh, V., Singh, C., & Singh, A. (2022). Review on pathophysiological aspects of sleep deprivation. *CNS & Neurological Disorders—Drug targets*. Bentham Science Publishers. https://doi.org/10.2174/1871527321666220512092718

Aldrich, R. S., & Cerel, J. (2020). Occupational suicide exposure and impact on mental health: Examining differences across helping professions. *OMEGA – Journal of Death and Dying*, 85, 23–37. https://doi.org/10.1177/0030222820933019

Andriessen, K., Krysinska, K., Kolves, K., & Reavley, N. (2019). Suicide postvention service models and guidelines 2014–2019: A systematic review. *Frontiers in Psychology* 1-22. https://doi.org/10.3389/fpsyg.2019.02677

Badge of Life (n.d.). https://badgeoflife.org/

Barber, C. W., & Miller, M. J. (2014). Reducing a suicidal person's access to lethal means of suicide: a research agenda. *American Journal of Preventative Medicine*, 47(3 Suppl 2), 264-72. https://doi: 10.1016/j.amepre.2014.05.028

Bell, C. M., Ridley, J. A., Overholser, J. C., Young, K., Athey, A., …Phillips, K. (2018). The role of perceived burden and social support in suicide and depression. *Suicide and Life Threatening Behavior*, 48(1), 87-94. https://doi: 10.1111/sltb.12327

Blosnich, J. R., & Bossarte, R.M. (2017). Premilitary trauma as a correlate of suicidal ideation among veterans. *Psychiatric Services* 68(8), 755–55. https://doi.org/10.1176/appi.ps.201700186

Bureau of Justice Assistance (n.d.). National Officer Safety Initiatives (NOSI), preventing suicide among law enforcement officers: an issue brief, 1-28. https://tinyurl.com/2s3wzevy

Calati, R., Romano, D., Magliocca, S., Madeddu, F., Zeppegno, P., & Gramaglia, C. (2022). The interpersonal-psychological theory of suicide and the role of psychological pain during the COVID-19 pandemic: A network analysis. *Journal of Affective Disorders*, 302, 435-439. https://doi:10.1016/j.jad.2022.01.078

Cerel, J., McIntosh, J. L., Neimeyer, R. A., Maple, M. Marshall, D. (2014). The Continuum of "Survivorship": Definitional Issues in the Aftermath of Suicide. *Suicide and Life-Threatening Behavior*, 44(6). https://doi.org/10.1111/sltb.120932014

Centers for Disease Control and Prevention [CDC] (2021). *Suicide Prevention.* http://www.cdc.gov/violenceprevention/suicide/

Centers for Disease Control and Prevention (2023). *Suicide Prevention.* https://www.cdc.gov/suicide/suicide-data-statistics.html

Centers for Disease Control and Prevention (2023a). *Suicide Data and Statistics.* https://www.cdc.gov/suicide/suicide-data-statistics.html

Civilotti, C., Acquadro Maran, D., Garbarino, S., & Magnavita, N. (2022). Hopelessness in police officers and its association with depression and burnout: A pilot study. *International Journal of Environmental Research and Public Health,* 19(9), 5169. https://tinyurl.com/5n9b5bub

Congress.gov (2020). S.2746 - Law enforcement suicide data collection act. *Public Law 116-143, 116th Congress 2019-2020.* https://tinyurl.com/2s3nmrwn

Dixon, S. S. (2021). Law enforcement suicide. *Aggression and Violent Behavior,* 61, 1359-1789. https://doi.org/10.1016/j.avb.2021.101649

Dube, S. R., Anda, R. F., Felitti, V. J., Chapman, D. P., Williamson, D. F., & Giles, W. H. (2001). Childhood abuse, household dysfunction, and the risk of attempted suicide throughout the life span. *JAMA,* 286(24), 3089–3096. https://doi:10.1001/jama.286.24.3089

Federal Bureau of Investigation (2022). Priva*cy impact assessment for the department of justice privacy impact assessment FBI/law enforcement suicide data collection.* https://www.fbi.gov

Garbarino, S., Guglielmi, O., Puntoni, M., Bragazzi, N. L., & Magnavita, N. (2019). Sleep quality among police officers. *International Journal of Environmental Research and Public Health,* 16(5), 885. https://doi.org/10.3390/ijerph16050885

Garverich, S., Carvalho, K., Ross, C., Baglivo, A., Farmer, J., Gully, M., ...Lincoln, A. (2023). I'm not going to tell him what I tell you. *Journal of Participatory Research Methods,* 4(1). https://doi.org/10.35844/001c.57646

Gibbons, M. J., Fan, M. D., Rowhani-Rahbar, A., & Rivara, F. P. (2020). Legal liability for returning firearms to suicidal persons who voluntarily surrender them in 50 US states. *American Journal of Public Health,* 110(5), 685-688.

Gibran, K. (2017). *The broken wings.* McAllister Editions.

Gradus, J. L., Qin, P., Lincoln, A. K., Miller, M., Lawler, E., Toft Sorensen, H., & Lash, T. L. (2010). Post-traumatic stress disorder and completed suicide. *American Journal of Epidemiology,* 171(6) 721–727. https://doi.org/10.1093/aje/kwp456

The Harris Poll (2022). *Public perception of mental health and suicide prevention survey results September 2022.* https://tinyurl.com/bdhhmrbh

Heyman, M., Dill, J., & Douglas, N. R. (2018). *The Ruderman white paper on mental health and suicide of first responders.* https://dir.nv.gov/uploadedFiles/dirnvgov/content/WCS/TrainingDocs/First%20Responder%20White%20Paper_Final%20(2).pdf

International Association of Chiefs of Police [IACP] (2014). *In IACP national symposium on law enforcement officer suicide and mental health: Breaking the silence on law enforcement suicides.* Washington, DC: Office of Community Oriented Policing Services.

International Association of Chiefs of Police [IACP] (2023). *National consortium on preventing law enforcement suicide 2023 report and recommendations.* https://tinyurl.com/5a5kudw3

Johnson, O. (2022). Silent No More: The fatal 10 of law enforcement suicide. Calibre Press. https://calibrepress.com/2022/11/silent-no-more-the-fatal-10-of-law-enforcement-suicide/

Johnson, O. (2020). Unpublished raw data on the demographics of police suicides for the years 2017 to 2021. Blue Wall Institute, Belleville, IL.

Johnson, O., Milliard, B., & Krawczyn, J. (2022). Chapter 1, Pre-employment eligibility and predicating self-harm in law enforcement personnel, 1-30, In Johnson O., Papazoglou K., Violanti J., Pascarella J. (Eds). *Practical considerations for preventing police suicide: Stop officer suicide* Springer.

Kennedy-Hanson, H. (2020). How employers can help first responders stay mentally and emotionally strong. *Kaiser-Permanente.* https://tinyurl.com/3jdv8j98

Krishnan, N., Steene, L. M. B., Lewis, M., Marshall, D., & Ireland, J. L. (2022). A systematic review of risk factors implicated in the suicide of police officers. *Journal of Police and Criminal Psychology, 37,* 939–951. https://doi.org/10.1007/s11896-022-09539-1

Law Enforcement Officers Relief Fund (LEORF) (2022). *Police Suicide Prevention.* https://leorf.org/2022/11/07/police-suicide-prevention/

Lopez-Cabarcos, M. A., Lopez-Carballeira, A., & Ferro-Soto, C. (2022). How to avoid a lack of work engagement among public police professionals. *European Management Review,* 1–13.

Lyra, R. L., McKenzie, S. K., Every-Palmer, S., & Jenkin, G. (2021). Occupational exposure to suicide: A review of research on the experiences of mental health professionals and first responders. *PLoS One, 16*(4), e0251038. https://doi.org/10.1371/journal.pone.0251038

Maple, M., Cerel, J., Sanford, R., Pearce, T., & Jordan, J. (2017). Is exposure to suicide beyond kin associated with risk for suicidal behavior? A systematic review of the evidence. *Suicide and Life-Threatening Behavior, 47*(4), 461-474. https://doi:10.1111/sltb.12308

McGill, K., Bhullar, N., Batterham, P. J., Carrandi, A., Wayland, S., & Maple, M. (2023). Key issues, challenges, and preferred supports for those bereaved by suicide: Insights from postvention experts. *Death Studies, 47*(5), 624-629.

Merriam-Webster. Upstream (n.d.). https://tinyurl.com/5dsk2n4u

Morrison, A.S., Ustun, B., Horenstein, A., Kaplan, S.C., Reis de Oliveira, I., Batmaz, S., Gross, J.J., Sadikova, E., Hemanny, C., Pires, P.P., Goldin, P.R., Kessler, R.C., & Heimberg, R.G. (2022). Optimized short-forms of the cognitive distortions questionnaire. *Journal of Anxiety Disorders, 92,* 102624, https://tinyurl.com/mry28529

National Action Alliance for Suicide Prevention (2023). *Safety*. https://tinyurl.com/yckb7cdu

National Institute of Mental Health (n.d.). ASQ suicide risk screening tool. bit.ly/45WJnLD

National Law Enforcement Suicide Mortality Database (n.d.). https://tinyurl.com/a6y9fbz7

National Wellness Survey for Public Safety Personnel Summary Report. November 2022.

Nelson, P. A., Cordingley, L., Kapur, N., Chew-Graham, C. A., Shaw, J., Smith, S., ...McDonnell, S. (2020). We're the first port of call: Perspectives of ambulance staff on responding to deaths by suicide. *Frontiers in Psychology*, 11, 722. https://tinyurl.com/mrxt3eww

Nissim, H. S. B., Dill, J., Douglas, R., Johnson, O., & Folino, C., (2022). The Ruderman white paper update on mental health and suicide of first responders. https://rudermanfoundation.org/white_papers/the-ruderman-white-paper-update-on-mental-health-and-suicide-of-first-responders/

Norton, T. (2022). Are correctional officers being ignored? *Responder Health*. https://responderhealth.com/blog/f/are-correctional-officers-being-ignored

Paoline, E. A. & Gau, J. M. (2023). Police Stress: the role of occupational and officer characteristics. *Policing: An International Journal*, 46(1), 194-208.

Pennings, S. M., Finn, J., Houtsma, C., & Green, A. (2017). Post-traumatic stress disorder symptom clusters and the interpersonal theory of suicide in a large military sample. *Suicide and Life-Threatening Behaviors*, 47(5), 538-550. https://doi:10.1111/sltb.12317

Podlogar, T., Ziberna, J., Postuvan, V., & Kerr, D. C. R. (2017). Belongingness and burdensomeness in adolescents. *Suicide and Life-Threatening Behavior*, 47(3), 336-352. https://doi:10.1111/sltb.12276

Police Executive Research Forum (2019). An occupational risk what every agency should do to prevent suicide amongst its officers. *Critical Issues in Policing Series*. https://www.policeforum.org/assets/PreventOfficerSuicide.pdf

Quinnett, P.G. (2023). The Certified QPR Pathfinder Training Program: A Description of a Novel Public Health Gatekeeper Training Program to Mitigate Suicidal Ideation and Suicide Deaths. *Journal of Prevention*. https://doi.org/10.1007/s10935-023-00748-w

Rajaratnam, S. M., Barger, L. K., Lockley, S. W., Shea, S. A., Wang, W., Landrigan, C. P., ... Czeisler, C. A. (2011). Harvard work hours, health and safety group. Sleep disorders, health, and safety in police officers. *JAMA*, 306(23), 2567-2578. https://doi: 10.1001/jama.2011.1851

Rouse, L. M., Frey, R. A., López, M., Wohlers, H., Xiong, I., Llewellyn, K., ... Wester, S. R. (2015). Law enforcement suicide. *Police Quarterly*, 18(1), 79–108. https://tinyurl.com/4rujepnb

Rubel, B. (2020). (3ed). *But I didn't say goodbye: Helping families after a suicide.* Griefwork Center, Inc.

Runyan, C. W., Brooks-Russell, A., Brandspigel, S., Betz, M., Tung, G., Novins, D., & Agans, R. (2017). Law enforcement and gun retailers as partners for safely storing guns to prevent suicide. *American Journal of Public Health*, 107(11), 1789-1794.

Shneidman, E. S. (1969). Prologue: Fifty-eight years. In E. S. Shneidman (Ed.), *On the nature of suicide*, 1-30. Jossey-Bass.

Stanley, I. H., Hom, M. A., Sachs-Ericsson, N. J., Gallyer, A. J., & Joiner, T. E. (2020). A pilot randomized clinical trial of a lethal means safety intervention for young adults with firearm familiarity at risk for suicide. *Journal of Consulting and Clinical Psychology*, 88(4), 372–383. https://doi: 10.1037/ccp0000481

Soomro, S., & Yanos, P.T. (2019). Predictors of mental health stigma among police officers: The role of trauma and PTSD. *Journal of Police and Criminal Psychology*, 34, 175–183. https://doi.org/10.1007/s11896-018-9285-x

Suicide Prevention & Response Independent Review Committee (SPRIRC) (2022). Preventing suicide in the U.S. military. 1-115.

Thompson, M.P., Kingree, J.B., Lamis, D. (2019). Associations of adverse childhood experiences and suicidal behaviors in adulthood in a U.S. nationally representative sample. *Child: care, health and development*, 45(1), 121–128. https://doi.org/10.1111/cch.12617

Turecki, G. & Brent, D. A. (2016). Suicide and suicidal behaviour. *The Lancet*, 387, (10024), 1227-1239. https://doi.org/10.1016/S0140-6736(15)00234-2

Uniform Crime Reporting (UCR) Program. Federal Bureau of Investigation (2016). Police employee data. 2016 crime in the United States. https://tinyurl.com/5n7xmh3e

Violanti, J. M., Owens, S. L., McCanlies, E., Fekedulegn, D., & Andrew, M. E. (2019). Law enforcement suicide: a review. *Policing: An International Journal* 42(2), 141-164. https://doi.org/10.1108/PIJPSM-05-2017-0061

Violanti, J. M., & Steege, A. (2021). Law enforcement worker suicide: an updated national assessment. *Policing*, 44(1), 18-31. https://doi: 10.1108/PIJPSM-09-2019-0157

Violanti, J. (2022). Police suicide: The hidden danger. In: O. Johnson, K. Papazoglou, J. Violanti, J., & J. Pascarella. (Eds) *Preventing police suicide: Stop officer suicide*. Springer. https://doi.org/10.1007/978-3-030-83974-1_3

Violence Policy Center. (2018). *Guns and suicide*. http://www.vpc.org/wp-content/uploads/2018/05/suicide-factsheet-2018.pdf.

Zimmerman, G. M., Fridel, E. E. & Frost, N. A. (2023). Examining differences in the individual and contextual risk factors for police officer, correctional officer, and non-protective service suicides. *Justice Quarterly*, https://doi:10.1080/0741 8825.2023.2188063

11 | GRIEVING ON THE JOB

DEFINITIONS

AMBIGUOUS LOSS - uncertain whether a person is dead or alive, and they cannot make sense of the loss situation.

DISENFRANCHISED GRIEF - cannot openly acknowledge the death; when loss is not sanctioned by society; or when the bereaved does not feel supported.

PALETTE OF GRIEF® - blending of physical, emotional, cognitive, behavioral, religious, or spiritual grief reactions after a final separation.

PROLONGED GRIEF DISORDER (PGD) - incapacitating feelings of grief.

OBJECTIVES

After reading and considering the content of this chapter, the reader should be able to:

- Describe Palette of Grief® reactions after a loss.

- Review 25 risk factors that complicate the grief process.

- Compare contemporary mourning models for coping with loss.

In My Experience & Lessons Learned

JASON PALAMARA

It was Sunday morning. I was on my first day tour after a "turn-around," second night tour. I had seven hours between the two and was never lucky enough to get the full seven. There was always an end of tour, last minute call to the squad or job broadcast over the radio where a unit was asking central dispatch for "the squad to respond." This usually meant my night was going to continue straight into the morning.

My partners and I had the grim assignment of responding to a residence that called to report the death of a newborn child. Not an accident or under suspicious circumstances; it was expected. The parents had brought their terminally ill newborn home to die surrounded by family. I stood in the living room with a sobbing mother holding her lifeless child in her arms.

The father was doing his best to keep it together on the other side of the room. What they were experiencing was traumatic stress, and I was experiencing secondary traumatic stress. Although I knew procedurally what to do, it was impossible to filter out immediate thoughts and emotions as I thought of my own children. Calls like this one are your quintessential "On the job training (OJT)." However, no amount of training could prepare me for the traumatic scene. It doesn't matter how many times I have experienced jobs like this; each one brings its own challenges.

I took photographs of the scene and of the deceased child. EMS arrived. We gently assisted in taking the child from his mother. After we obtained information from the parents and completed paperwork, we were off to our next assignment. But the images from the morning were etched in my mind. I thought about how the family lived through a traumatic loss. I will never forget that moment in time—a dead infant, a mother sobbing, a father doing his best to hold on, and my feeling of helplessness, which brought me back to memories of my own children as infants.

I believed that what happened at work should stay at work, and what occurred in my family life was not to be brought into work. I am a human being that happens to be a cop, not a cop that is a human being. I am a son, brother, husband, and father first whose job is a police officer; not a police officer who happens to be someone's son, brother, husband or father. When

240

I was not on the job, I needed to be mindful of who I was in the lives of those who cared about me most and make time for them.

It was not customary to get home and say "Hey hun, I had to take pictures of a dead infant today. How was your day?" It's not the culture to pull a partner aside and say, "Hey man, you okay after that job we just went to?" I never considered how the job was damaging me on the inside—making it easier for me to isolate, remain alone with my darkest of thoughts, and holding on to the false belief that there was no one else who could relate to me and what I had experienced. What came out of that filter was what my family received. I had nothing left for them when it was time to take off the uniform.

Several cases like this in a short period of time demanded the same, if not more of my attention. This culminated in a personal rock bottom due to the stress and lack of skills in how to deal with my experiences. My unhealthy behavior and poor coping methods ultimately gave me pause, and compelled me to change course and explore what I could do differently.

When Detective Jason Rivera and Wilbert Mora were murdered by being shot while investigating a domestic dispute in a Bronx apartment on January 21st, 2022, I felt helpless. Although retired, I became a listening ear to a good friend who attended their funeral. Although I wanted to be back on the proverbial battlefield and in the fight, I was a now spectator—or so I thought. I still had control over allowing myself to process my hurt by being present to listen to my fellow officers when they needed me.

My friend, Kevin, called as he was leaving Det. Rivera's funeral. We spoke about the cold weather and how it reminded him of us standing for hours at the funeral of Det. Daniel Enchautegui in December of 2005. We felt like our toes were going to freeze. Sharing memories with Kevin about our time together on the job helped me process my own grief. And for a few minutes, Kevin and I were the listening ears we both needed at that moment.

As a peer, you may be the only person a bereaved LEO lets in. As a crisis counselor, I received calls from many individuals struggling with a loss. As their own family and friends may also be grieving the same loss or dealing with their own struggles, many callers have shared with me their unwillingness to lean on them. They tell me, "I don't want to be a burden or bother to them." And so they turn to someone outside of their network for help.

But a trained peer knows about the issues to explore, questions to ask, and grief reactions. A fellow LEO—especially someone who has training in health and wellness—may be just who a person in crisis needs, perhaps the only someone, who can provide a sense of clarity and sense where the person suffering cannot otherwise find comfort.

I am present as they metaphorically unpack their story and walk with them on their journey. I know that there is no one way to grieve. I have lived the blue life and am in a position to connect my fellow LEOs to higher levels of care if they need it. Those providing therapy for our tribe must be equipped to do so. Although well intentioned, some counselors fall short and say the wrong thing, such as: "I am excited to work with you. You are my first cop." or "In your seventeen years as a trooper have you ever experienced trauma?" or "How many people have you killed?" These are actual statements my clients heard while in therapy.

Where there is a small window in which a LEO may reach out for help, it is imperative that cultural competency is not a term used lightly. A peer is paramount in establishing a level of trust that allows those specially trained to provide therapy to walk through that door before it closes. As a detective, I would often find myself knocking on the door to an apartment with my partner to speak with a witness about a case. Most times, a resident would open the door, yet leave the chain engaged allowing us only a small view inside until we had earned their trust and were let in. Often a peer can bridge the trust gap between another LEO hesitant in accepting help and those providing mental health services.

As LEOs, we like to ask questions and explore before we open up, especially to those we feel don't get us. It is important to have a peer to walk with us while navigating our grief. Whether you are a peer, mental health professional, or chaplain who supports officers and their families, it is important to know how grief may be experienced differently within the law-enforcement profession and by first responders. As cops, we are accustomed to responding to and handling jobs that involve death or near-death situations. Even more routine is how we must complete these jobs and move on to the next one. We pivot to assist the next person in need and answer the next call in the queue. Compartmentalization is a skill set we begin to perfect as the years pass.

We put our thoughts and grief for the victims away as we work towards the next call for help. When we return to our lives outside of work, we often keep what we have experienced from our family, and don't process our grief. Unfortunately, when we experience a loss in our personal life, we tend to operate by the same standards we use while in uniform. Like most of my brothers and sisters, I have experienced the death of one of our own in the line of duty. I have felt anger, sadness, loss, injustice, shock, and disbelief.

In retirement, I sometimes feel survivors' guilt for having made it to this stage in life while a young officer's life has been cut short. I've cried and still do when I know another hero has fallen. There have been times that I couldn't process my next thought, was unable to eat, and felt impending doom. Would this happen to me? Would I find myself on the losing side of a fight for my life? When an officer is injured in the line of duty and is "likely to die," as we would refer to it in the police department, we grieve, yet the process is delayed until the anticipated final word of their death is shared.

When one of us takes their life, my heart breaks for the officer who experienced such pain that it made them feel like dying was their only option. As a Christian, my comfort is found in knowing that God awaits us after we are done in this life. Whatever your belief, you do not have to grieve alone. While writing this book, I have worked through the losses that I had never processed that were locked up inside of me for years. Talking with my wife and Barbara about my losses, as well as writing them down, has been therapeutic. It could have been helpful to practice this all along.

We navigate through grief in our own way. Although I have grieved for those whom I have lost, I also find myself grieving for those that are still here. This anticipatory grief is possible as I am aware of what is to come as life moves on. I have found and re-discovered healthier ways to manage those thoughts. I no longer use alcohol as a means of avoidance.

Now I focus on the time I have with those in my life and the shared memories we create. I look back on my losses and share them so others may find their strength restored. I have been blessed with this opportunity. I have found meaning in what for a long time was internal chaos. Most times, I was laser focused on my investigations and career, sometimes in order to block out the rest in my life. Although there are days I stumble, I continue to develop my sea legs.

While in uniform, I grieved for my brothers and sisters who died a Line of Duty Death (LODD). As an older officer, I grieved for the loss of being a young cop. I grieved for the past relationships that I had with my children and family. To grieve is to experience reactions to loss and to miss what is gone. When I retired, I grieved the loss of being a cop. I remember missing *me*. I used to miss the version of myself that had the hunger and drive to become a cop, especially towards the end of my career exhausted and far from where I had started.

Without realizing it, I was grieving the version of myself that I, and others, used to be proud of. When grief, trauma, and stress overwhelm us, we must reach out and talk to someone. It is at this point where we are losing too many of our brothers and sisters in blue. Are you at this point? If you are overwhelmed with grief, trauma, or stress, I implore you to recognize that you may be reading this for a reason. Maybe it's because you were meant to help yourself or someone else. Either way, at the very least, use this moment as your catalyst for growth.

I process grief through a blend of both intuitive, as well as instrumental patterns. It can be helpful to identify your characteristics so things are not unfamiliar when you find yourself on the receiving end of a death notification. As an intuitive type of griever, I experience an overwhelming feeling of sadness and find it difficult to stop being tearful when I think of a LEO and the pain they were suffering before taking their life. I think of my own mortality and have trouble concentrating.

In contrast, with an instrumental pattern, I often ask a great deal of questions. I look to find ways to get involved and things I could do to honor the person who has died. Although I need to support those left behind, I have often slipped back into my shell and found immediate comfort in its silence.

There are more times than I wish to remember, as a rookie cop, when I found myself sitting with a deceased victim for hours on end waiting for the Medical Examiner to arrive. Most of us have experienced death at some point. As cops, we experience it in a very in-depth way. We see it, hear it, smell it, and feel it in ways that most never experience. This stays with us. I grew very disconnected from loss because of this hands-on experience. This habit of disconnecting helps insulate us in our work. However, it also acts as a barrier between experiencing trauma and navigating through it in a healthy way.

I once received a call in my role as a peer counselor from a man who said that he was going to kill himself. It was difficult to hear him over the sound of gusting wind on his end of the call. He told me that he was walking from his car along the pier towards the ocean so he could jump. The wind grew louder with every step he took. I remained calm in my intervention role while I tapped into my detective skills to gather information to identify his location. There were points throughout the twenty minute call where I felt progress had been made. "Thank you for listening and everything you did. But, I am going to do now what I set out to do." These were his last words to me before the line went dead.

This call occurred on the morning of my birthday. While my family was celebrating my life, I had just spoken to a man who had shared with me he wanted to end his own. I never found out what happened to him. I had assumed the worst, and believed I was the last voice he ever heard. I grieved for the loss of his life while my family was celebrating my life. After the man had disconnected our call, I called a peer to unpack what had happened. "The call was emotionally grueling. I was the one now in crisis, unable to provide myself the advice and counsel I was trained to offer others in crisis. I was deeply and emotionally involved in this stranger's struggle, and I grieved him—and the emotional distress and crisis I was unable to help him avoid.

I find meaning in being able to use this experience to help the next person I meet who needs support. It remains a privilge to be someone who others would turn to in their time of need.

My Story & Evidence-Based Practices

BARBARA RUBEL

"The friend who can be silent with us in a moment of despair or confusion, who can stay with us in an hour of grief and bereavement, who can tolerate not knowing, not curing, not healing and face with us the reality of our powerlessness, that is a friend who cares."

— Henri J.M. Nouwen

Thanatology

As a thanatologist, the first part of my career was helping those who were bereaved. The second part of my career has been providing education and information to first responders on managing non-death related loss and traumatic death experiences. Telling people that I am a thanatologist rarely goes down well. A thanatologist studies death, dying, and bereavement and ways to cope with the grief process. The typical response is, "Barbara, why do you want to work with people who are grieving?" or "What a sad job you have." I always respond the same way. I share how we all experience loss. Many of us need someone to talk to about what happened. It's not a sad job listening and providing education and information. Rather, it is a rewarding one.

I received my Bachelor of Science in Psychology and a Master's degree in Community Health with a concentration in thanatology, both from Brooklyn College. Since death is prevalent, those who are involved in the field of thanatology may hold the key to discovering and effecting comforting measures on behalf of officers (Sugimoto et al., 2021). However, some mental health professionals have little knowledge of thanatology. When an officer is struggling with grief and they reach out for help, that professional must know how to interact with, communicate, and build a connection with an officer who is grieving.

For example, police chaplains who are culturally competent step in and do an outstanding job in grief's aftermath. I was comforted by a police chaplain who came to the hospital after my father's suicide. Being on complete bedrest, I could not attend my father's funeral. The chaplain asked about my father's career as a sergeant and helped me to find meaning in his life. He made me realize how I will always be a part of a blue family, even after my father's death.

Years later, at my mother's funeral, four NYC police officers, including a policewoman, and three members of the armed forces carried my mother's casket to her gravesite. The plot was designated for officers who belonged to a police fraternal society, Shomrim, which provides burial and perpetual care services in the society's dedicated cemetery in NY. The large granite obelisk erected in 1949 was the backdrop to her casket. As I thanked each officer, I knew that although both of my parents were dead, I was still part of the blue family.

Palette of Grief® in Law Enforcement

You may describe grief as a shadow, a journey, a tidal wave, or getting hit with a ton of bricks. What you are doing is using figurative language. I'd like to give you a little background about how I coined the phrase Palette of Grief® (Parekh de Campos et al., 2022). For artists, a palette holds and blends a range of paint colors; in the domain of loss, it holds and blends grief. Palette of Grief can include a blending of grief reactions —emotional, cognitive, behavioral, physical, religious, or spiritual—after a final separation.

The concept of the Palette of Grief came to me a few weeks after my father's suicide. As I waited for my newborn triplets to wake up, I was watercolor painting and spilled a glass of water on my palette, which caused the colors to mix and change in hue and shape. I realized that grief reactions often blend, sometimes in ways that are confusing, and all over the place, just like my palette. When I speak to officers about loss, many think that there are stages of grief. It bothers me when they tell me that they are still in the bargaining stage, or have returned to the anger stage, and that they are not grieving correctly. I believe that there are no stages of grief. Rather, grief is a process that ebbs and flows throughout life.

> **LAW ENFORCEMENT CONSIDERATION & PERSONAL INSIGHT**
>
> What metaphor would you use to describe your grief?

Palette of Grief® Reactions

Common emotional, cognitive, behavioral, physical, religious and spiritual grief reactions:

- **EMOTIONAL:** angry, cynical, despair, impulsive, frustrated, guilty, irritability, sadness, self-doubt, bitterness, stigma, self-blame, loneliness, regret, overwhelmed, anxiety, worried, relief, yearning, fear, intense sorrow, shame, and emotionally shocked.
- **COGNITIVE:** trouble accepting the death, avoidance, flooded by thoughts, trouble concentrating, confused, intrusive visual images,

mental disorganization, difficulty trusting others, forgetful, attempt to make sense, and repeatedly ask, "Why?".

- **BEHAVIORAL:** carry special objects, increased substance use, diet changed, preoccupied with deceased, risk taker, seek out certain places, careless, scream in the car, alienated from friends, avoid social situations, and changed work performance.
- **PHYSICAL:** restless, oversensitivity to noise, exhaustion, sighing a lot, lack of energy, muscle weakness, frequent colds, constipation, nauseated, cold chills, hives, eye strain, grind teeth, dry mouth, lost energy.
- **RELIGIOUS AND SPIRITUAL:** search other faiths, prayer, feel their presence, see or hear the deceased, enlightened, hopeless, changed sense of purpose, rituals, continued bonds, profound coincidences, difficulty making meaning.

CASE NOTES

Ken Harker, Retired Chief of Police in Indiana, retired 22 years, notes, "Dead babies, children, family and friends, being shot at, having to fight for your life, tragic accidents with mangled bodies and burned bodies, suicides, murders, and the list goes on! It does take a toll and plays back over and over in your mind. The events we experience as Police Officers or First Responders sometimes causes us to question our feelings and emotions. We all need help from time to time. However, it's not always easy to ask for the support or assistance that we need. If asking for help is something you struggle with, you might be seeking inspiration to take the first step.

"The danger is tying your self-worth and feeling shame that you have to ask for help. One of the best things I was able to do as an Officer was to be able to talk and communicate with some of my brother officers who were my partners and shared or went through the same horrific incidents with me. I think we helped each other by listening and sharing our thoughts. If you find you can't help yourself, there's no shame in asking others for help. Sometimes, asking for help is just as heroic as giving it. Asking for help is never a sign of weakness. It's one of the bravest things you can do. And it can save your life. If you feel like you still are troubled don't be afraid to seek professional help such as a therapist. Remember that asking for help is a strength and that you deserve to get the support you need" *(K. Harker, personal communication, January 21, 2023).*

Factors that Impact the Palette of Grief

According to the International Association of Chiefs of Police (n.d.),

"There are many sources of grief and loss, in addition to death, that officers may face throughout their careers. Police may also experience a loss of their role and identity due to injuries and aging, which may lead to changes in duties and assignments, advancement, and retirement. They may experience grief in response to these career transitions as well as changes in their personal lives" (p. 1, para 2).

Being that officers are an understudied population regarding bereavement, this chapter highlights several factors that can influence their grief, such as pre-event factors, exposure, and the aftermath of a death.

Psychological Proximity

Psychological proximity refers to how dependent the bereaved person was on the deceased and on each other, and the quality and closeness of the relationship.

Anticipatory Grief

Grief is influenced by how a bereaved individual emotionally prepares for the death and how the anticipatory loss (e.g., cancer) was managed while the deceased was alive. There is no anticipatory grief for a LODD,

Unsuccessful Coping Response

Positive coping styles include reframing problems, maintaining a positive attitude, focusing on faith, humor, social support, and finding solutions through problem engagement. Avoidance coping styles include blaming others, denying the death occurred, or self-medicating.

Concurrent Stressors

* **HEALTH STRESSORS:** diabetes, mental illness

- **SELF-INDUCED STRESSORS:** need for control
- **ENVIRONMENTAL STRESSORS:** traffic congestion
- **RELATIONAL STRESSORS:** family conflicts, aging parents
- **JOB STRESSORS:** lack of family-friendly policies
- **ONLINE STRESSORS:** social media replaying the death

Stability of Life

Stability of life (e.g., secure, reliable, established) will affect the grief process. Instability can be sparked by retirement, lack of healthy relationships, financial problems, and not being physically or emotionally well.

Religion, Spirituality, and Culture

The duration of reactions is expected based on religion, spirituality, and culture, which is a shared set of beliefs, values, and practices that structure behaviors and the way people express bereavement.

Attachment

An attachment style is a pattern of behavior that stems from the way in which the bereaved bonded with their parents as a child. Over fifty years ago, John Bowlby, a psychoanalyst, described four adult attachment styles: secure, avoidant attachment, anxious attachment, and disorganized. Bowlby's research has been supported by many experts in psychiatry and traumatology.

Attachment styles influence one's relationships throughout their lifetime and how they manage loss. When present attachment bonds are severed, past traumatic attachment wounds may be triggered (Dellmann, 2018). Some research has challenged theories on attachment style and complicated grief indicating that further research is needed to better understand grief and attachment orientation. Being that infants grow into adults, their secure, avoidant, ambivalent, and disorganized attachment can be identified in relation to loss. Attachment-related patterns are:

- **SECURE ATTACHMENT:** An infant with secure attachment will be distressed if separated from a parent, but will seek comfort and be comforted once they return. As a bereaved adult who had loving parents, they are resilient and can accept loss. They can experience personal growth rather than lose a sense of who they are now. They probably have long-lasting and healthy relationships and will seek out comfort from those close to them.

- **AVOIDANT ATTACHMENT (DISMISSIVE ATTACHMENT OR ANXIOUS AVOIDANT ATTACHMENT):** An infant ignored or separated from their parent avoids them when they return. Disengaged parents could have left them home alone a lot or were only present when they were teaching them. Being ignored, the child may have had no boundaries. As an adult, they are self-sufficient, emotionally guarded, and feel that they are better off by themselves. Without emotional connection as a child, they avoid emotional conversations, do not get close to or comfort others, have difficulty forming supportive relationships, and don't let their guard down. Although they may cope well, they are likely to suppress their feelings and appear okay.

- **ANXIOUS-AMBIVALENT ATTACHMENT (PREOCCUPIED ATTACHMENT OR ANXIOUS AMBIVALENT ATTACHMENT):** An infant with an anxious-ambivalent attachment would be very upset if separated from a parent and would not want to be comforted once they return. They feel insecure as their caregivers are not consistent in their care. As adults, they may have difficulty breaking the physical bond with the deceased and handling loss. If others show them kindness in their grief, they may have difficulty receiving it. They fear being abandoned and hurt by others, are angry, and can't move on.

- **DISORGANIZED ATTACHMENT (UNRESOLVED TRAUMA):** An infant with disorganized attachment will have erratic reactions if separated from a parent. When the parent returns, the child may freeze up. If parents were abusive or angry, a child in this unpredictable environment will find it hard to adapt as an adult. When fear and trauma is unresolved, adults can continue to believe that relationships are dangerous. As an adult, although they want to have close relationships, they may avoid sharing their loss and push empathetic people away while they struggle with intense emotions, especially during a time of sorrow.

Past Experiences, Pre-Existing Trauma, and Childhood Trauma

If officers had traumatic experiences as a child, they could have higher health and well-being challenges as adults. Negative effects as a bereaved adult may possibly increase with the number of Adverse Childhood Experiences (ACEs) that they have experienced.

**LAW ENFORCEMENT CONSIDERATION
& PERSONAL INSIGHT**

What challenge did you face as you attempted to make meaning of loss?

Manner of Death

In 2020, most police officer deaths were due to the coronavirus, followed by suicide, and line of duty (Nissim et al., 2022). The manner in which a person dies can be classified into several causes: a natural death, which is ordinary and expected; an unnatural death (e.g., accident), which is unintentional and unplanned; a suicide or a homicide; and the circumstances (e.g., a crime scene). Death is undetermined if there is insufficient evidence, and the coroner cannot determine the manner of death.

Responsibility and Accountability for the Death

Distribution of responsibility for a death can include more than one person; accountability depends on who hastens the death and who is ultimately responsible. An officer told me that he was furious at a crowd who did not provide help to an individual who had died from a gunshot wound. Although the shooter was responsible for the death, the crowd was accountable.

Place of Death

Possible places can include a highway or a park and can occur in the officer's neighborhood. An officer told me that he no longer goes to a grocery store after a death occurred there. His wife gets upset when he drives out of the way to get groceries. She could not grasp why he was upset, being that he did not know the victim.

Method of Death Notification

How the bereaved individual is told of the death will impact grief. They may be alone, hear it over the radio, or are told of a death with strangers waiting in an emergency room.

Finding the Body

Predictors of bereavement severity include finding the body, especially if it is that of a child.

Traumatic Death

A traumatic death is a distressing event with a personal impact that is interpreted in such a way that it overwhelms the person. It does not have to be violent or sudden.

Violent Death

Violent deaths can occur due to suicide, being crushed or trampled, and can be caused by the intentional use of physical force hastened by human intervention. They can result from a severe blow, stabbing, explosion, or gunfire. Bereavement symptoms include insomnia, anxiety, anger, avoidance of reminders, and fear (Rheingold & Williams, 2018).

Sudden Death

The period of infirmity leading up to death is a time to prepare for death (Block, 2018). With a sudden death (e.g., fire, drug overdose, heart attack), there is no period of preparation because the death did not occur over time.

Preventable Death

A preventable death is avoidable and unnecessary, as in the case of an alcohol-related car crash, issues of blame and culpability can develop.

Multiple Losses

A factor that can predict prolonged mourning is when a person has experienced multiple losses at the same time or close together (Worden, 2018). It's also called 'bereavement overload,' which causes individuals to question whether they grieve for everyone the same, grieve for one person more than another, delay grief of one and focus only on the other, or avoid dealing with one death to cope with the other (Kastenbaum, 1969)

Untimely Death

An untimely death occurs at an inopportune time and sooner than anyone had expected.

Age of the Deceased

Although death usually happens in old age, it can occur at any point in the life span. However, when a young child dies, it is a profound loss.

Ambiguous Loss

Ambiguous loss can occur when the bereaved is uncertain whether their loved one is dead or alive, and they cannot make sense of the situation (Boss, 2012). It relates to the nature of the loss (Carolan & Wright, 2017). Two types of ambiguous loss are physical presence and psychological absence (e.g., Alzheimer's disease, traumatic brain injury, dementia) or psychological presence and physical absence (e.g., missing persons, kidnapping).

Ambiguous losses, whether death related or non-death related, can complicate the grief process (Boss, 2022). LEOs may experience ambiguous loss after spending years working on a missing person case and the lack of answers. They may have a close friend with whom they have lost contact through immigration, or are divorced, and their relationship is ruptured, but not erased.

CASE NOTES

Pauline Boss, a retired family therapist, professor emerita of family social science at the University of Minnesota, is the author of *The Myth of Closure: Ambiguous Loss in a Time of Pandemic and Change* (2022). Dr. Boss notes, "Ambiguous loss can be classified in two categories, psychological and physical. In 1973, I focused on families where fathers were so busy at work that they did not spend that much time with their children. These fathers were psychologically absent but physically present. I then focused on the wives of fighter pilots missing in action during the Vietnam War. In comparison, the fighter pilots were physically absent but psychologically present.

"Ambiguous loss is an unclear loss and makes grieving a difficult and lingering experience. I personally lived with ambiguity during the pandemic disruption as my social networks were disrupted. Sadly, many families had loved ones die from COVID, and they had no rituals of mourning. Many people are still unaccounted for from the Maui fire, and bodies or DNA evidence may never be found" *(P. Boss, personal communication, August 27, 2023).*

Grief Style (pattern)

There are intuitive and instrumental patterns of grief (Martin & Doka, 2021). Grief pattern is based on personality and culture, and not based on gender. An intuitive pattern of grief expression occurs when feelings are intensely experienced with behaviors, such as crying, shouting, and withdrawing. An instrumental griever more often expresses grief cognitively without emotional displays, uses active problem solving, expressing grief through actions. Bereaved individuals may have a blended pattern (Martin & Doka, 2021). Intuitive grievers have significantly more 'feeling' in how they process grief, while instrumental grievers prefer 'thinking' (Gamino et al., 2020).

Mental Health and Wellness Factors

Poor physical health, personality, depression, bipolar disorder, alcohol abuse, schizophrenia, obsessive-compulsive disorder, PTSD, chronic pain, intellectual disabilities, and trauma impact grief. The Substance Abuse and Mental Health Services Administration (SAMHSA) has identified eight dimensions of wellness, which are emotional, environmental, financial, intellectual, occupational, physical, social, and spiritual (Kobrin, n.d.). So, the needs of each dimension should be met in the context of loss.

Disenfranchised Grief and Perceived Support

When over 200 LEOs lost their lives to COVID-19, there were few mourning customs due to social distancing measures, and those bereaved experienced disenfranchised grief. Over 30 years ago, Ken Doka coined the phrase, "disenfranchised grief," which occurs when a person cannot openly acknowledge a death; when it is not sanctioned by society; when mourning publicly is avoided; or when they don't feel supported (Doka, 1989). After a stigmatized death, grief can be disenfranchised due to a perceived lack of social support.

CASE NOTES

Kenneth J. Doka, PhD, Senior Vice-President, The Hospice Foundation of America, and prolific author, notes, "While Law Enforcement Officers are often witnesses to both horrendous crimes and accidents—and often have a duty to notify relatives about such deaths, the impact of the death is rarely noted. In effect, their grief is disenfranchised—dismissed as 'part of their job.' Moreover, while the effects of these secondary traumas are ignored, so is the grief of the family members as such law enforcement agents cannot help but bring the trauma home—whether openly or more subtlety in their behaviors. In addition, families must cope with their own grief and anxiety, recognizing the dangers their loved ones face—again a grief disenfranchised" *(K. Doka, personal communication, November 2, 2023).*

Secondary Losses

Secondary losses (e.g., economic difficulties, changes in routines, loss of a confidant, loss of identity) are the result of a primary loss. Because lost companionship or family role are often overlooked, these secondary losses can turn out to be serious problems (Zhai et al., 2020).

Make Meaning

There is an interconnection between finding meaning in life and one's personal worldview (Vähäkangas et al., 2022). Basic assumptions about the world are changed when making meaning of a loss, which is reconstructed through self-narratives (Neimeyer, 2020). An officer who makes meaning by valuing relationships would say, "I appreciate peer support because other cops get it."

Prolonged Grief

The more factors that influence grief, the more complicated grief will become with clinically significant emotions that cause distress. Prolonged grief disorder (PGD) is an incapacitating feeling of grief, such as intense yearning, longing and sorrow, and being preoccupied with thoughts of the deceased person (American Psychiatric Association, 2021). The duration exceeds expected social, cultural, or religious norms. Studies have found higher rates of PGD in parents, spouses, and those who lost loved ones to substance overdose, homicide, suicide, or accidents (Thieleman et al., 2023; Wilson et al., 2018).

When the bereaved has difficulty adjusting to the loss and cannot accept the death, grief gets disrupted. PGD only affects 7% to 10% of the bereaved (Kakarala et al., 2020), and is more prevalent in females. Although mood disorders can co-occur with PGD, it is unlike depression. PGD symptoms are centered on the death, whereas depressive symptoms involve several areas, and are not only due to a death. Grief symptoms are sadness, yearning, intrusive thoughts related to the deceased, avoiding feelings, places, and activities that remind them of the deceased, and physiological dysregulation due to disconnectedness from interpersonal contact (Papazoglou et al., 2020).

257

Prolong Grief Disorder Symptoms

Intense symptoms include disabling yearning or longing that continues twelve months or more after the death (Prigerson et al., 2021). If at least three of eight symptoms occur to a clinically significant degree, mostly every day for at least the past month, the officer is probably experiencing PGD. The American Psychiatric Association (2021) has outlined the symptoms:

1. **IDENTITY DISRUPTION:** part of themselves has died along with the deceased.
2. **MARKED SENSE OF DISBELIEF:** cannot accept that the person is dead for a long period of time.
3. **AVOIDANCE:** over rely on suppressing painful thoughts or avoid places that remind them of the deceased.
4. **INTENSE EMOTIONAL PAIN:** permanent separation is too much to handle.
5. **DIFFICULTY MOVING ON:** unable to plan or pursue interests as future-oriented thinking is difficult without the deceased.
6. **EMOTIONAL NUMBNESS:** separated from others, difficulty focusing, unable to feel joy.
7. **LIFE IS MEANINGLESS:** life has no significance or purpose, may feel hopeless.
8. **INTENSE LONELINESS:** emotionally isolated, detached, don't talk to those who want to support them.

Unhealthy coping (e.g., drug and alcohol addiction, eating disorders) are self-destructive and problems that affect the bereaved (Sherman & Neimeyer, 2023). Based on the World Health Organization (2022) criteria, I have adapted questions to ask a bereaved LEO or their family member after 12 months have passed to see if they are struggling with PGD:

- Are they longing and persistently preoccupied with thoughts of them?
- Are they experiencing numbness or intense emotional pain?
- Are they having difficulty accepting the death?
- Has a part of themself died?
- Are they unable to experience a positive mood?
- Are they having difficulty engaging socially?

- Have they stopped doing activities?
- Has their grief exceeded expected social, cultural, or religious norms for their culture and context?
- Has the disturbance caused impairment in personal, family, social, educational, occupational, or other areas of functioning?
- Are they persistently preoccupied with the circumstances of the death?
- Have they preserved the person's belongings exactly as they were before their death?
- Are they alternating between preoccupation and avoidance of reminders of the deceased?
- Are they having problems coping?
- Are they unable to recall positive memories of the deceased?
- Are they having difficulty trusting others, and socially withdrawing?
- Is life meaningless?
- Have they increased substance use?
- Are they having increased suicidal thoughts?

Above all, when a LEO is experiencing PGD, they should be referred to a bereavement therapist.

Ways Officers Can Manage Prolonged Grief

Bereavement interventions include support groups, online support, bereavement counseling, and therapy. Bereaved individuals who pursue mental health services, whether alone or in groups, report higher levels of post-traumatic growth (Ryan & Ripley, 2021). Throughout this book, I speak directly to those who are providing support to officers and their families. Nevertheless, I know that officers also find the content valuable in their own life. If you are a bereaved officer, my hope is that this section on evidence-based practices provides some insight into finding healthy strategies to manage what you are going through.

Coping With Emotional Reactions

If your grief reactions lean to the emotional, sharing your story is one way to manage reactions by reframing the words you use to describe the situation. "I'm alone in my grief" becomes "I'm not alone; other officers are grieving too." Keep a journal to manage emotional numbness or the feeling that life has no meaning. Process your grief through a guided imagery exercise, or therapeutic writing. Keep a grief diary where you monitor your feelings, and the points in the day where grief was at its highest intensity and the related triggers to those emotions.

> **LAW ENFORCEMENT CONSIDERATION & PERSONAL INSIGHT**
>
> Do you think your peers may ignore your feelings because they can't handle your grief and fear that if they validate your feelings, you may get more emotional?

Coping with Cognitive Reactions

If grief reactions lean to the cognitive, reframe your thoughts with information and awareness. Reading about grief provides cognitive reassurance. Explore ways to manage your thoughts, especially when your mind is racing, you feel preoccupied, or confused. When given little information about the death, digesting the reality of the event is more difficult. Maybe you're hearing negative messages in your head like, "I should be getting more done" or "I should be better by now." Some thoughts—like despair and emptiness—are hard to tolerate and lead to uncomfortable feelings.

Think positively to increase the ability to manage reactions. If thinking, "My life is empty without them," then your feelings will likely reflect that thought. Separating thoughts from feelings is challenging. Reconstruct these messages into, "It's OK to feel whatever I'm feeling because there's no set-in-stone way to feel when grieving."

> **LAW ENFORCEMENT CONSIDERATION & PERSONAL INSIGHT**
>
> When you think about your loss, what life lessons have sprung from it?

Coping with Behavioral Reactions

If grief reactions lean to the behavioral, you may want to keep a special object that belonged to the person who died. Share the meaning of this object with others. Some officers may need to avoid reminders of the loss, whereas others feel comforted by trips to the cemetery. Discuss activities with a peer or police chaplain. Pursue interests and volunteer work to feel less alone. Commit an act of kindness on their birthday. Donate time to a charity. Create a memorial or a scholarship fund in their name, which can fill up time, and lead to a meaningful outcome.

LAW ENFORCEMENT CONSIDERATION & PERSONAL INSIGHT

Do you have an object that belonged to the deceased that holds special meaning to you?

Coping with Physical Reactions

If your grief reactions lean to the physical, get active, and move your body as it creates a healthy way to sort through difficult feelings. You may feel a part of yourself died with your loved one. Persistent emotional pain is not uncommon. Engaging in regular activities may seem unthinkable. To move grief physically, explore relaxation skills like meditation and breathing. Physical activities like dancing or working out at the gym can distract your mind from the loss. Consider going outside, walking, horseback riding, hiking, swimming, running, or gardening. Planting a tree can move your body and honor the memory of the deceased. Concentrate on self-soothing techniques. If you want to try yoga or find a karate class, map out the steps needed, so you can follow through on this physical activity.

LAW ENFORCEMENT CONSIDERATION & PERSONAL INSIGHT

If you feel spiritually connected to the person who died, what advice would they give you?

Coping with Religious and Spiritual Reactions

If your reactions lean to the religious or spiritual, explore a deeper connection to your beliefs and culture. If you had a healthy relationship, explore ways to continue the spiritual bond. While adjusting to a world in which they are physically gone, look at ways to make meaning of your loss. Make a monetary donation to a charity. Light a candle in their memory. Prayer, meditation, listening to uplifting music, or being near the spiritual energy of flowing water is comforting.

Wayne Dyer said, "give yourself a gift of five minutes of contemplation in awe of everything you see around you. This five-minute-a-day regimen of appreciation will help you to focus your life in awe" (BrainyQuote, n.d.). Moments of awe promote creativity, curiosity, open-mindedness, optimism, prosocial behaviors, learning, and connectedness (Thompson, 2022).

LAW ENFORCEMENT CONSIDERATION & PERSONAL INSIGHT

Make a list of five things you feel grateful for in life.

What Do Bereaved Men Want?

Traumatic deaths while on duty can emotionally impact the officer when off duty. A critical incident, a mass trauma, a dead body at a crime scene, or a LODD can bring to the surface other past death scenes. Whether they use a peer crisis hotline or speak with someone on a peer mentoring program, it is okay to say that they are not okay. The problem is that mostly women reach out for support, not men. Studies show that bereaved men:

- Don't want to hear phrases like "you seem depressed" or "you should get help."
- Use laughter as a coping mechanism, such as gallows humor to manage the pain of loss.
- Appreciate when officers struggling with grief talk about their experience and become role models.
- Prefer to get grief information online or via a hotline rather than in person.

- Hope that if they ask for grief support, they won't lose control in front of others.
- Need to find messaging about mental health in places that they hang out, such as the gym, coffee shop, a bar, house of worship, or sports club.
- Presume they can manage loss and need to identify easy steps to do on their own to cope.
- Want to know that their chief and organization are onboard with their getting bereavement support.
- Want to know that their grief due to an animal crime is a normal reaction.

A few LEOs shared their thoughts about grief:

- "Although hard for me to be exposed as grieving, a few brothers pulled me aside and shared their story and that helped."
- "I was numbing myself with scotch, which wasn't a good grief counselor. Don't use grief as an excuse. You are better that that!"
- "The Chief believes that a chain is only as strong as its weakest link. He'll think I'm breaking the chain by talking about grief."
- "I was proud of myself. No B.S. I told the group of my brothers and sisters that I was struggling with grief and thought that if I admitted it, I would be branded weak. I looked around the room, and they were positively shaking their head, like they got it, and I felt relief."

Mourning Models for Coping with Mourning

Empirically proven theories of mourning include Four Tasks of Mourning, the Dual-Process Model, Meaning Reconstruction, and Continuing Bonds Theory. A police chaplain or bereavement specialist can be of assistance when working through any of the models listed below.

Four Tasks of Mourning Model

Abnormal grief reactions occur when people are unable to complete four tasks of mourning (Worden, 2018). The first task is to *accept the reality of the loss*; the second task is to *process the pain of grief*, the third task is to *adjust to a world without the deceased*, and the fourth and final task is to *find an enduring connection with the deceased while embarking on a new life.*

The Dual-Process Model

The dual-process model focuses on oscillation to cope with grief (Stroebe & Schut, 1999, 2001, 2021). Oscillation is like an imaginary spring between the loss-oriented (LO) approach (cope with loss, e.g., relocate deceased, denial) and the restoration-oriented (RO) approach (cope with stressors secondary to loss, e.g., financial problems, take on new roles). If one type of coping is used disproportionately over the other, the bereaved can experience higher levels of distress.

Meaning Reconstruction

The bereaved revise basic assumptions about their world and reconstruct their relationship according to what has been lost (Neimeyer, 2001). Having an unclear sense of who they are without the deceased can cause identity confusion. Meaning making looks at grief as an active process through a self-narrative. Meaning reconstruction is accomplished through stories marked by loss, which aids in thinking, feeling, and acting through an account of what happened, weaving it into one's life story (Neimeyer, 2000).

Continuing Bond

The continuing bonds model looks at ways to maintain a spiritual connection with the deceased. The bond continues by including the deceased in everyday life, such as writing them a letter, or creating a ritual during the holidays (Rheingold & Williams, 2018). Continuing bonds are now looked upon as an ordinary aspect of bereavement in practically all grief models and have been integrated into numerous techniques of professional grief support (Klass & Steffen, 2018).

THE NEXT STEP

This chapter bolstered your knowledge of evidence-based interventions to help bereaved LEOs and their families. Organizations need to develop a formal department wellness policy that includes managing the grief process, and supervisors need to be in favor of it. The next chapter provides an overview of individual psychological resilience to manage organizational stress. Chapter 12 discusses ways to boost resilience through language, emotional intelligence, and coping strategies. Also, Chapter 12 explains homeostasis and self-regulation to manage a maladaptive stress response and concentrates on post-traumatic growth.

REFERENCES

American Psychiatric Association. (2021, September 23). *APA offers tips for understanding prolonged grief disorder* [Press release]. https://tinyurl.com/ycy5na5t

Block, E. (2018). Living, dying, after death: Achieving a "good" death in the time of AIDS orphan care. *Death Studies*, 42(5), 275-281. https://doi:10.1080/0748118 7.2017.1396396

Boss, P. (2012). Resilience as tolerance for ambiguity. In D. S. Becvar (Ed.), *Handbook of family resilience*, 285-297. Springer.

Boss, P. (2022). *The myth of closure: Ambiguous loss in a time of pandemic and change.* W.W. Norton & Company.

Bowlby, J. (1969). *Attachment. Attachment and loss: Vol. 1. Loss.* New York: Basic Books.

Dyer, W. (n.d.). *Brainy quote.* https://tinyurl.com/4k9wrhyz

Carolan, M., & Wright, R. J. (2017). Miscarriage at advanced maternal age and the search for meaning. *Death Studies*, 41(3), 144-153. https://doi:10.1080/074811 87.2016.1233143

Dellmann, T. (2018). Are shame and self-esteem risk factors in prolonged grief after death of a spouse? *Death Studies*, 42(6), 371-382. https://doi:10.1080/074 81187.2017.1351501

Doka, K. J. (1989). Disenfranchised grief. In K. J. Doka (Ed.), *Disenfranchised grief: Recognizing hidden sorrow* (pp. 3–11). Lexington Books.

Gamino, L. A., Sewell, K. W., Prosser-Dodds, L., & Hogan, N. S. (2020). Intuitive and instrumental grief. *OMEGA – Journal of Death and Dying*, 81(4), 532–550.

International Association of Chiefs of Police [IACP] (n.d.). *Grief and loss in law enforcement: Helping officers and agencies recover and heal guidance for agency leaders*, 1-3. https://www.theiacp.org/sites/default/files/Grief%20and%20 Loss%20Leaders_Final.pdf

Kakarala, S. E., Roberts, K. E., Rogers, M., Coats, T., Falzarano, F., Gang, J., Chilov, M., Avery J., Lacour, O., Morina, N., Spaaij, J., Nickerson, A., Schnyder, U., von Känel, R., Bryant, R. A., & Schick, M. (2020). Prolonged grief disorder among refugees in psychological treatment—Association with self-efficacy and emotion regulation. *Frontiers in Psychiatry*, 11, 526. https://doi:10.3389/ fpsyt.2020.00526

Kastenbaum, R. (1969). Death and bereavement in later life. In A. H. Kutscher (Ed.), *Death and Bereavement*, 28-54. Charles C. Thomas.

Klass, D., & Steffen, M. (Eds.). (2018). *Continuing bonds in bereavement: New directions for research and practice.* Routledge.

Kobrin, M. (n.d.). Substance Abuse and Mental Health Services Administration (SAMHSA). *Promoting wellness for better behavioral and physical health.* https://mfpcc.samhsa.gov/ENewsArticles/Article12b_2017.aspx

Martin, T. L., & Doka, K. J. (2021). Grief and bereavement in contemporary society. In The influence of gender and socialization on grieving styles. In R. A. Neimeyer, D. L. Harris, H. R. Winokuer, & G. F. Thornton (Eds.). (2021), *Grief and bereavement in contemporary society: bridging research and practice* (1st ed), 69-80. Routledge. https://doi:10.4324/9781003199762

Neimeyer, R. A. (Ed.). (2001). *Meaning reconstruction and the experience of loss.* American Psychological Association.

Neimeyer, R. A. (2020). What's new in meaning reconstruction? Advancing grief theory and practice. *Grief Matters*, 23(1), 4-9. https://search.informit.org/doi/10.3316/informit. 439384113866066

Nissim, H. S. B., Dill, J., Douglas, R., Johnson, O. & Folino, C., (2022). *The Ruderman white paper update on mental health and suicide of first responders.* https://rudermanfoundation.org/white_papers/the-ruderman-white-paper-update-on-mental-health-and-suicide-of-first-responders/

Nouwen, H. J. M. (n.d.). Henri Nouwen Society. *The friend who cares.* https://henrinouwen.org/meditations/the-friend-who-cares/

Papazoglou, K., Blumberg, D. M., Collins, P. I., Schlosser, M. D., & Bonanno, G. A. (2020). Inevitable loss and prolonged grief in police work: An unexplored topic. *Frontiers in Psychology,* 11. https://doi.org/10.3389/fpsyg.2020.01178

Parekh de Campos, A., Boysen, R., & Coyle-Saeed, S. (2022). *Loss, grief, and bereavement,* 5th ed. Elite Learning. Colibri Healthcare.

Prigerson, H. G., Kakarala, S., Gang, J., & Maciejewski, P. K. (2021). History and status of prolonged grief disorder as a psychiatric diagnosis. *Annual Review of Clinical Psychology*, 17(1), 109-126.

Rheingold, A.A., & Williams, J.L. (2018). Module-based comprehensive approach for addressing heterogeneous mental health sequelae of violent loss survivors. *Death Studies*, 42(3), 164-171. https://doi:10.1080/07481187.2017.1370798

Ryan, A. P., & Ripley, J. (2021). Factors contributing to post-traumatic growth following bereavement. *OMEGA – Journal of Death and Dying*, 0(0). https://doi.org/10.1177/00302228211051528

Sherman, A. L., & Neimeyer, R. A. (2023) Grief Impairment Scale: A biopsychosocial measure of grief-related functional impairment. *Death Studies*, 47(5), 519-530. https://doi:10.1080/07481187.2022.2113605

Stroebe, M. S., & Schut, H. (1999). The dual process model of coping with bereavement: Rationale and description. *Death Studies*, 23, 197-224.

Stroebe, M. S., & Schut, H. (2001). *Meaning making in the dual process model.* In R. Neimeyer (Ed.), Meaning reconstruction and the experience of loss, 55-73. American Psychological Association.

Stroebe, M., & Schut, H. (2021). Bereavement in times of COVID-19. *OMEGA – Journal of Death and Dying*, 82(3), 500-522. https://doi:10.1177/0030222820966928

Sugimoto, J. D., & Oltjenbruns, K. A. (2001). The environment of death and its influence on police officers in the United States. *OMEGA – Journal of Death and Dying*, 43(2), 145–155. https://doi.org/10.2190/5MXX-TY46-AYTQ-0X8W

Thieleman, K., Cacciatore, J., & Frances, A. (2023). Rates of prolonged grief disorder: Considering relationship to the person who died and cause of death. *Journal of Affective Disorders*. https://doi:10.1016/j.jad.2023.07.094

Thompson, J. (2022). Awe: Helping leaders address modern policing problems. *Journal of Community Safety and Well-Being*, 7(2), 53–58.

Vähäkangas, A., Saarelainen, S. M., & Ojalammi, J. (2022). The search for meaning in life through continuing and/or transforming the bond to a deceased spouse in late life. *Pastoral Psychology*, 71, 43-59. https://doi:10.1007/s11089-021-00979-w

Wilson, D. M., Cohen, J., MacLeod, R., & Houttekier, D. (2018). Bereavement grief: A population-based foundational evidence study. *Death Studies*, 42(7), 463-469. https://doi:10.1080/07481187.2017.1382609

Worden, J. W. (2018). *Grief counseling and grief therapy: A handbook for the mental health practitioner* (5th ed.). Springer.

World Health Organization [WHO]. (2022). *ICD-11 for mortality and morbidity statistics: 6B42 prolonged grief disorder.* https://icd.who.int/browse11/l-m/en#/http://id.who.int/icd/entity/1183832314

Zhai, Y., & Du, X. (2020). Loss and grief amidst COVID-19: A path to adaptation and resilience. *Brain, Behavior, and Immunity*, 87, 80-81. https://doi.org/10.1016/j.bbi.2020.04.053

12 | RESILIENCE AND POST-TRAUMATIC GROWTH

DEFINITIONS

PSYCHOLOGICAL RESILIENCE - the process of adapting, bouncing back, and overcoming quickly in the face of difficult challenges and sources of stress.

POST-TRAUMATIC GROWTH (PTG) - a positive change that can occur due to a struggle with a difficult life circumstance.

OBJECTIVES

After reading and considering the content of this chapter, the reader should be able to:

- Describe post-traumatic growth after a psychological struggle.
- Select eight-character strengths to build psychological resilience.

In My Experience & Lessons Learned

JASON PALAMARA

When you ask a police officer why they want to be a cop, the most common answer is, "I want to help people." That was my answer too, but there was more to it than just that for me. The job—like my time in the military—fit my personality. The structure, discipline, honor, and the selfless life of service to those that need it most—qualities that define both the military and the police department—spoke directly to me. They were a definition of the service I wanted to be to my community.

Moreover, when a LEO believes they have lost their ability to be of service to themselves, we can and should step in to help them learn how to tap into these very qualities and look inward. Reminding them why they took the test to become officers in the first place; helping them connect with the very qualities that enabled them to be an effective officer is the first step. They are living a life they have dedicated to discipline and honor, to serving those who are unable or prevented from serving themselves. We can help them understand that the structure they have created in their professional work can be parlayed into a comprehensive strategy for strengthening their own mental and emotional health.

As a rookie, I paid little to no attention to my mental and emotional health as it didn't seem to advance my focus on being the best cop that I could be. It wasn't until I nearly lost my marriage and destroyed my relationship with my children that I finally accepted the fact that a change in my perspective was needed. I decided that unless I changed and focused on my mental and emotional growth, nothing else in my life would change or grow. But it was a long road to that realization. A road that I hope to shorten for you by sharing my experiences and learnings here.

When I look back upon those experiences, I find that I began with the right attitude and perspective—somewhere along my journey, however, I lost my way and was too proud to ask for the help I needed.

It makes me laugh when I think about where I started. Just a few weeks before entering my police academy class, I was running to my local high school to climb and jump over the eight-foot fence as if I was chasing a suspect. Day after day, for weeks, I would complete my sprint in preparation for what I expected to have to do on the job. (At least this was more practical than when I believed watching the movie Top Gun would prepare me for what to expect when I joined the Navy.) Back before I had started my first day at the academy, I looked at the problem before me and decided I was deficient in certain skills, and took the steps I needed to develop the skills I believed were important for my professional success.

But as the years passed, I stopped being the owner of my struggles. I developed an attitude best described as, everything will work out once I get promoted or all of my problems will be solved once I get the transfer. This attitude, if nothing else, was consistent in failing me every time. Only when I owned the solutions to my problems did they ever resolve themselves. I started to develop more of an internal rather than an external locus of control. Once I decided that what happened in my life was not happening to me but rather was happening for me, did I find a new faith—in myself, in others, and ultimately in my return to faith in God. For a long time, I had the false belief that I was not worthy of asking for His help. It took time to understand that the person I had become is exactly who God wants to help.

And through my faith, I also found the growth I needed. I learned that I was not alone with my struggles, that it was okay to ask for help in managing them, and that only through them could I experience the kind of growth necessary to be of service to myself—mentally and emotionally, but also to others, to my fellow LEOs, and to anyone else who feels as though they have reached the end of their personal rope.

I needed to learn to accept that growth takes time. My good friend and partner, Pete Liota, told me, as a rookie detective, that when you rush you make mistakes. It is easy to become a victim to the hurried lifestyle of living blue, to become so stuck in the responsibilities and demands of the job that we end up living a reactive rather than proactive personal life. And living a proactive life means preparing for the inevitable traumas we are going to face in life, and as LEOs, on the job. Those traumas need not result only in post-traumatic stress. There is opportunity for our traumas to yield post-traumatic growth.

Post-traumatic growth for a LEO is the positive direction taken due to lessons learned from a traumatic job-related experience. This specific variety of growth makes all the difference in whether or not you allow yourself to live a healthy life. As I think back on my years as a cop with the New York City Police Department, I know that I would not be who I am today—capable of managing my mental and emotional health in a growth-oriented manner—without having had those traumatic experiences, and learning how to choose post-traumatic growth over post-traumatic stress.

Leveraging one another—our unique tribe of LEOs—is one of the most effective low-risk/high-reward strategies we can employ in our pursuit of that growth. Our shared experiences and understanding of those experiences as LEOs (e.g. coming upon a multi-vehicle accident with fatalities) is rarely understood by non-first responders. Too often this results in our not extending our trust beyond the boundaries of our LEO tribe. No different than the brotherhood or sisterhood familiar to those who are on a sports team, in a dedicated club or organization, part of single company in a branch of the military—we know and trust that our LEO tribe always has our back. While we need to continue having one another's back through retirement, we should also be open to seeking out the best possible resources. Extending our trust to those who may not be in the LEO community, but who have demonstrated a commitment to post-traumatic growth, results in broadening the pool of those we call "our tribe."

As effective as our tribe can be, we need to prepare for managing our traumas alone when we need to rely solely on ourselves for a period of time. Having a plan for how we are going to deal with a trauma builds up our level of resiliency to the trauma. Our resilience allows us to endure. It gives us time to manage the trauma, to process the trauma, to recover from the trauma—and ultimately to grow from the trauma.

One of my colleagues lost a lifelong friend, a fellow LEO and Marine Veteran, to suicide. I have always admired this colleague for his commitment to personal growth and wellness, and for nurturing a degree of emotional safety for and with his friends, family, and colleagues. It was the very preparedness that allowed him to navigate the awful tragedy of losing a friend to suicide. He decided that he wanted to share his friend's memory with those that had never met him, to keep his friend alive by continuing to honor the life he lived. That decision gave birth to a new life mission for him, and, ever since, he has been helping fellow LEOs who are suffering with personal struggles to develop their own resilience to trauma. He continues a life of living blue, serving his tribe, and using his own experiences with trauma and his emotional preparedness for traumas to teach his tribe how to be more resilient to trauma. That's post-traumatic growth.

You cannot have growth without first being prepared for it.

I remember when my partner, Kevin Lynch, and I were assigned to work the West Indian Day Parade in East New York, Brooklyn the morning after we attended a colleague's wedding. While putting on our uniforms that morning, Kevin realized he forgot his service weapon at home. Jokingly, Kevin said, "I'll just jump behind you if anything happens." We eventually reported to our post, both of us sufficiently armed (Kevin having borrowed the service weapon of a colleague going home for the day). Ducking for cover is not a smart, or long-term, strategy for life's dangers. We must prepare.

Imagine the following absurd scenario: Your sergeant assigns you to work a protest in a busy part of town on a freezing cold day in December. Once at your post, you realize that, not only do you not have your gun, you have only a pencil and pad on your belt, and somehow you are only wearing flip flops and shorts. Not exactly prepared for the possible situations you may face while on your detail. The situation is absurd for many reasons, not the least of which is because you would never allow it to happen. The idea of showing up to your detail that unprepared is too absurd for fiction, let alone a LEO. And yet, we often show up to life outside of the job as a LEO as unprepared as our absurd scenario. It's possible for us to practice extreme preparedness in our jobs, and yet show up to the rest of our life wearing flip flops when we should have laced up our boots.

Once I began extending my on-the-job preparedness to my life outside of the job, my life began to change for the better.

Preparation in my marriage, for example, took the shape of date nights scheduled without the kids around. They could be as simple as just sitting at the same table together and asking my spouse how her day was (and actually being interested in her answer). I forced myself to learn how to include her in my life often spent away from her. I stopped assuming she wasn't interested or would feel burdened with what I shared about my job. As a result, we grew more resilient together. I looked to do the same with my children, including myself in their lives with more interest and com-mitment. I stopped isolating myself alone with my traumas. And a strange thing happened—I realized that both my wife and my children were also living blue along with me. While I wasn't paying attention, they had been developing the resilience and preparedness I needed, too.

What you do to prepare today may not seem valuable until you need it. The first time you put on a pair of boots, they feel uncomfortable and stiff. Overtime, the boots adjust to each foot. The first time the front of the boot is banged or bumped, and our toes do not ache by being stubbed, we are grateful to be wearing them. After wearing the boots for the rest of the day, not stubbing your toes, you realize that you didn't need to question your purchase of them. Being prepared comes with acquiring the skills to do your job, arming yourself with knowledge that makes you ready to manage the chaos and pain. Working on resiliency prepared me for my shifts, equipped me for the challenges I faced, and helped me to manage the emotional aftermath.

In Barbara's FABULOUS Framework, she talks about the importance of identifying and understanding what our character traits are as LEOs. For example, through her framework model, I learned that my negative job experiences had been leading me to focus my attention only on my negative personality traits—and failing to admit that I had positive personality traits, too. Recognizing unhealthy behaviors is the first step in changing them. I joined the military and became a cop because of traits I had yet to fully identify or put into practice. But in time, I learned that some of my positive traits include confidence, resourcefulness, courage, and reliability. I look to remind myself of my positive traits when I feel myself growing negative. I also remind myself that what I believe to be positives can also become negative. For example, when we hit tough times, I told my wife, "I'll figure it out." Although I had confidence in my resourcefulness and was reliable for my family, I needed to know how my strengths could become my weaknesses.

Near the end of my LEO career, I made a shift towards prioritizing healing, growth, and asking for help. Although this shift should have happened sooner, I am grateful for the relationships I made while seeking out those who seemed to be on a similar path as myself. I believe it would be valuable to a new recruit if police training included learning how to discover one's inherent traits, their strengths and weaknesses, and how to best manage them while living blue and wearing the badge. That kind of preparedness would help build the resiliency needed to be successful on the job, and in life. The result would be the recruit becoming a better version of themselves by the time they trade their badge for a retired ID card.

My Story & Evidence-Based Practices

BARBARA RUBEL

"All thinking begins with wondering."
— Socrates

Individual Psychological Resilience

F ew studies focus on an officer's perceptions, personal views, and reactions to stress and trauma even though they operate in constantly changing and occasionally harsh environments (Fleischmann et al, 2018). When exposed to traumatic environments and risks, it is possible to overcome them with the help of psychological resources, known as resilience (Hendricks, et al., 2023). Psychological resilience is the ability to recover after a trauma and is the process that helps to balance negative emotions with positive ones while choosing coping strategies that enable a gradual recovery (Laura, et al., 2016). We need to stay curious as we build our psychological resilience.

Managing Organizational Stress

Police health promotion programs decrease stress. Organizations can focus on coping strategies along with lifestyle factors, such as physical exercise and hobbies (Galais, 2021). Social support, acceptance, and problem solving are effective coping strategies in officers (Kaur et al, 2013). Bureaucracy is an organizational stressor. Management can redesign work, increase flexibility, autonomy, and discretion for scheduling work, offer different shift structures with stipulated working hours, rewrite responsibilities and work routines, and increase the number of officers on duty (Acquadro Maran et al., 2022). Strategies that decrease organizational stress are quality sleep, music, nutrition, organization of the work environment, a support group, peer-to-peer support, and exercise (Papazoglou et al., 2021).

Three protective factors against burnout in officers are organizational identification, meaningful work, and organizational justice (Correia, et al., 2023). Organizational justice ensures that resources such as pay and workload are evenly distributed, decisions are made fairly, and there is respectful and honest communication about the procedural details. Organizational justice interventions focus on emotional and cognitive demands of police work, influence at work, self-care to prevent exhaustion, and predictability for preventing disengagement (Correia, et al., 2023).

Resiliency Training

If we fail to hire LEOs who are resilient, we could have physically and mentally exhausted officers who may not be able to provide safe and effective policing to the public (Reid, 2023). According to the Georgia Peace Officer Standards and Training Council (n.d.), resiliency training improves work performance and overall health and creates balanced thinking that supports enhanced creativity and improved academics and sound decision-making.

The Institute for Justice Research and Development (n.d.) maintains that resiliency training helps officers identify calming techniques to use when experiencing stressful work situations and their aftereffects. Officer resilience training teaches learned optimism, enhances an understanding of signature character strengths, shows how to use deliberate breathing, and clarifies ways to manage difficult conversations (IACP, n.d.).

For example, the NJ Resiliency Program for Law Enforcement (NJRP-LE) is a training program that encourages a positive culture for LEOs. NJRP-LE provides officers with strategies to withstand, recover, and grow from stress, trauma, and changing demands of their work (State of New Jersey, 2019). In 2019, the NJ Attorney General issued the "Officer Resiliency Directive," which is a first-in-the-nation statewide resiliency program to support LEOs in NJ.

All NJ law enforcement agencies must appoint a "Resiliency Program Officer" (RPO) trained in helping officers handle stress. They provide training in their department and serve as a confidential resource for officers. The Chief Resiliency Officer (CRO) oversees the statewide program and provides training for RPOs and ensures that officers have access to the latest resources. RPOs then provide training to officers within their law enforcement agencies (State of New Jersey, 2019).

Evidence-Based Practice Elements that Boost Resilience

Language to Boost Resilience

When my mother was retiring from the police force, she would often use phrases like, "It could be worse." My father, a sergeant, would say things like, "It is what it is." They used short-phrase, thought-terminating clichés.

A police captain whose best friend was retiring from the force jokingly said, "What doesn't kill you makes you stronger." I question how that was helping his friend. Thought-terminating clichés usually put an end to a conversation, especially a conversation about mental health. Although well-meaning, they can prevent an officer from opening up or dismiss a traumatic experience.

CASE NOTES

Dr. Trish Mahan, OTD, MS, OTR/L, CHC, CPC, ELI-MP, CDTS, registered occupational therapist, notes, "Be mindful of the language you use to express your emotions. The words and terms we use to describe our emotions are often limited to our expressive vocabulary. It can be difficult to label and discuss energies and feelings when our vocabulary bank is low in inventory. When we expand our emotional vocabulary, we learn to recognize the various states of energy associated with those labels. Release emotional clutter and intensity via expressive journaling. Become familiar with how you express yourself and then modify as desired. Consider for example, do you use catastrophic language to describe a situation or story?

"'Ughh, this traffic is such a nightmare! Today is starting out to be such a disaster! This is why I hate my job; the commute is destroying my quality of life and it is such a terrible way to start my day!' If you find yourself using this type of descriptive language often, you may feel consumed by your worst fears. The first thing to do is to recognize that you are using language that may be exacerbating the situation and contributing to heightened emotional responses that increase anxiety and stress in the body and mind. Then, take a step back and try to replace the language to reframe the situation. "The traffic is really frustrating this morning (deep breath). I will stay calm and make a conscious choice to be mindful and arrive at work with gratitude that I am ready to experience the day" *(T. Mahan, personal communication, December 27, 2023).*

No one wants to be labeled as weak, have their file flagged as they attempt to cope with emotional upheaval, or hear others talk about them in a negative way. Coping behaviors are effective when leadership is supportive and fosters a resilient work environment (Labrague, 2021). Supervisors can help them to withstand traumatic situations and bounce back by enhancing their problem-solving skills, and being supportive.

> **LAW ENFORCEMENT CONSIDERATION & PERSONAL INSIGHT**
>
> What has someone said to you that impacted your feelings of self-worth, impacting your level of resilience?

"Get over it!" Words can build psychological resilience, or they can hurt. Language helps an officer to make sense of their feelings—"I feel like I am thriving in spite of the hard times." Words that command staff, supervisors, and officers use with each other shape how they see each another, especially those who are struggling with depression—"You are adapting to all this change well and I'm proud of you."

> **LAW ENFORCEMENT CONSIDERATION & PERSONAL INSIGHT**
>
> Perhaps you want to have a conversation with someone who will keep the conversation confidential. Maybe you want someone to listen to you without judgement, allowing you to speak without interruption. What do you want?

Although officers need to model and talk about positive coping strategies around one another, they may have a particular bias against those who are struggling with mental health issues, which permits widespread use of offensive terminology (e.g., crazy, different, unhinged), which must stop.

Emotional Intelligence to Boost Resilience

Emotional Literacy

Command staff and supervisors can adopt a positive approach to well-being and engagement by looking at their teams, and promoting skill building and competence in emotional literacy and coping to increase resilience

(Tehrani, 2022). Emotional literacy is an understanding of emotions and having the skill to express feelings. Emotional literacy is to recognize and understand emotions and normal reactions to trauma and know how to deal with them, which helps officers take charge of the mental challenges of police work and to have a clear mind to make safe decisions, keep healthy relationships, and remain strong on the job (Laura, et al., 2016).

Emotional Intelligence

Where emotional literacy focuses on naming and expressing feelings, emotional intelligence (EI) is the ability to manage emotions in positive ways. EI is a set of skills that enables individuals to regulate their emotions by accurately perceiving, expressing, and managing their emotions and others' (Salovey and Mayer, 1990). Magny and Todak's (2021) reviewed police research studies on EI and found scant attention on this topic. However, one study did find a connection between an officer's EI and their job satisfaction and well-being (Brunetto et al., 2012). Four dimensions of EI are:

1. **SELF-AWARENESS:** emotional self-awareness, accurate self-assessment, self-confidence;
2. **SOCIAL AWARENESS:** empathy, service orientation, organizational awareness;
3. **SELF-MANAGEMENT:** self-control, trustworthiness, conscientiousness, adaptability, achievement drive, initiative; and
4. **RELATIONSHIP MANAGEMENT:** developing others, influence, communication, conflict management, leadership, change catalyst, building bonds, teamwork and collaboration (Goleman, 2001).

Coping Strategies to Boost Resilience

Resiliency, considered a distinct group of characteristics, is expressed by being persistent, flexibly adapting to life demands, taking remedial actions in difficult situations and being tolerant of negative emotions and failures (Ogińska-Bulik, 2015). Coping strategies are usually related to contending with a perceived threatening circumstance (Martínez ct al., 2020).

We need to understand the harmful coping strategies LEOs use to deal with their job, so better wellness programs and services can be designed to help them build resilience (Bradley, 2020). For resilience training programs to have a positive effect on a LEO's mental health, increase job satisfaction, and build resilience, they need to target positive coping skills from within the department or through peer networks, and improve a leader's ability to increase fairness (Stogner et al., 2020).

Alexander Castellanos, Police Captain, Miami Florida, notes, "I was the tactical commander for 5 years in the Miami-Dade County police department. I oversaw swat, K9, bombs, the incident management team and the rapid deployment force. As a result, I have been involved in command and control of the most critical incidents in law enforcement, including the surfside building collapse.

"I can tell you that for the frontline officers, tactical and specialized units, there is no escape from the stressors of law enforcement. Therefore, it is the responsibility of the managers in those units to be ever so vigilant and for the officers to take it upon themselves to self-invest. Our department allows for swat and K9 officers to exercise on duty!!! I cannot stress this enough. Departments must allow time for all officers to at least have 30 minutes during work hours to undertake physical activity" *(A. Castellanos, personal communication, January 18, 2023).*

Resilient officers are analytical as they investigate the problem causing their stress and find solutions using their coping strategies. They cope with low mood and anxiety in different ways, such as active help-seeking within the profession, avoidance, substance use, handling their issues outside of the workplace, or physical exercise (Beer et al., 2022). Physical exercise promotes resilience after major life stressors (Szuhany et al., 2023). Although most studies found that alcohol is a preferred stress reliever in LEOs, exercising is their main stress reliever (Ermasova et al., 2020).

Even small amounts of physical activity can reduce anxiety and improve depression symptoms (Reed, 2021). A significant reduction in anxiety, sleep issues, and impact of mental health and improvement in overall well-being was found in those who participated in a workplace physical activity program of walking 10,000 steps daily (Hallam et al., 2022). LEOs need to feel comfortable talking about their stress, their mental health status, and be aware of preventable wellness resources, healthy lifestyle choices, and coping skills (Newell et al., 2022). Ways LEOS can build resilience are:

- Choose self-care and mindfulness techniques (e.g., yoga, meditating, walking).
- Recognize ways to stay connected to their family.
- Explain how they make meaning of their career of service when faced with public persecution.
- Examine ways to put character traits into practice to gain a sense of control when subjected to injustice.
- Relate how to use emotional regulation skills, such as engaging in positive self-talk, when dealing with public persecution.
- Give examples of ways to frame trauma to manage their stress.
- Apply spiritual and religious beliefs when they feel lost.
- Use information-seeking skills to get emotionally well.

Five leading indicators of resilience are self-care, active problem-solving, positive outlook, meaning and purpose, and social support (Payne, 2019). Resiliency requires a holistic approach to wellness with a focus on an officer's body, mind, and spirit (Goerling, 2012).

CASE NOTES

Former United States Secret Service Agent Samantha Horwitz hosts A Badge of Honor Podcast with Retired NYPD Detective and firefighter John Salerno. Samantha notes, "Many guests have shared the same sentiment on healing within our police officer communities, the top brass must recognize and implement brain health initiatives within their departments. I have learned that to cope with LEO stressors, LEOs must communicate that they are stressed, feeling overwhelmed, or burnt-out to a trusted and confidential source.

"Whether it's peer support, the chaplain, their spouse, or a co-worker, they have got to let it out. Getting well and staying well is personal, not one size fits all. LEOs should explore stress reducing activities, which include non-traditional therapy like kayak fishing, equine therapy, or group programs. When it comes to our overall wellness, ultimately, it's up to us to take action and not wait for our departments to provide it" (S. Horwitz, personal communication, July 24, 2023).

Janssens (2021) did a review of the literature on resilience and found that it's mostly studied in relation to physical and mental health variables. No study has focused on resilience in relation to a LEO's professional functioning. However, a study did suggest several recommendations to improve resilience and promote wellness in Internet Crimes Against Children (ICAC) Task Forces and affiliated agencies (Mitchell et al., 2022), such as, providing more awareness for new staff working on traumatic cases around the mental health impact of the job and strategies to promote well-being; supplement standard EAPs and mental health access with information about warning signs; offer access to strategies to stay healthy (e.g., flexible work hours, exercise opportunities, family events); and prioritize wellness awareness for incoming Commanders to better support their team and promote well-being strategies.

Homeostasis

The human body self-regulates to adjust to an event. If the body cannot regulate, the balance shifts in the nervous system, which can cause a maladaptive stress response. A LEO must be in a calm, stable, healing state, a state of balance, otherwise called homeostasis. Keeping boundaries, feeling safe, eating a healthy diet, exercising, and stress management improves homeostasis. But, if that is not taking place, they may feel anxious, unable to maintain intimate relationships, or have issues with mood or addictive tendencies.

Self-Regulation to Manage Maladaptive Stress Response

Self-regulation is the ability to calm down to manage one's state of mind, physiology, and emotions in a stressful situation. To boost resilience, emotional intelligence, and decision making, attention needs to be paid to what is going on in the body. If a LEO is responding to a traumatic incident, they may automatically react, and ignore or suppress what is bubbling to the surface, or they may attempt to exert control over it by monitoring their body and getting in touch with what they are feeling.

This moment-to-moment self-awareness during a stressful event helps them maintain a sense of control as they focus on their behavior. Self-awareness is the ability to be aware of traits, thoughts, emotions, and what is going on in the body that drives behaviors, such as values and motivations, and how it impacts and influences others (Carden et al., 2021).

Chapter 3 went into detail on how the brain informs the nervous system of a threat. Unconscious biological states produce three stages of response: social engagement, fight or flight, or freeze/shutting down. Self-awareness on how these three states relate to social behavior, helps LEOs to self-regulate.

Although their heart may race and they may begin to sweat, they can self-regulate. They can focus on the intensity of their emotions and get in touch with whether the intensity is aligned with the current traumatic scene or if something else has triggered their reactions. Those who are skilled at self-regulating are inclined to act in accordance with their values, can cheer themselves when feeling down, can openly communicate, are flexible, see the good in others, and view challenges as opportunities (Hampson et al., 2016).

> **LAW ENFORCEMENT CONSIDERATION & PERSONAL INSIGHT**
>
> On a scale from 1 to 5 (1 very bad – 5 great), how would you rate your daily mood?

Using Grounding Techniques to Self-Regulate

Grounding is a way for LEOs to calm themself in the present moment by focusing on those things around them instead of their thoughts or feelings. Grounding techniques can bring their body back to homeostasis, where all their body systems are functionally well. Tightly grabbing the back of a chair, touching their keys, or clenching their fists are all grounding techniques that can distract them from emotional pain. Here's an example of a grounding technique that I used the week of September 11th. As a hospice bereavement coordinator, I held the hand of a patient who took her last breath. She was my age and had the same number of children. Her death hit me hard.

Later that day, I drove to a support group that I was facilitating. Several newly bereaved members attended. After the death of my patient and facilitating the support group, all I wanted to do was go home, curl up into a ball and eat ice cream. Instead, I headed out to teach a masters level class on health crisis intervention at Brooklyn College. During the drive home, I felt overwhelmed by thoughts of my patient, bereaved group members, and my students traumatized by the 9/11 attacks. I gripped the steering wheel and forced myself to focus on the cars, lights, and buildings around me. Without realizing it, I was grounding myself in the present—the only place I could be.

> **LAW ENFORCEMENT CONSIDERATION & PERSONAL INSIGHT**
>
> What grounding technique have you used as a distraction?

I used a mental grounding technique at a recent wellness conference. The speaker shared a traumatizing case study with gruesome details, and then asked the attendees to do a grounding technique using our five senses, called 5-4-3-2-1. I took a breath, and named five things I could see, four things I could feel, three things I could hear, two things I could smell and one thing I could taste. I noticed the stage, lectern, tables, chairs, and a few officers leaving through the back door. I felt the seat cushion, my pen, a glass, and folder. I heard sounds coming from the ballroom and focused on smell and taste. The grounding technique helped me to feel less stress and stay in the present rather than thinking of the details of the case study.

During the break, I struck up a conversation with a psychotherapist. We talked about a category game he used as a grounding technique with first responder clients. He asked them to think about songs from the 90s or TV programs that have gone off the air. I shared with him a few songs and TV programs, totally forgetting about the gruesome details of the last hour. A few days later, I was a keynote speaker. During the break, an attendee shared a horrific story. I walked into the parking lot, recalled songs from the 90s and old TV shows, and I felt grounded. Try it the next time you find yourself in a stressful situation—you'll be amazed how well it works!

Character Traits

Police culture is frequently depicted as a male-dominant environment with traditionally masculine traits like stoicism or a 'suck it up' attitude (Bullock

& Garland, 2017). Conformity to traditional masculine gender norms may deter men from seeking help. Supervisors can encourage them by mentioning how it takes strength to take a wellness class or get a checkup. Supervisors can reduce the "tough-guy" talk and focus on traits that define behavior and attitudes. Certain types of people choose law enforcement, like Jason and my parents.

My father, a sergeant, was a problem-solver and had a need for protection. My mother, a policewoman, was highly moral, and could easily take charge of a situation. Some LEOs are competitive and goal driven. Positive traits are teamwork, and empathy, while negative attributes are cynicism and suspicion. Problem solving, coping and positive thinking can boost resilience (Alonso-Tapia, 2019). Resilient officers use coping methods such as planning, self-control, social support, and careful actions (Fedorenko et al., 2020). They can bounce back or rise above a challenging experience.

Officers who have been affected by their job may describe their traits as untrusting, cynical, or suspicious. Traits can become a weakness, such as being pessimistic, self-critical, or hard-driving. Traits with a negative connotation are unkind, impatient, abrasive, quarrelsome, or selfish. During a training, I asked attendees to share character flaws of their supervisors. Attendees, not sitting with supervisors, shouted out, "blunt, stubborn, impatient, and socially awkward". I encouraged them to take a wellness course or get a checkup being that studies show that supervisor behavior impacts employee psychological well-being.

Although withdrawal, being passive-aggressive, or avoidant seem harmless at first, these behaviors can lead to self-directed violence. Clinical interventions need to be tailored and targeted to increase their service uptake and the effectiveness of treatments (Seidler et al., 2016). Promoting and finding services should be based on the traits of the officers themselves (Lane et al., 2022).

LAW ENFORCEMENT CONSIDERATION & PERSONAL INSIGHT

What character traits drew you into policing?

FABULOUS FRAMEWORK TO BUILD RESILIENCE

The FABULOUS framework for wellness in chapter 3 focuses on burn-out and in chapter 5, the framework focuses on moral injury. In contrast, the framework in chapter 12, focuses on traits that encourage a LEO to take a class on wellness, get a checkup, speak to a peer mentor, or do what they need to do to focus on their well-being. The main objective of the FABULOUS framework is to establish the eight guiding principles of resilience and the essential elements through a step-by-step approach to move towards wellness. The eight elements are:

- Flexibility to build a resilient mindset and be less rigid to adapt to work-life challenges.
- Attitude to evaluate stressors and behave positively because of being engaged and a good fit for the job.
- Boundaries to balance, monitor, and maintain limits of acceptable workplace behavior.
- United to cultivate personal and professional relationships that increase well-being.
- Laughter to maintain a sense of humor and to manage a stressful workplace.
- Optimism to think positively and realistically and to anticipate the best possible outcome.
- Understanding of job satisfaction and compassion satisfaction to gain gratification from the job.
- Self-compassion to express kindness to oneself every day, even on the worst days possible.

Character Traits:

Adaptable, Agreeable, Authentic, Boldness, Brave, Calm, Charismatic, Charming, Cheerful, Careful, Compassionate, Confident, Conscientiousness, Content, Cooperative, Creative, Curious, Daring, Dependable, Determined, Devoted, Disciplined, Driven, Eager, Efficient, Empathetic, Energetic, Extraversion, Fair, Firm, Generous, Gentle, Gratitude, Happy, Hard-working, Honesty, Honorable, Hopeful, Humble, Humorous, Idealistic, Independent, Integrity, Kind, Logical, Love, Loyal, Mature, Motivated, Open-minded, Optimistic, Organized, Outgoing, Passionate,

Patient, Perseverance, Playful, Pleasant, Practical, Principled, Proud, Punctual, Quiet, Realistic, Reflective, Relaxed, Religious, Rescuer, Resourceful, Respectful, Restrained, Self-aware, Self-regulation, Sensitive, Skillful, Social intelligence, Spiritual, Tactful, Tenacious, Tolerant, Trusting, Vitality, Warrior, Wise, Zest.

Instructions

Choose one trait from the above list. Apply that character strength for each of the eight elements. Then, indicate how you express each trait, or how you put the trait into practice.

- **FLEXIBILITY.** Example: Critical thinker. "I identified and solved a problem a victim faced by developing solutions and improving the situation."
- **ATTITUDE.** Example: Brave. "Even when others felt differently, I spoke up for what was right."
- **BOUNDARIES.** Example: Self-control. "I recognized when I was triggered by someone yelling and escalating."
- **UNITED.** Example: Collaborative. "I combined my efforts with others."
- **LAUGHTER.** Example: Zest. "I started my day with a sense of excitement."
- **OPTIMISM.** Example: Realistic. "I treated the situation as temporary and had high expectations that everything would be OK."
- **UNDERSTANDING JOB SATISFACTION.** Example: Kindness. "I offered support which made me feel good."
- **SELF-COMPASSION.** Example: Open-minded. "I noticed a negative thought about myself when I handled a situation poorly, kept a balanced view and realized others screw up, too."

I asked LEOs to share their character traits and how they put them into action. These are their responses:

- **TAKE INITIATIVE:** I know the steps I need to take.
- **REALISTIC:** I know what I can and cannot manage.
- **CONSCIENTIOUS:** I need to be honest that I am struggling with certain thoughts.
- **GOOD JUDGMENT:** I realized that I had a drinking problem and got help.

- **AWARENESS:** I have learned from my mistakes and am working on stopping myself from making them.
- **PROBLEM SOLVER:** I am coming up with ideas on developing healthy habits.
- **GRATEFUL:** I am thankful for my family.
- **SELF-COMPASSIONATE:** I focus on what I have learned from the mistakes that I have made.
- **RESPONSIBLE:** I want to be the best person that I can be around my family.
- **TAKE A PROACTIVE APPROACH:** I am headed toward a cliff and am working on changing direction.
- **CONFIDENT:** I am making the right decision.
- **APPRECIATIVE:** I have learned a lot from my supervisor and need to put what they taught me into action.
- **MOTIVATED:** I realize what is not working and will focus on what I can try.

Post-traumatic Growth

Resilience is the ability to bounce back. Post-traumatic growth (PTG) is the ability to bounce forward. PTG is to use adaptive coping strategies to manage traumatic experiences by reflecting on them and making meaning. PTG describes a positive change that occurs because of a traumatic struggle, and is the consequence of the psychological struggle that follows in its aftermath (Tedeschi & Calhoun, 2004). Tedeschi and Calhoun (1996; 2004; 2014) coined the term as enduring psychological struggle following a difficult experience, but whose functioning surpasses what was present before the trauma (Joseph, 2011).

Five domains of PTG are 1. personal strength not identified prior to the event; 2. new possibilities and a new way of life; 3. relating to others and connection to one's surroundings; 4. appreciation of life; and 5. intensifying spiritual change (Tedeschi & Calhoun, 2014).

A significant predictor of PTG is deliberate rumination; in other words, reexamining the trauma to understand the cause and meaning of it (Calhoun et al., 2000; Calhoun & Tedeschi, 2014; Zhou et al., 2015). According to PTG theory, social support helps people create narratives about their traumatic experiences, which makes them face certain difficulties and reframe them as positive experiences. (Tedeschi & Calhoun 2004). Although less significant than social support, resilience, adaptive coping behaviors age, gender, and faith are small predictors of PTG. Also, less significant, though a predictor of PTG, is gratitude (Jang & Kim, 2017).

Studies show that 50% of those who experience a trauma can experience PTG through increased compassion and enhanced relationships. After a major life crisis or trauma, an individual can experience a positive change in their life (Calhoun & Tedeschi, 2014). For example, military troops who have experienced PTG readjust to military life and show functional improvement, increasing the combat power of their unit (Tedeschi, 2011; Tsai et al., 2016). Also, LEO peer-led programs help them to achieve PTG (Donovan, 2022). Peer interactions assist with processing trauma, managing organizational stressors, increasing well-being and relational safety with peers, and encouraging disclosure that leads to PTG (Donovan, 2022).

IN MY EXPERIENCE & LESSONS LEARNED

If you have experienced post-traumatic growth, what was that like for you?

THE NEXT STEP

While coping strategies boost a LEO's resilience and grounding techniques help them to self-regulate, there comes a time in their career when they sign off for the last time. In Chapter 13, we look at ways to prepare for retirement.

REFERENCES

Alonso-Tapia, J., Rodríguez-Rey, R., Garrido- Hernansaiz, H., Ruiz, M. & Nieto, C. (2019). Coping, personality and resilience: prediction of subjective resilience from coping strategies and protective personality factors. *Behavioral Psychology* 27(3), 375–389. bit.ly/3r3CVDg

Acquadro Maran, D., Magnavita, N., & Garbarino, S. (2022). Identifying organizational stressors that could be a source of discomfort in police officers: A thematic review. *International Journal of Environmental Research and Public Health*, 19(6). https://doi:10.3390/ijerph19063720

Beer, O. W. J., Beaujolais, B., Wolf, K. G., Ibrahim, A., & Letson, M. M. (2022). How children's advocacy centers law enforcement officers cope with work-related stress. *Policing and Society*. https://doi:10.1080/10439463.2022.2127712

Bradley, Kelly D. (2020). *Promoting Positive Coping Strategies in Law Enforcement: Emerging Issues and Recommendations*. Washington, DC: Office of Community Oriented Policing Services.

Brunetto, Y., Teo, S. T. T., Shacklock, K., & Farr–Wharton, R. (2012). Emotional intelligence, job satisfaction, well-being and engagement: Explaining organisational commitment and turnover intentions in policing. *Human Resource Management Journal*, 22(4), 428–441. https://doi.org/10.1111/j.1748-8583.2012.00198.x

Bullock, K., & Garland, J. (2017). Police officers, mental (ill-) health and spoiled identity. *Criminology & Criminal Justice*, 18(2), 173–189.

Calhoun, L. G., Cann, A., Tedeschi, R. G., & McMillan, J. (2000). A correlational test of the relationship between post-traumatic growth, religion, and cognitive processing. *Journal of Traumatic Stress*, 13(3), 521–527.

Calhoun, L. G., & Tedeschi, R. G. (2014). *Handbook of post-traumatic growth*. Research and practice. Routledge.

Carden, J., Jones, R. J., & Passmore, J. (2022). Defining self-awareness in the context of adult development. *Journal of Management Education*, 46(1), 140–177.

Correia, I., Romão, Â., Almeida, A.E., & Ramo, S. (2023). Protecting police officers against burnout: Overcoming a fragmented research field. *Journal of Police and Criminal Psychology*. https://doi.org/10.1007/s11896-023-09584-4

Donovan, N. (2022). Peer support facilitates post-traumatic growth in first responders: A literature review. *Trauma*, 24(4), 277–285. https://doi:10.1177/14604086221079441

Ermasova, N., Cross, A. D., & Ermasova, E. (2020). Perceived stress and coping among law enforcement officers. *Journal of Police and Criminal Psychology*, 35, 48–63. https://tinyurl.com/3rbhr6f9

Fedorenko, O., Dotsenko, V., Okhrimenko, I., Radchenko, K., & Gorbenko, D. (2020). Coping behavior of criminal police officers at different stages of professional activity. *BRAIN*, 11(2), 124–146. http://doi:dx.doi.org/10.18662/brain/11.2/78

Fleischmann, M. H., Strode, P., Broussard, B., & Compton, M.T. (2018). Law enforcement officers' perceptions of and responses to traumatic events. *Policing and Society*, 28(2), 149–156. https://doi:10.1080/10439463.2016.1234469

Galais, P., Fragkou, D., & Katsoulas, T. A. (2021). Risk factors for stress among police officers: A systematic literature review. *WORK: A Journal of Prevention, Assessment & Rehabilitation*, 89(4), 1255–1272. https://doi:10.3233/WOR-213455

Georgia Peace Officer Standards and Training Council (n.d.). *Why resiliency training matters*. https://gapostcouncilresiliencytraining.org/home/

Goerling, R. J. (2012). Police officer resilience and community building. *ASBBS Proceedings*, 19(1), 394.

Goleman, D. (2001). Emotional intelligence: Perspectives on a theory of performance. In C. Cherniss & D. Goleman (eds.), *The emotionally intelligent workplace*. Jossey-Bass.

Hallam, K. T., Peeters, A., Gupta, A., & Bilsborough, S. (2022). Moving minds. *Current Psychology*. https://www.frontiersin.org/articles/10.3389/fpsyg.2018.02793/full

Hampson, S. E., Edmonds, G. W., Barckley, M., Goldberg, L. R., Dubanoski, J. P., & Hillier, T. A. (2016). A Big Five approach to self-regulation. *Psychology, Health & Medicine,* 1(2), 152–162.

Hendricks, R., Keilp, J.G., Lesanpezeshki, M., Muqkurtaj, R., Ellis, S.P., Galfalvy, … & Mann, J.J. (2023). Deconstructing resilience in patients at high risk for suicidal behavior. *Journal of Affective Disorders*, 323, 320–326. https://doi.org/10.1016/j.jad.2022.11.041

Institute for Justice Research and Development (n.d.). *Resiliency behind the badge*. https://tinyurl.com/bddf6ayp

International Association of Chiefs of Police (IACP) (n.d.). *Law enforcement agency and officer resilience training program*. https://www.theiacp.org/projects/law-enforcement-agency-and-officer-resilience-training-program

Jang, H., & Kim, J. S. (2017). A meta-analysis on relationship between post-traumatic growth and related variables. *Korean Journal of Counseling*, 18(5), 85–105.

Janssens, K. M. E., van der Velden, P. G., Taris, R., & Veldhoven, M.J.P.M. (2021). Resilience among police officers. *Journal of Police and Criminal Psychology*, 36, 24–40. https://doi.org/10.1007/s11896-018-9298-5

Joseph, S. (2011). *What doesn't kill us: The new psychology of post-traumatic growth.* Basic Books.

Kaur, R., Chodagiri, V. K., & Reddi, N. K. (2013). A psychological study of stress, personality, and coping in police personnel. *Indian Journal of Psychological Medicine,* 35(2). 141–147.

Labrague, L.J. (2021). Psychological resilience, coping behaviours and social support among health care workers during the COVID-19 pandemic. *Journal of Nursing Management,* 29(7), 1893–1905. https://doi.org/10.1111/jonm.13336

Lane, J., Le, M., Martin, K., Bickle, K., Campbell, E., & Ricciardelli, R. (2022). Police attitudes toward seeking professional mental health treatment. *Journal of Police and Criminal Psychology,* 37, 123–131. rebrand.ly/s8qi1gm

Laura, U., Friedhoff, S., Cochran, S., and Pandya, A. (2016). *Preparing for the unimaginable: How chiefs can safeguard officer mental health before and after mass casualty events.* Washington, DC: Office of Community Oriented Policing Services. rebrand.ly/ev3ilb8

Magny, O., & Todak, N. (2021). Emotional intelligence in policing. *Policing: An International Journal,* 44(6), 957–968. https://tinyurl.com/y9fkdvmv

Martínez, J. P., Méndez, I., Ruiz-Esteban, C., & Fernández-Sogorb, A. (2020). Profiles of burnout, coping strategies and depressive symptomatology. *Frontiers in Psychology,* 11(591), 1–7. https://doi:10.3389/fpsyg.2020.00591

Mitchell, K. J., Gewirtz-Meydan, A., O'Brien, J., & Finkelhor, D. (2022). Practices and policies around wellness: Insights from the Internet Crimes Children Task Force network. *Frontiers in Psychiatry,* 13, 1–12. https://doi.org/10.3389/fpsyt.2022.931268

Newell, C. J., Ricciardelli, R., Czarnuch, S. M., & Martin, K. (2022). Police staff and mental health. *Police Practice and Research,* 23(1), 111–124. https://doi:10.1080/15614263.2021.1979398

Ogińska-Bulik, N. (2015). The relationship between resiliency and post-traumatic growth following the death of someone close. *OMEGA – Journal of Death and Dying,* 71(3), 233–244. https://doi.org/10.1177/0030222815575502

Papazoglou, K., Kamkar, K., & Thompson, J. (2021). Law enforcement wellness. *Journal of Community Safety & Well-being,* 6(4), 168–173. https://doi.org/10.35502/jcswb.209

Payne, B. (2019). Enhancing resilience. *The Foreign Service Journal.* rebrand.ly/03mn5qc

Reed, P. (2021). U.S. Department of Health and Human Services. *Physical activity is good for the mind and the body. Health and wellbeing matter.* Health.gov https://tinyurl.com/3rskv968

Reid, E. J. (2023). The impact of pre-hire fitness scores on resilience and burnout among New Castle county patrol-level police officers. *Doctoral Dissertations and Projects*. 4170. https://digitalcommons.liberty.edu/doctoral/4170

Rubel, B. (2019). *Loss, grief, and bereavement: Helping individuals cope.* (4th ed.). SC Publishing, Western Schools.

Salovey, P., & Mayer, J. D. (1990). Emotional intelligence. *Imagination, Cognition, and Persona*, 9, 185–211. https://doi: 10.2190/DUGG-P24E-52WK-6CDG

State of New Jersey. (2019). *Attorney General Law Enforcement Directive No. 2019-1*, 1–6. https://www.nj.gov/oag/dcj/agguide/directives/ag-directive-2019-1.pdf

Szuhany, K. L., Malgaroli, M., & Bonanno, G. A. (2023). Physical activity may buffer against depression and promote resilience after major life stressors. *Mental Health and Physical Activity*, 24. https://doi.org/10.1016/j.mhpa.2023.100505

Seidler, Z. E., Dawes, A. J., Rice, S. M., Oliffe, J. L., & Dhillon H. M. (2016). The role of masculinity in men's help-seeking for depression: A systematic review. *Clinical Psychology Review*, 49, 106–118. https://doi:10.1016/j.cpr.2016.09.002

Socrates. (n.d.). *Quotefancy*. rebrand.ly/d4l35q6

Stogner, J., Miller, B.L., & McLean, K. (2020). Police stress, mental health, and resiliency during the COVID-19 pandemic. *American Journal of Criminal Justice*, 45, 718–730. https://doi.org/10.1007/s12103-020-09548-y

Tedeschi, R. G., & Calhoun L. G. (1996). The post-traumatic growth inventory: Measuring the positive legacy of trauma. *Journal of Traumatic Stress*, 9(3), 455–471.

Tedeschi, R. G., & Calhoun L. G. (2004). Post-traumatic growth: Conceptual foundations and empirical evidence. *Psychological Inquiry*, 15(1), 1–18. https://tinyurl.com/yk9rm4ya

Tedeschi, R. G. (2011). Post-traumatic growth in combat veterans. *Journal of Clinical Psychology in Medical Settings*, 18(2), 137–144.

Tehrani, N. (2022). The psychological impact of COVID-19 on police officers. *The Police Journal*, 95(1), 73–87. https://doi.org/10.1177/0032258X211039975

Tsai, J., Sippel, L. M., Mota, N., Southwick, S. M., & Pietrzak, R. H. (2016). Longitudinal course of post-traumatic growth among U.S. military veterans. *Depression and Anxiety*, 33(1), 9–18. https://doi.org/10.1002/da.22371

Zhou, X., Wu, X., & Chen, J. (2015). Longitudinal linkages between post-traumatic stress disorder and post-traumatic growth in adolescent survivors following the Wenchuan earthquake in China: a three-wave, cross-lagged study. *Psychiatry Research*, 228(1), 107–111.

13 | LIFE BEYOND LAW ENFORCEMENT

DEFINITIONS

COMPASSION SATISFACTION - internal strength that acts as a shield against compassion fatigue, increasing motivation and satisfaction from helping others.

PRE-RETIREMENT - a transitional stage of preparation before retiring that involves financial, emotional, and social wellness that establishes a healthy retirement.

OBJECTIVES

After reading and considering the content of this chapter, the reader should be able to:

- Plan for retirement with a long-term wellness strategy.
- Recognize eight elements of resilience that enhance the ability to take action to secure a healthy retirement.

In My Experience & Lessons Learned

JASON PALAMARA

My police department career began with the entire world loving us. I was a recruit during the attacks of September 11th, 2001. My first job was responding to Ground Zero. I left the job with what seemed like pure vitriol from the world expressing the exact opposite towards my tribe. I have seen the highs and the lows. What I have learned is that when we are under attack, we activate our self-preservation skills. We close our law-enforcement doors, rally the troops, and protect our own. We adopt the us versus them mindset, a preservation mindset that becomes part of our cop DNA. For a while, this mindset began to infect me as a man, husband, and father.

I closed my doors. I thought I would go it alone and would 'figure it out'. My frame of reference was confined to what I allowed in. As cops, we can relate to looking down towards our sights when firing our weapon. We lose vision of what is to the left and right of us. Until I broadened my line of sight and allowed it in, my focus stayed the same. Although frozen at the beginning of the retirement process and unsure of my first step, I figured it out.

Start where you are! Whether attending a pension seminar, reading a book on rolling over your pension to an IRA, or listening to a podcast on the subject matter, begin your forward motion with an open mind. I have learned from author and coach, John C. Maxwell, that it is okay to make a mistake as long as you are failing forward. Be intentional in learning about your options and be patient with yourself.

All day, I was sitting in my financial advisor's office, waiting for my pension counselor to call to discuss my options. What I got was five minutes that determined the rest of my life. I retired during the Covid-19 pandemic. The normal retirement procedure was virtually modified to accommodate my needs which took the human element out of the retirement process. On an emotional rollercoaster, retirement and my transition, were like experiencing the loss of a loved one.

Throughout this period, I was a peer support member for the department and volunteered as a crisis intervention counselor. At that point, I was more drawn towards the mental health of fellow cops than what I had been doing for the last almost twenty years. It is often said in the police department that you will know when it is time to retire. I began to feel it. Although I was no longer satisfied with my job and started to feel more connected to other interests, the decision to retire was a difficult one. I tried to keep a positive attitude, and I was okay with not knowing all the answers.

Once you decide to retire, there are permanent decisions you need to make. Compressed uncertainty in a short period of time is what creates stress. I surrounded myself with people who knew more than I did about finance. I was not afraid to ask questions. Asking another cop for their advice is helpful, but it is a perspective from their lived experience that will guide their advice. Everyone wants to give advice. I learned the value of keeping boundaries during this process. We are cops, not financial experts. Ask an expert! Read books about the process. Put yourself in a position of options designed around what is best for you and your family.

After years as a detective, I had confidence in my skills and ability to conduct a great investigation. I had developed one skill that was more important than any other—the ability to ask for help and realize when I needed to seek out those that were better at something than I was—financial institutions, advisors, and those that specialize in the retirement of law enforcement and the first responder community. If part of my investigation concerned fraudulent documents, I sought out an expert in that unit. If I was planning an interview of a sex offender, I would seek the advice of a detective in the Sex Crimes Unit. I was prepared for any situation if I surrounded myself with those that made me better at what I did.

As cops, we leave a job that was filled with life and death experiences; that has sacrificed our colleagues; that has seen tragedies, and seen miracles, like babies being born, lives saved, and hopes restored. I didn't have to say goodbye. I had control to continue the relationships I maintained while in uniform. Rather than losing my identity, I was rediscovering who I was before I took the oath and introduced myself to a new me. I remained connected to 'the job' as I began to connect with my new world. Meeting someone new can be intimidating, especially if it's the person staring back at you in the mirror.

As a Cold Case Homicide detective, I had the distinct privilege of confronting evil for those no longer able to speak for themselves. While writing this, I received a text message from a former colleague and friend in Cold Case, Det. Carlos Vazquez. He just finished assisting the NYPD's Regional

Fugitive Task Force in extraditing someone wanted for the homicide of a victim in a cold case that I had investigated before retiring. He shared with me that the family had asked for me, which makes me realize that I am now a part of their loss narrative. It makes me also realize that what we leave behind as we transition to civilian life can be lasting hope for others in their loss. I am touched that they remembered me.

I remember all my cold cases. September 25th is the National Day of Remembrance for Homicide Victims. It is a day to commemorate murder victims and surviving members. It is a day to remember. On this day and any other, you can take a moment to remember the value that you have provided to others in navigating their trauma. As you enter a new chapter of life, you can make meaning of what you have done as it lays the foundation for what you have yet to start. I am grateful to have had the opportunity to work in this prestigious unit alongside some amazing detectives.

Any good, long-lasting relationship takes time. It is forged through rough patches. Embrace the bumps. As author, David Meltzer often says, the pain you feel at times, should be viewed as just an indication that you haven't finished learning the lesson in front of you. Look back on your career and what you have learned from the job while being curious about what tomorrow brings. You didn't start on day one knowing everything about the profession.

You learned along the way. Remember this as you approach what you have worked hard to achieve. You can't expect to be a retirement expert on day one. Embrace this journey just like you did when you were wet behind the ears, and the leather of your duty belt hadn't yet weathered and cracked. This is how I kept my sense of humor, remembering to laugh; mostly at myself. You are once again a rookie. A Retirement Rookie™. Only this time, it comes with "time on the job" built in!

Once I decided it was time to retire, I was assigned a pension counselor who helped me make good decisions to protect my "financial" health. However, on day one, I should have been assigned a financial counselor and a behavioral/mental health counselor who would have helped me to make good decisions and protect my emotional and financial health. If it is part of the new hire process, it would not be looked at as taboo to reach out.

After I retired, I got a call from a district attorney regarding an upcoming trial about one of my cases. This made me realize how much I had missed detective work and cold case investigations. It was the most rewarding work I had ever done. The pandemic and unrest in the city in late 2020, put my office in a holding pattern regarding going out on cases and doing interviews. I began to contemplate what life looked like out of uniform for me and my family.

I received a call from my old partner and friend, Detective Steven Litwin (Ret.). Steve and some of my old colleagues from Cold Case had been assigned to the details formed following a recent verdict stemming from the trial of an officer whose arrest of a suspect had resulted in his death.

Steve told me about the protesting crowd he encountered the night before. The crowd shouted at the officers to finish their shift, go home, and kill themselves. Someone shouted their joy when hearing that an officer had recently taken their life, stating that they had laminated the article and hung it on their wall. Steve and his fellow cops stood shoulder to shoulder as the crowd yelled that they should be embarrassed for causing their families and the community damage and should look at themselves as garbage for their profession.

Steve, now retired, is a veteran detective with over forty years with the NYPD. He is an empathetic and compassionate human being. What troubled us both was that words from the crowd were an intentional effort to de-humanize officers. Although I felt helpless listening to Steve, I began to realize I could focus on those moments throughout my career that empowered me rather than focusing on the negative public perceptions of the police.

Retirement can be difficult. Although you no longer wear the uniform standing shoulder to shoulder with fellow cops, you are not out of the game. I am optimistic that if you talk about what you are going through, other cops will too. Name some of what you experience so it's not so unfamiliar to you. If you experience a stressful situation, talk about it, so the feelings don't live inside and begin to grow. Let it only own space in your head for a short time. Look at situations like these for what they are and not the entirety of our existence.

You can still make a difference in retirement. Be a listening ear to a fellow cop that may need to unpack their day. When we give, we receive. We are told to ask for help, but often don't know when we need it. Speaking to one another can assist in revealing when we need it. What I learned towards the end of my career should have been acquired on day one. I continue to serve and give back to the community that helped transform me into who I am today. In writing about my lived experience and knowledge, I hope it becomes the catalyst you need to make a change in your life and provides you with a few tools for when you get bumped off your stride.

I gave everything I had when I put on my gun belt. However, when the people closest to me needed that same attention, it was too watered down to be effective. I shielded the ones closest to me from most of what I experienced on the job. If I had included them in my world, yet still shielded them from the worst of it, it would have prevented us from feeling isolated from each another.

I want better for you, your family, and your relationships. There is no point at which progress from pain is unreachable. Trauma endured in uniform is difficult to handle. Rather than erasing it, think of it as a past that you keep close enough to foster growth but not so close that it deprives you of your future. Don't get weighed down by your experiences. Be grateful that you play a small part in the lives that touched yours while in service. Each time I look for a lesson in life, I attempt to make meaning in it, whether good or bad.

I was not married when the September 11th attacks occurred. That experience helped grow my relationship with my wife in ways we could have never imagined. I understood and appreciated how precious life was, and how quickly it could change. I found the positive during painful situations. No matter what obstacles you are facing or will face in your career and in life, develop the mindset that you can progress from it. I struggled through balancing work and home worlds. I share my story and experiences that were forged from the fire, so you might gain greater confidence.

I have made mistakes. The difference now is the kindness or self-compassion I show myself when I do. They say it is better to break up with someone in person. Well, I sent an email instead. How impersonal after a twenty-year relationship! A request for a retirement appointment thirty days before I was looking to separate from service was the procedure. "There will be no changes permitted once your name appears on the Finest Message. If you need to change anything, you will be required to complete the application withdrawal process."

That was the first response email I received. Next came, 'Give it all back'! The Discontinuance of Service form listed every item issued over my career that was to be returned prior to being allowed to retire. Forms focused on will preparation and notifying the retiree that upon their death, they were entitled to a department funeral. While I am making plans to live, post-retirement, I am also making plans surrounding my death.

Although stressful, I was excited to start a new stage of life with my family that for many years was a long-distance relationship. The last day was spent walking through NYPD Police Headquarters with my family and partners. As Evelyn and Steve accompanied my wife and I on what seemed like a reverse scavenger hunt, I returned my department issued phone, radio, shield, and ID card and was given my last gift, a new ID card that had "RETIRED" emblazoned across it. I kept tradition and placed my shield on a commemorative retirement pillow. A career laid to rest.

It was in my control to make this day one in which I would share and celebrate with those that mattered most to me. I retired on my wife's birthday. There were many special events missed throughout the years. That day was going to be the start for me to reverse that trend. Rather than that day being about me, it was about us, what we had achieved, and overcame together, and one we would celebrate together. I made the conscious decision to surround myself with my wife and those who helped me navigate my exit strategies and next steps.

Things are as good as the effort we put into them. I dove in and began to create coincidences that grew in ways I could have never imagined. My brother, Anthony, told me to prepare for a professional life post NYPD and to prepare my resume, put together my LinkedIn profile, and be intentional and strategic about utilizing it as a networking tool at least a year out. During the pandemic, while restricted at the end of my career as a detective, I explored further education and volunteerism. I studied CBT, became a crisis intervention counselor with a crisis center because of my work as peer counselor with the NYPD's Peer Support Program, and became a certified life coach, teacher, speaker, and trainer with the John C. Maxwell Team.

My friend Bob asks, "How is your heart today?" instead of, how are you today? I have learned to focus on what makes my heart happy and have found my purpose. If there was something that I could learn that would help me help someone else be happy than I hungered for it. I was intentional about maintaining an attitude of curiosity. I remained flexible, realizing when to take a break from trying to figure it all out.

Although I was unhappy for a long time, I found happiness again in helping others. My new purpose took shape. I remained optimistic by reminding myself that if I could navigate a career in law-enforcement, I would be able to do the same now in my current job helping my fellow Veterans and first responders get connected to care by those that understand our LEO culture.

I first met Barbara on LinkedIn. I read her book *But I Didn't Say Goodbye: Helping Families After a Suicide* and reached out to her with an idea to write a book together. I was a detective, and she was the daughter of two cops. My hope was to inspire one another, so we could create a wellness book for law enforcement professionals and those who support their well-being.

Barbara continues to assist me in stepping outside of my comfort zone, comfort that has been curated because of *living blue* for so many years. It was time for me to challenge what was comfortable. I'm grateful to have found someone who was willing to challenge me. However, I think I challenged her, as well. Her parents were cops over fifty years ago, and as she shared her stories, she faced her own traumas and fears.

The song *Dear Rodeo* by country music singer, Cody Johnson, focuses on thinking about one's past, attachments, the wild times, and missing it all when you leave it behind. The song reminds me of the years I spent in police work facing my own traumas and fears. My wife says that we are now cowboys and ranchers because we own a few chickens, listen to country music, attend rodeos, and like to watch bull riding. Recently, we attended the Professional Bull Riders (PBR) Series. As I watched each rider hold on to their 2,000 lb. bull, I drew parallels to my law enforcement career, which is my rodeo and the NYPD, my bull. Like the rider and bull, the job bucked me off many times. Yet, I kept getting back on, not for eight seconds, but for an entire career.

In bull riding, each rider prepares themselves before giving the sign to their team that they are ready to exit the chute, a steel structure where the bull and rider get ready to interact. The rider's team ensures that the rider is safely seated. One person puts their boot on the bull, and another grabs the rider's vest to ensure they don't fall off. As the crowd cheers, the rider attempts to hold on to the rope for eight seconds. After the riders and the bull are judged, the team dusts them off, and prepares them for their next ride.

While on the job, there were times when I tried to stay mounted, but was bucked off. I didn't always stop to acknowledge who was at my chute looking after me as I got ready to be released into the ring or those who cheered for what I had accomplished. It took years before they came back into view. Take the time to find those who have supported you and invite them back into your life.

Being retired, I have stepped out of the ring. The chute is ready for the next rider who faces their eight seconds on the bull. They need to prepare, train, and hold on tight until they decide to retire. I will always be in love with being a cop. When it is your time to retire, I hope you keep loving the reason you joined in the first place. Use the memories you have collected as you begin this new period of your life.

My Story & Evidence-Based Practices

BARBARA RUBEL

"Life is like riding a bicycle. To keep your balance, you must keep moving."

— Albert Einstein

Why Would Anyone Want to be a Cop?

Although policing is risky, demanding and unpredictable, millions of people choose to work in the police services, so there must be some appeal to the profession (Elntib et al., 2021). The top ten reasons for joining a specific law enforcement agency are 1. department or community's size; 2. benefit package; 3. pension plan; 4. starting salary; 5. being an exciting place to work; 6. professional reputation or prestige; 7. community where they lived at the time; 8. promotional or career mobility opportunities; 9. the first agency to offer them a job; and 10. the community's level of crime or call activity (Oliver, 2023).

A policing poll of 10,000 officers found that only 7% would recommend becoming a cop (Calibre Press, 2020). A study found a 45% increase in retirement rate, 5% decrease in hiring, and 18% increase in resignations in 194 departments in 2020–21 compared to the previous year, and agencies with fewer than 250 sworn personnel had the largest increase in retirement (PERF, 2021). Although perceptions of public hostility can be tempered by proactive measures to enhance organizational justice for LEOs, many are resigning or retiring early (Mourtgoa et al., 2021). Unfavorable public perceptions, low recruiting rates, defunding, and lack of mentorship have generated the rise of a police exodus (Axtell et al., 2022).

Pre-Retirement

CASE NOTES

Medina Baumgart, Psy.D., ABPP, Board Certified in Police and Public Safety Psychology, American Board of Professional Psychology, notes, "Policing is a demanding profession that takes a tremendous toll on officers. This cumulative impact does not magically resolve itself when you retire. Training your brain and body to operate under different conditions is an intentional process that takes time. As a living and breathing human being, chances are that you will experience moments of discomfort or uncertainty as you approach and settle into retirement. Many of these experiences are normal and temporary.

"Your training, coupled with your experiences, have shaped your brain and body to function from a threat-based perspective as a means of officer safety. This threat-and-protect mindset, and its accompanying behaviors, become an automatic part of your life over the course of your career. It is important to recognize that this protective stance runs counter to living well in retirement, which involves connecting with others and with a new mission and purpose" *(M. Baumgart, personal communication, May 20, 2023).*

Pre-retirement is a transitional stage of preparation before retiring that involves financial, emotional, and social wellness. Preparation is key to their smooth transition to their next stage in life. Stress is a strain on emotions, thought processes, and/or physical conditions that threatens the capability to cope with a situation (Bheemaiah & Venkataiah, 2022). LEOs are able to manage their stress when they recognize that vulnerability is tempered by resilience. Personal resilience in the pre-retirement phase is the ability to combine traits with peer support and organizational resources to retire well.

CASE NOTES

Brandon Standley, Chief of Police (Retired), Bellefontaine, Ohio Police Department, notes, "I retired as a Chief of Police in April 2023. As I reflect on my 28 years of service (last 12 as Chief), I realized a few important points regarding wellness. I would encourage each person to find their own methods of staying healthy using good eating habits, work outs, and regular medical check-ups. Back in 2020, we lost a beloved narcotics detective to an enlarged heart at just 42 years of age. He died in his sleep after working the overnight shift.

"As tragic as this loss was, it made me realize that his 'fit' appearance still didn't protect him from unexpected medical crises. By keeping a regular plan in place, this can certainly help prevent other medical issues from appearing. Retirement always seemed unreachable, but through my faith and my family, I succeeded. Financial planning is only worthwhile if you are healthy enough to enjoy it!" *(B. Standley, personal communication, July 10, 2023).*

FABULOUS Framework to Manage Retirement

Wellness is a state of being healthy, especially when it's a goal that's actively pursued (Merriam-Webster, n.d.). As noted in a previous chapter, the main objective of the FABULOUS framework for wellness is to establish eight guiding principles of resilience and the essential elements through a step-by-step approach to move towards wellness. Accordingly, what follows is an eight-part wellness framework that could jumpstart an officer's pre-retirement goals. Pre-retirement indicates the time between a decision to retire and the actual day they hand in their badge.

The FABULOUS framework incorporates research evidence and practical benefits of resilience (Rubel, 2019). The previous chapters focus on the LEO's career. In this chapter, the focus is on how the framework promotes wellness during retirement planning. Officers may have chosen law enforcement because they had a desire to help, a person close to them encouraged them, they always wanted to do it and had a calling, or they had related experience (Hilal & Litsey, 2020). Let's unpack each of the eight elements starting with flexibility.

1. Flexibility

The first element is **FLEXIBILITY**. LEOs need a flexible mindset as they disengage from work. Their mind might race as they move between tasks at work and tasks related to retirement. They might hold multiple thoughts in their mind at the same time. There is a lot to consider as they problem solve. Generally, in the pre-retirement phase, LEOs need to shift their thought patterns and focus on certain things that they may have been putting off for years. They may speak with those who have already retired, and incorporate their perspective on managing pre-retirement planning. They need an open mind as they consider the suggestions offered to them.

This is the time when they must practice thinking creatively. In a perfect world, their supervisor is normalizing conversations about well-being and helping them implement pre- and post-retirement support methods (Smith et al., 2021). As they disengage, they may have a supervisor who is not supportive. It's a toss of a coin. Not all supervisors share the dream. LEOs need to create action-oriented wellness strategies as their mindset could influence their success as they face the next chapter in life. They can:

- Expose themself to sunlight to increase serotonin while sitting at a computer.
- Incorporate grounding techniques such as counting backward from 10 to 1, deep breathing, or crossing their arms over their chest and slowly alternate tapping their fingers on their upper arms when overwhelmed.
- Splash cold water on their face and hands to reduce cortisol, a stress-causing hormone.

- Recognize where their body is holding onto stress (e.g., tingling, sweating, dry mouth, tight shoulders, upset stomach) and move their body to release endorphins.
- Try a meditation or breathwork activity after they calculate how much they need for living expenses.
- Emotionally regulate by rethinking a challenging situation they are facing in retirement (e.g., healthcare costs).
- Reframe negative self-talk about finances into a positive statement.

CASE NOTES

Karen DiRienzo, LICSW, mental health clinician, Burlington Police Department, MA, notes, "I have had the opportunity to talk with many retired officers who shared their transition to retirement. One grieved the loss of 'the hunt' for the criminal offender, one spoke of missing being part of the team, and one discussed the need to address his trauma now that he didn't have those working hours to hide behind it. The need to find a sense of purpose for their next chapter was a common thread for all of them" *(K. DiRienzo, personal communication, April 26, 2023).*

Fred Rogers said, "Often when you think you're at the end of something, you're at the beginning of something else." Officers need to evaluate all aspects of their life as they figure out what their something else looks like. During the transition, they focus on being prepared for life after law enforcement.

LAW ENFORCEMENT CONSIDERATION & PERSONAL INSIGHT

What worries you most about retirement?

I spoke with a few LEOs while gathering research for this chapter. After they retired, they became a police recruiter, cybersecurity specialist, and an expert witness. Other careers to consider where a LEO can use their skills include being a bodyguard, a loss prevention specialist, a corporate security manager, or a security guard.

After my father retired, he began his second career as a security guard at Pace University in NY. A few months later, we were on our way to Coney Island and heard a siren behind us. He pulled over and the officer walked up to his window noting that he recognized him at the light and wanted to say hello. After they talked for a few minutes, my father drove towards Nathans for a hotdog. He turned to me and slowly said, "He called me Sarge. Did you see that? He called me Sarge." The officer made his day.

While writing this book, Jason received a text message from a former colleague, who had finished assisting the NYPD's Fugitive Task Force in extraditing someone wanted for the homicide of a victim in a cold case that Jason had investigated. Jason was told that the family had asked for him. He was touched that they remembered him. Although Jason nor my father thought much about how they wanted to be remembered, it is meaningful to be remembered by those who you have worked with and those you have helped.

CASE NOTES

Mike Schentrup, Captain (Retired), Gainesville, FL, notes, "I retired in October 2021. In 12 months leading up to it, my family lost 6 people very close to us, including 3 who were about my age. My parents had just moved in with me and they were both in their mid-80s. I realized life was too short and no matter how much money I could make, it could not buy time. As a father, husband, and son, I retired. I was fortunate to be able to retire from the PD on my own terms. I had a small police training company to work on and help grow, which gave me lots of purpose, but also lots of control over my own destiny" *(M. Schentrup, personal communication, May 4, 2023).*

---

2. Attitude

The second element is **ATTITUDE**, to evaluate stressors and behave positively because of being engaged, and a good fit for the job. Fit encompasses the ability to manage the demands of the job, having the right skills for the job, and where values match the department. Winston Churchill said, "Attitude is a little thing that makes a big difference" (BrainyQuote, n.d.).

(Ginting et al., 2022). Also, there is a certain attitude in how LEOs define themselves. If you ask them about their work, most will say, "I am a police officer" rather than "My job is a police officer."

CASE NOTES

Jessica Flores, Law Enforcement Transition Specialist, founder of Next Shift, LLC, knows firsthand what it means to lose the career she thought she'd always have and the only one she ever wanted. Jessica notes, "After just 10 years in the field, where I served as a patrol officer, a detective, and lastly as a sergeant, a nagging injury to my dominant hand required surgery and ultimately ended my career. I felt robbed by being forced to 'retire' early and not being able to medically retire with any benefits, since we couldn't prove the injury was an on duty injury.

"I felt so lost and so alone, like no one understood, and sat in that pity party mindset for about two years before deciding I needed to rediscover my identity, redefine my purpose, and reignite my passions to ensure the rest of my life was the best of my life. It was my Next Shift.

"As you shift into a life of retirement, realize that you are much more than, 'just a cop.' That phrase has gotten far too many of us stuck in a mindset that not only doesn't serve us but keeps us from reaching our true potential. Your law enforcement career may be over, but your life is just beginning. You are starting over with knowledge and experience to pull from for that Next Shift in life. As you spend time with those you love, do the things you love, lean into who you are behind the badge" (*J. Flores, personal communication, July 24, 2023*).

Attitude refers to disposition about persons and places, and is significantly impacted by retirement planning. Suggestions from LEOs who have recently retired on how to keep a positive attitude are:

- "Look at the job market at least 18 months out."
- "Try a college class or corporate training course."
- "Prepare a resume. It's an essential part of a job application."
- "Consider hours: part-time or full-time."
- "Evaluate volunteering options. Consider a hotline or animal rescue."

■ "Don't do what I did. You should start day one to save for that rainy day."

■ "Include your family in the retirement process."

Attitude about Money, Workplace Spirituality, and Physical Health

While LEOs plan for retirement, they assess and address several factors which are influenced by their attitudes. Positive attitudes focus on being open to new information and willingness to identify their needs in relation to things, such as money, workplace spirituality, and physical health.

Attitude About Money

Financial counselors, specialists, and advisors often emphasize that attitude is a significant factor for saving goals and retirement planning (Kerdvimaluang et al., 2022). There are several things that create a positive attitude about money: an up-to-date budget, cutting costs, dedicated savings, having saved and invested well, and financial literacy. From the first day on the job, a LEO should set a budget and keep track of monthly expenses, and not wait until the pre-retirement phases to do so.

To create a personal finance ecosystem that influences financial well-being, it is important to focus on being in control, having financial skills, having access to financial products, and identifying one's values, culture, and choices (National Endowment for Financial Education, 2022).

CASE NOTES

Courtney B. is a veteran wife and current police wife. Courtney and her husband had years of credit card debt, car payments and student loans. She developed a plan of action and was able to live a life that was not weighed down by financial anxiety. Courtney is the owner of Heroes Financial Coaching and helps first responders and military families take control of their money and lower their financial stress through coaching and department trainings. She shares 5 top money tips for cops:

1. Don't buy the truck the day you get the job offer. It will only cause you stress when you have to make the huge monthly payment on your

income. Save up so you can afford it comfortably. Bulletproof your money.

2. Don't get into debt. Build your budget. Make a solid plan for your money, which is a tool that will do what you tell it to do. Use it to better your life.

3. Don't forget to get life insurance. Get the right amount of term life insurance to care for your loved ones. A good starting place is 10–12 times your annual income.

4. Don't sacrifice family time by picking up overtime just so you can buy more junk that you don't need. Your children will remember the times that you spent with them rather than the times that you were gone.

5. Don't overspend. Live on less than you make. Save and invest for your future so you can retire comfortably. Become the hero in your financial journey. *(Courtney, Heroes Financial Coaching, August 13, 2023).*

Attitude About Workplace Spirituality

Religion is an organized practice, and is not the same thing as spirituality, which is the ability to make meaning in life and being a part of something greater than oneself. A positive attitude is influenced by workplace spirituality, which is an inner sense of connectedness and completeness with one's job that intersect mindfulness and meaningful work (Yadav et al., 2022). Workplace spirituality focuses on the beliefs and values within the police culture. There is a relationship between workplace spirituality and gratification, which centers on duties, fellow officers, supervisors, and organizational policies, and how all of it impacts life.

Workplace spirituality is the positive energy and connection felt toward the department and their role. It comprises value congruence, emotional bonds, and being appreciated by leaders and fellow LEOs. It involves one's emotions around work and the connection to something bigger than themself.

In retirement, workplace spirituality shifts from everyday routines and working together to changed relationships with a spouse and children, new routines, and a new identity. Once retired, they can reflect on what they are most grateful for (e.g., years of service, health), and what they are able to accomplish in retirement. They can reflect on their mission and purpose.

> **LAW ENFORCEMENT CONSIDERATION & PERSONAL INSIGHT**
>
> What are you grateful for?

Attitude About Physical Health

Attitude is the way LEOs look at their physical health. Although they can suffer mentally from disorders related to depression, anxiety disorder, or substance use (Carleton et al., 2018; Haugen et al., 2017; Velazquez & Hernandez, 2019), they may also be suffering physically. Sitting in a vehicle can cause the chronic stress of discomfort and pain in the lower back and hips at the end of a shift due to wearing a handgun, radio, and handcuffs on their duty belt (Hsiao, 2023).

Chronic physical conditions can happen after years of violent encounters, assaults, or falls. A study showed that LEOs sustain injuries to their upper body, as well as soft tissue sprains, physical problems, and muscle pain (Lyons et al., 2017). For example, several incidents on the job caused my father to have severe back pain. In retirement, he suffered with deteriorating disks, and killed himself. Perhaps years of wearing a duty belt aggravated his symptoms.

3. Boundaries

The third element is **BOUNDARIES**. We first learn about this core emotional need as a child. Boundaries help a child to be disciplined and safe. Specifically, physical, emotional, mental, material, sexual, time, and spiritual limits need to be defined as a child and throughout life. If a child was not given clear and flexible boundaries, then their boundaries might not be healthy as an adult. Boundaries helped them to feel loved as a child. They gave them the ability to self soothe their nervous system, which we focused on in Chapter 2.

> **LAW ENFORCEMENT CONSIDERATION & PERSONAL INSIGHT**
>
> How healthy were your boundaries as a child?

If their emotional needs were not met as a child, it shapes how their nervous system reacts to a trauma during their shift. If they were given healthy boundaries as a child, they knew not to cross the street, touch a hot stove, or talk to strangers. If the adults in their life were consistent in helping them maintain limits, they taught them to trust that borders kept them safe. What happens when clear boundaries are not communicated? For example, what happens when a LEO lives and works in a community where neighbors ask them about ongoing cases?

Detective Sergeant Timothy J. Hoover, South Brunswick, NJ Police Department, notes, "When living and working in the town you were born and raised in, you develop strong ties with many people who inevitably become interested in your high-profile cases. It is important to set boundaries in these relationships where it is understood that confidential information on active investigations cannot be divulged" *(T.J. Hoover, personal communication, March 8, 2023).*

What happens when during the pre-retirement phase, friends take them off track from reaching their goals, which makes it difficult to protect their savings? They may not be able to pay off their mortgage because they allowed boundaries to be undermined by a relative who needed a loan. They need to pay attention to future financing, how they will pay for healthcare, save money, maintain an income stream, downsize or relocate. Here are a few suggestions from retired officers:

- "Being that you may be on the Internet scrolling through sites on retirement, cap the time you spend on these sites. Tomorrow is another day."
- "Recognize those things that can get in the way of your set financial goal. Prioritize who you will lend money to. My sister kept asking for money. It was okay while on the job. Now, I set my boundaries with her."
- "Evaluate if you can financially support your adult children. They will ask for money!"
- "Make sure you talk to your spouse about your need for private time because they may expect you to spend more time with them."

April Switala, Police Sergeant, Bloomfield Township Police Department, Michigan, mental health trainer/advocate, notes, "Most of us in law enforcement have an innate drive to fix things and make them right. When we deal with victims or survivors of trauma, we want justice for them; to help fix that horrible illogical event. This exposure could turn into our own trauma injury. Throughout your career maintain healthy boundaries. This is not selfish but a self-sustaining necessity. Always have someone you can share with and talk openly" *(A. Switala, personal communication, February 14, 2023).*

4. United

The fourth element is being **UNITED**, which means growing together or bound in close association. It is about connection and safety. Erik Erikson, known for his theory on psychological development said, "Life doesn't make any sense without interdependence. We need each other. The sooner we learn that, it is better for us all" (A Z Quotes, n.d.). Being that LEOs who hang out with friends less regularly are more likely to announce their decision to retire early, police organizations should encourage them to stay social in their personal life (AlKaabi et al., 2022).

Although a LEO may have no plans on getting sick or hurt, they may face a medical retirement and the decision to retire is made for them. They don't want to resign; don't want their employment to be terminated; don't want the gathering and a piece of cake; don't want to clean up their locker or be given a retired I.D. Yet, the end date has come. The process can be a positive experience if they have a structure that supports their well-being.

Whether forced into retirement or it is their own choice, LEOs could still feel connected to those who continue to serve. For example, retired Assistant Chief Steven Smith was forced into retirement when a drug addict shot him with a sawed off 12 gauge shot gun. Smith (2022) notes,

"There is not a day goes by that I don't miss being in the field and running calls with my guys. Sometimes, even almost 8 years later, if I see a cruiser running code, I'm heartbroken that I'm not there doing it anymore. More times than not it, still brings tears to my eyes. . . When you leave voluntarily, or in my case forced to medically retire, something that you loved so much you leave a part of yourself" (para 1–3).

Agencies need to ensure that all members of a command are familiar with the stressors associated with pre-retirement and its impact on everyone in the department. They need to provide guidance to LEOs as they figure out what life might look like once they retire. Although retired and no longer standing shoulder to shoulder with fellow LEOs, they do stand with them as retired members of the force and may always maintain that connection. That's what *living blue* is all about.

CASE NOTES

David Giroux, Deputy Chief of Police, Commander, Office of Wellness and Safety, Arlington County Virginia Police Department, notes, "Agencies dedicate a significant amount of time providing training on tactical and operational skills to keep their officers physically safe and well during their careers. They need to dedicate comparable time and resources to keeping their officers mentally safe and well during AND after their careers" *(D. Giroux, personal communication, January 3, 2023).*

---

5. Laughter

The fifth element is **LAUGHTER**. A sense of humor is associated with increased mental well-being, lower levels of loneliness, less headaches, and cognitive flexibility (Curran et al., 2021). Whether listening to a comic or funny story, many people find stand-up comedy amusing. Whether observational humor, where something funny was unplanned or self-defeating humor, where you poke fun at yourself, the most important thing is to keep a sense of humor.

Greater reliance on the use of humor as a coping mechanism among recruits in the police academy predicted a reduction in emotional distress after they graduated from the academy (Tuttle et al., 2022). Studies on humor have been largely focused on how LEOs use gallows humor to disengage from a circumstance that involves death and tragedy (Saroglou & Anciaux, 2004). Ask yourself:

- Have I thought about taking courses on fun things such as scuba diving or flying?
- Have I focused on my travel goals and going on a big adventure?
- Does the thought of mountain biking or off roading enthuse me?
- Will I try military fitness, or running a marathon?
- Would I like to rent an RV and take a cross-country trip?
- Does learning boxing or a martial art energize me?
- What games would I like to play with my children?

Laughter can reduce anxiety symptoms such as irritability, restlessness, and fatigue. Having fun is just as important as good health. Having purpose and the right amount of control to feel balanced is key to retiring well. Also, retirees often mention needing an outlet to plug into to relieve stress.

CASE NOTES

Clee Tilman, host of the podcast, Black & Blue, notes, "Throughout my 17 years in this field, preceded by three years in the army, I have witnessed both the highs and lows that come with this career. Divorce, depression, alcoholism, custody battles, and various other challenges have affected many of my colleagues. It is time we acknowledge the toll this profession can take on us mentally, spiritually, and emotionally. As a podcast host, I interview law enforcement personnel and first responders. I have gained valuable insights from retirees and those who have triumphed over their struggles.

"The most common advice I receive is the importance of having an outlet outside of the job, physical exercise, writing books, photography, or digital marketing. Having something else to look forward to, something that allows us to identify with ourselves beyond our careers, is vital. Taking care of our own well-being is not a sign of weakness, but rather a testament to our strength and commitment to serving our community" *(C. Tilman, personal communication, September 7, 2023).*

6. Optimism

The sixth element is **OPTIMISM,** which is an attitude and personality trait that influences health and ways to cope. Optimism is defined as "the generalized, relatively stable tendency to expect good outcomes across important life domains" (Scheier & Carver, 2018, p. 1082). It is also a protective factor against burnout. Optimism is linked to well-being and a longer lifespan. Optimists are significantly more successful than pessimists in aversive events and when important lifegoals are impaired.

> **LAW ENFORCEMENT CONSIDERATION & PERSONAL INSIGHT**
>
> If your department wanted to help you remain optimistic about finances by bringing in consultants to provide one-on-one financial consultations, would you want to meet with them?

Retirement impacts wellbeing as LEOs focus on financial issues, loss of social networks, psychological counseling, and seeking other interests and hobbies (Carney, 2019). They can remain optimistic if they use positive phrases. Rather than saying, "I'll never lose weight" say, "Today, I'll eat healthier." Rather than complaining about things that get in their way, they can consider ways to increase optimism. They can learn a new hobby, start a wellness podcast for first responders, become a peer mentor, or stay in touch virtually with their brother and sister officers. It comes down to their motivations. Here are a few questions that they can ask themselves:

- Do I believe that things will turn out the way I want them to in retirement?
- Although retirement is a challenge, do I feel as though I will succeed?
- Do I feel prepared to structure my own day?

Whether they are thinking about the answers, whispering them, or yelling them from the rooftop, they need to remain optimistic. These questions help those in the pre-retirement phase to remain confident that they will have enough money to live comfortably throughout retirement.

CASE NOTES

Retired Fire Lt. David Dachinger, notes, "When thinking of retirement, reach the finish line with gratitude. There are no guarantees we'll have a linear path from hire to retire. We may intend to have a 25-year career, but a career-ending physical injury, officer-involved shooting, or cumulative post-traumatic stress resulting in burnout can change everything in an instant.

"Gratitude is a powerful way to stay positive and resilient throughout the good and bad days. Start a daily gratitude practice. It only takes a few minutes. On your drive into work, verbally or mentally list 3 things you are grateful for (examples: 'I'm grateful my job has great healthcare insurance,' 'I'm grateful that Tim is my riding partner today,' 'I'm grateful I get to drive a badass Cruiser or Fire Engine or Ambulance.' Don't end your career being bitter and complaining, strive to be part of the solution and not the problem" *(D. Dachinger, personal communication, March 24, 2023).*

7. Understanding Job/Retirement Satisfaction

The seventh element is **UNDERSTANDING JOB/RETIREMENT SATISFACTION.** Job satisfaction is the level to which LEOs like their career. It refers to a subjective evaluation that they make of their role as a whole or with respect to motivating factors. These factors are compensation, competitive pay, recognition, quality of supervision, workplace relationships, fair treatment, and incentives (Ali & Anwar, 2021). Factors that affect job satisfaction are career opportunities, job influence, teamwork, and job challenge (Riyadi, 2020). Employees are likely to stay in organizations where their capabilities, contributions, and efforts are appreciated (Febrianti & Se, 2020).

Although rewards and incentives can motivate a LEO to stay in their job, satisfaction needs to be viewed through the lens of social context, such as organizational values, culture, leadership, management, and department influence (Anwar & Shukur, 2015). LEOs experience a positive emotional state when they accomplish their goals and feel respected by other officers. They need to have trust in leadership and be satisfied with their union/police fraternal organization. Job satisfaction is also influenced by positive interactions with the public.

Understanding Retirement Satisfaction

Retirement satisfaction is the level of satisfaction and how happy a retiree feels at a certain stage of life due to physical and mental conditions and economic status (Honarvar et al, 2022). Retirement satisfaction influences life satisfaction, and this effect lasts for a long time (Gorry et al, 2018). Leaders and police unions need to educate officers on their benefits at the police academy, and throughout their career. On day one, their agency should educate them about having disability insurance or a second retirement fund. LEOs should talk about their benefits with their family while they are still employed.

CASE NOTES

Mike Roche, retired law enforcement officer and U.S. Secret Service agent, author of *The Blue Monster*, husband and father, notes, "We receive a considerable amount of our identity from our occupation. In the insular world of law enforcement, we develop few relationships outside our profession. It is imperative as you approach retirement and lose that identity that you identify folks that you can establish common bonds and have areas of mutual interests such as fishing, golfing, cooking, or whatever interests you would like to pursue.

"The essential element is that hopefully as you cross the finish line, your family is there to greet and support you. They will be the ones that judge you for what you have done for them over the previous twenty or thirty years. The camaraderie of the profession will dissipate quickly after retirement. The phone calls will decrease, and your former colleagues will often be too busy to keep up. I have witnessed this over and over as an observer of retirees and sadly watched as many found companionship with vices not conducive to good health. Limit your time sucking social media and maintain fitness and nutrition to ward off the toxic effects of a career of stress. Life is fragile. Embrace each day" *(M. Roche, personal communication, January 12, 2023).*

8. Self-Compassion

The eighth element is **SELF-COMPASSION**. Kristen Neff defined self-compassion as an interactive system of ways to turn compassion inward. Elements of self-compassion are being kind and understanding, rather than judgmental or critical, to be a part of common humanity that makes mistakes, to connect with others in failure rather than isolating through suffering, and mindfulness, to keep the experience in perspective with a balanced view, and don't ignore or exaggerate what happened (Neff, 2011).

Salary, living near family and friends, health benefits, community support of police, commuting distance, and specialty assignment opportunities might have been the factors that an officer considered when they applied to their agency (Police1 Staff, 2023). As they struggled with making the right decisions, they showed themselves compassion. As they enter the pre-retirement phase, a LEO's focus shifts to the future. For example, they may be upset that they do not have enough money to retire well. LEOs may have failed at saving as much money as they had hoped. Many LEOs who did not focus on finances on day one are in the same boat and need to continue to show themselves compassion.

CASE NOTES

Jeff Ladieu, retired Captain, NH State Police, Business Development Manager, Off Duty Management, notes, "In looking at the stressors embedded into the law enforcement profession, the weight bearing struggles, at times, can become excruciating. From the constant exposure to carnage and grief, to family outings and children's birthday parties, the endless back and forth of these worlds incites invisible scars and mental anguish. The suffering and battle-hardened wounds never fully heal yet linger with those not willing to accept.

"As the radical stigma runs deep through the veins of our brothers and sisters, we still need to have a strong voice echoed through our precincts... When drowning in the murky waters of the political abyss, find the sun and swim towards it. When feeling lost, don't waste time with the obscure nature of grid north, or the political pulls of magnetic north, sight-in on your true north as this direction will always bring you home.

"Retirement is another chapter turned in the pages of this profession. We still need to maintain and manage these demons that surface time and time again... This is the norm, balance, and price one pays for their selfless service and honor to the public, but having known all the lives saved and communities we've touched makes it all worth it. Always remember those that have served, those that have fallen, and those yet to be... God bless" *(J. Ladieu, personal communication, March 13, 2023).*

In summary, the FABULOUS framework for wellness, which incorporates research evidence and practical benefits of resilience, can be applied throughout one's law enforcement career, and well into retirement.

CASE NOTES

Dr. Travis Yates, Chief Executive Officer, author of *The Courageous Police Leader: A Survival Guide for Combating Cowards, Chaos, and Lies,* notes, "Leaders must offer support for the difficult job that their law enforcement personnel are tasked with. Stress should never be higher on the inside of the profession than the outside and that is predominantly what we are seeing. If leaders aren't careful, they will use training, programs, and wellness units as an excuse to not actually practice the very tasks required to provide a supportive and well-rounded environment for their personnel. Talk is cheap and it's time to start doing. Leaders need to treat their officers like athletes and not just care about their mental and physical condition at the beginning of their career, but take the necessary steps throughout that ensure that cops leave the profession just as healthy as when they entered it" *(T. Yates, personal communication, October 1, 2023).*

A Note from the Authors

Thank you for reading all the way to the end. We are grateful that you took the time to read *Living Blue* and hope that you found the chapters valuable. We offered you education and information. Being that we are not healthcare providers, we recommend that you consult your primary care physician for specific conditions. We hope that you now understand the issues facing LEOs and their families, and link practice to science. If you are interested in having us speak to your group, details are on "About the Author" pages.

REFERENCES

Ali, B. J., & Anwar, G. (2021). An empirical study of employees' motivation and its influence job satisfaction. *International Journal of Engineering, Business and Management*, 5(2), 21–30. https://doi.org/10.22161/ijebm.5.2.3

AlKaabi, F. A. M., & Davies, A. (2022). Future-proofing organizational knowledge management and human resourcing: Identifying early retirement predictors in a modern police force. *Policing: A Journal of Policy and Practice*, 16 (4). https://doi.org/10.1093/police/paac005

Anwar, G., & Shukur, I. (2015). The impact of training and development on job satisfaction: a case study of private banks in Erbil. *International Journal of Social Sciences and Educational Studies*, 2(1), 65-72. https://www.research-gate.net/profile/Ahmet-Demir-19/publication/314712257_Optimizing_Human_Resources_Capacity_and_Performance_of_Newroz_Telecom_Company_by_Proposing_Queuing_Theory/links/58c4e80aa6fdcce648e51467/Optimizing-Human-Resources-Capacity-and-Performance-of-Newroz-Telecom-Company-by-Proposing-Queuing-Theory.pdfX

Axtell, K., Llamas, J., Llamas, M., & Roma, A. (2022). The anatomy of a crisis: Law enforcement leaders' perspective on police enforcement. *The Scholarship Without Borders Journal*, 1(2). https://doi:https://doi.org/10.57229/2834–2267.1011

Bheemaiah, P., & Venkataiah, P. (2022). A theoretical framework of stress management—contemporary approaches, models and theories. *International Journal of Advanced Research in Engineering and Technology* (IJARET) 13(1), 11–20. https://doi.org/10.17605/OSF.IO/94NMF

Calibre Press. *10,000 officers respond to policing poll: Only 7% would recommend becoming a cop. Police1 by Lexipol*. The Calibre Column. (June 30, 2020). https://www.police1.com/police-jobs-and-careers/articles/10000-officers-respond-to-policing-poll-only-7-would-recommend-becoming-a-cop-Ee-749RbuTcMG7bm5/

Carleton, R. N., Afifi, T. O., Turner, S., Taillieu, T., Duranceau, S., LeBouthillier, D. M., Sareen, J, Ricciardelli, R., MacPhee, R. S., Groll, D., Hozempa, K., Brunet, A., Weekes, J. R., Griffiths, C. T., Abrams, K. J., Jones, N. A., Beshai, S., Cramm, H. A., Dobson, K. S., … Asmundson, G. (2018). Mental disorder symptoms among public safety personnel in Canada. *The Canadian Journal of Psychiatry*, 63(1), 54–64.

Carney, C., Bates, L., & Sargeant, E. (2021). Exploring the impact of retirement on police officers wellbeing. *Police Practice and Research*, 22(1), 257–273. https://doi:10.1080/15614263.2019.1658584

Churchill, W. (n.d.). *BrainyQuote*. https://www.brainyquote.com/quotes/winston_churchill_104164

Curran, T., Janovec, A., & Olsen, K. (2021). Making others laugh is the best medicine: Humor orientation, health outcomes, and the moderating role of

cognitive flexibility. *Health Communication*, 36(4), 468–475. https://doi:10.108
0/10410236.2019.1700438

Einstein, A. (n.d.) https://www.goodreads.com/quotes/29213-life-is-like-riding-a-
bicycle-to-keep-your-balance

Elntib, S., & Milincic, D. (2021). Motivations for becoming a police officer: A
global snapshot. *Journal of Police and Criminal Psychology*, 36, 211–219.
https://doi.org/10.1007/s11896-020-09396-w

Erikson, E. (n.d.). *A Z Quotes*. https://www.azquotes.com/quote/90641

Febrianti, N.T., & Suharto, S., & Wachyudi, W. (2020). The effect of career development and motivation on employee performance through job satisfaction
in Pt Jabar Jaya Perkasa. *International Journal of Business and Social Science
Research*, 1(2), 1–12. https://doi.org/10.47742/ijbssr.v1n2p3

Ginting, S., Hartijasti, Y., & Rosnani, T. (2022). Analysis of the mediation role of
career adaptability in the effect of retirement planning for attitude formation of retirement in credit union employees West Kalimantan. *International
Journal of Social Science Research and Review* 5(4). https://doi:https://doi.
org/10.47814/ijssrr.v5i4.249

Gorry, A., Gorry, D., Slavov, S. N. (2018). Does retirement improve health and
life satisfaction? *Health Economics*, 27(12), 2067-2086. https://doi:10.1002/
hec.3821

Haugen, P. T., McCrillis, A. M., Smid, G. E., & Nijdam, M. J. (2017). Mental health
stigma and barriers to mental health care for first responders: a systematic
review and meta-analysis. *Journal of Psychiatric Research*, 94, 218–229.

Hilal, S., & Litsey, B. (2020). Reducing police turnover: Recommendations for the
law enforcement agency. *International Journal of Police Science & Management*,
22(1), 73–83. https://doi.org/10.1177/1461355719882443

Honarvar, M., Rasouli, J., & Amirzadeh-Iranagh. J. (2022). Predictors of retirement
satisfaction in the older adults of Urmia: a cross-sectional study. *BioMed Central Geriatric*, 22(1), 557. https://doi: 10.1186/s12877-022-03259-1

Hsiao, H. (2023). Assessment of challenges in patrol vehicles and with equipment
among law enforcement officers. *Applied Ergonomics*, 108, 103946. https://doi.
org/10.1016/j.apergo.2022.103946

Kerdvimaluang, N., & Banjongprasert, J. (2022). An investigation of financial
attitudes and subjective norms influencing retirement planning. *The EUrASE-
ANs: Journal on Global Socio-Economic Dynamics*, 1(32), 67–76. https://doi.
org/10.35678/2539-5645.1(32).2022.67-76

Lyons, K., Radburn, C., Orr, R., & Pope, R. (2017). A profile of injuries sus-
tained by law enforcement officers: A critical review. *International Journal of
Environmental Research and Public Health*, 14(2), 142. https://doi:10.3390/
ijerph14020142

Meltzer, D. (2023). https://dmeltzer.com.

Mourtgoa, S. M., & Nix, A. J. (2021). Elevated police turnover following the summer of George Floyd protests: A synthetic control study. *Criminology and Public Policy*, 21(1). https://doi.org/10.1111/1745-9133.12556

National Endowment for Financial Education (2022). *The personal finance ecosystem*. https://www.nefe.org/initiatives/ecosystem/financial-well-being.aspx

Neff, K. (2011). *Self-Compassion: The proven power of being kind to yourself*. William Morrow.

Oliver, P. (2023). Law enforcement recruitment, why it matters, and key management decisions, Part Two. *History and Government Faculty Publications*. 373. https://digitalcommons.cedarville.edu/history_and_government_publications/373

Police Executive Research Forum [PERF] (2021). PERF special report. *Survey on police workforce trends*. https://www.policeforum.org/workforcesurveyjune2021

Police1 Staff (2023). Using the survey data to improve recruitment, retention and morale at your agency, *What cops want in 2023*, 25–34.

Rubel, B. (2019). *Loss, grief, and bereavement: Helping individuals cope*. (4th ed.). SC Publishing, Western Schools.

Riyadi, S. (2020). The influence of leadership style, individual characteristics and organisational climate on work motivation, job satisfaction and performance. *International Journal of Innovation, Creativity and Change*, 13(7), 662–677.

Rogers, F. (n.d.). https://quotefancy.com/quote/807392/Fred-Rogers-Often-when-you-think-you-re-at-the-end-of-something-you-re-at-the-beginning

Saroglou, V. & Anciaux, L. (2004) Liking sick humor: coping styles and religion as predictors. *Humor-International Journal of Humor Research* 17(3), 257–277.

Scheier, M. F., & Carver, C. S. (2018). Dispositional optimism and physical health: A long look back, a quick look forward. *American Psychologist*, 73(9) 1082–1094. https://doi:10.1037/amp0000384

Smith, E., Dean, G., & Holmes, L. (2021). Supporting the mental health and well-being of first responders from career to retirement: A scoping review. *Prehospital and Disaster Medicine*, 36(4), 475–480. https://doi:10.1017/S1049023X21000431

Smith, S. (2022). What happens when your career is over? December 19, 2022. *Responder Health*. https://responderhealth.com/blog/f/what-happen-when-your-career-is-over

Tuttle, B. M., Merten, M. J., Gardner, B., Bishop, A. J., & Croff, J. M. (2022). Emotional distress among police academy recruits: Humor and coping. *The Police Journal*, 95(3), 492–507. https://doi.org/10.1177/0032258X211018494

Velazquez, E., & Hernandez, M. (2019). Effects of police officer exposure to traumatic experiences and recognizing the stigma associated with police officer mental health. *Policing: An International Journal*, 42(4), 711–724.

Wellness (n.d.). https://www.merriam-webster.com/dictionary/wellness

Yadav, S., Tiwari, T., & Yadav, A. K., Dubey, N., Mishra, L. K., Singh, A. L., & Kapoor, P. (2022). Role of workplace spirituality, empathic concern and organizational politics in employee wellbeing: a study on police personnel. *Frontiers in Psychology*, 13, 881675. https://doi:10.3389/fpsyg.2022.881675

ABOUT THE AUTHORS

Jason Palamara, a Navy Veteran, began his career of public service in 1997 when he joined the U. S. Navy. Jason served in Operation Noble Anvil, Southern Watch, and Allied Force aboard the USS Theodore Roosevelt earning the Armed Forces Expeditionary Medal, Armed Forces Service Medal, Navy Meritorious Unit Commendation, Navy Sea Service Ribbon, and Navy Unit Commendation.

After leaving the Navy, Jason joined the NYPD two months before the attacks of 9/11. He, along with the rest of his recruit class, responded to Ground Zero as their first assigned job. Jason started his career as a uniformed patrol cop earning both the Cop of The Month and Cop of the Year awards, then moved on to multiple plain clothes units, and the 84th Precinct Detective Squad where he was promoted to detective. In 2015, Jason was assigned to the Cold Case Homicide Squad where he earned The Distinguished Law Enforcement Hero of The Year award for the identification, apprehension, and indictments of two separate serial killers within twelve months closing two cold cases both over a decade old.

He retired after twenty years of service with the NYPD. Towards the later part of his career, Jason was a peer support counselor with the NYPD's Peer Support Team. He serves as a volunteer crisis intervention counselor and is a John C. Maxwell certified life coach, speaker, and trainer. Jason is also the Director of Veteran & First Responder Engagement for a behavioral healthcare company. Jason is the co-founder of *Living Blue* Apparel, whose mission is to connect and support heroes and those that live alongside them through their apparel. Visit their website at: livingblueapparel.com. Jason is a son, brother, husband, and the father of three children who have all lived blue alongside him.

If you would like to have Jason as your speaker or for training, visit the "contact" page on his website: jasonpalamara.org.

Barbara Rubel, MA, BCETS, DAAETS is a nationally recognized keynote speaker who motivates audiences to create wellness in their life through a vicarious trauma-informed approach. Barbara has presented to over 1,000 organizations since 1991. She is a leading authority and award-winning author on managing burnout, secondary traumatic stress, compassion fatigue, and vicarious trauma.

Utilizing a variety of theory and practice, Barbara educates first responders about ways to cope when exposed to traumatic loss. Her father was a sergeant and her mother was a police officer in Brooklyn, New York. Three weeks prior to Barbara giving birth to triplets, her father, died by suicide. Her story was featured in the Emmy award winning documentary, *Fatal Mistakes, Families Shattered by Suicide* narrated by Mariette Hartley.

As a Board-Certified Expert in Traumatic Stress and Diplomate with the American Academy of Experts in Traumatic Stress, Barbara gives audiences practical wellness strategies to manage moral injury and empathic distress fatigue. She received a Bachelor of Science in psychology and a Master of Arts degree in community health, with a concentration in thanatology, both from Brooklyn College. Thanatology is a multi-disciplinary field dedicated to understanding grief and bereavement.

Barbara is the author of, *But I Didn't Say Goodbye: Helping Families After a Suicide (3ed)*. (2020). She wrote four editions of the 30-hour CE course, *Loss, Grief, and Bereavement: Helping Individuals Cope (4ed)*, Elite, and is the reviewer for the 5th edition. Barbara wrote the CE course, *COVID-19 Loss, Grief, and Bereavement* (2020) and co-authored the Department of Justice, Office for Victims of Crime (OVCTTAC) Training Curriculum, *Compassion Fatigue*. She is a contributing writer to *Thin Threads*; *Fresh Grief*; *Coaching for Results*; and *Keys to a Good Life*. You have seen her work in Newsweek, Good Housekeeping, Family Circle, Health, Shape, FOX Business, and TODAY.

Reach out to Barbara at <u>barbararubel.com</u>

www.ingramcontent.com/pod-product-compliance
Lightning Source LLC
Chambersburg PA
CBHW031139020426
42333CB00013B/444

9 781892 906052